Sanskrit Studies
Vol. 2, Saṁvat 2063-64
(CE 2006-07)

Sanskrit Studies

Vol. 2, Saṁvat 2063-64
(CE 2006-07)

Edited by
Wagish Shukla

Special Centre for Sanskrit Studies
Jawaharlal Nehru University
New Delhi

in association with

D. K. Printworld (P) Ltd.
New Delhi

Cataloging in Publication Data — DK
[Courtesy: D.K. Agencies (P) Ltd. <docinfo@dkagencies.com>]

Sanskrit studies vol. 2, Saṁvat 2063-64 (CE 2006-07)
/ edited by Wagish Shukla.
xii, 307 p., 23 cm.
Contributed articles.
Includes passages in Sanskrit (roman)
Includes bibliograhical references.
Includes index.
ISBN 8124604339

1. Sanskrit philology — Study and teaching.
I. Shukla, Wagish (1946-).

DDC 491.25 22

ISBN 81-246-0433-9
First published in India in 2007

Published by:
Special Centre for Sanskrit Studies
Jawaharlal Nehru University
New Delhi - 110 067.

in association with

D.K. Printworld (P) Ltd.
Regd. Office: 'Sri Kunj', F-52, Bali Nagar
New Delhi-110 015
Phones: (011) 2545-3975; 2546-6019; *Fax*: (011) 2546-5926
E-mail: dkprintworld@vsnl.net
Website: www.dkprintworld.com

Printed by: D.K. Printworld (P) Ltd., New Delhi

Editorial Committee and Faculty Members
Special Centre for Sanskrit Studies
Jawaharlal Nehru University

Editorial

It is a pleasure to place the second volume of *Sanskrit Studies* before the readers. The publication aims at periodically bringing out a collection of articles from scholars across disciplines in Indian mind with Sanskrit as the epicentre. The first volume under the skilled editorship of Prof. Kapil Kapoor fulfilled this task admirably and it is with some apprehension at not being able to reach up to that level of academic management that I approach my readers.

Vedic studies continues to be an inexhaustible source of new and significant insights into the Indian mindset and we have articles in this area from reputed scholars as Tatiana Elizarenkova on the Charms of Atharvaveda and G.U. Thite on Schools of Vedic Interpretation. In addition we have a strong argument that the *Ṛgveda* is Pre-Harappan by N. Kazanas.

In the field of Indian philosophy, we have very significant contributions by Victoria Lysenko on the Atomistic Formulations in Indian Thought and by Makarand Paranjape on The Philosophy and Aesthetics of Rasa. A very crucial point has been raised and discussed by Bina Gupta on the question of Comparative Philosophy; the discipline as understood in East and as well in West being examined with modern tools.

History, another subject of the intellectuals which supposedly did not exist in India, is touched upon in their contributions by some authors. Walter Slaje discusses the last Buddhist of Kashmir on the basis of an indigenous History treatize as recorded by Jonarāja. R. Nagaswamy brings before us an account of the Pallava King Mahendra Vikrama Varman, an important name in Sanskrit literature. Panchanan Bhoi touches upon the question of historical writing in India, a subject of hot controversy, and examines the bricks in this connection.

Science, a subject of modern ideas, considered even by the Western historians, has been construed differently in India. Prof. M. Krzysztof Byrski in his provocative article, invites us to look at Dharmaśāstra as a Natural Science, while the article by Prof. Pankaj Joshi informs us about how India stood in the ancient times in the context of the modern discipline of Science.

Sanskrit was never delimited to the political and geographical boundaries of India as Dr Lokesh Chandra writes about Sanskrit in China.

The Indian Society has been a difficult area of study for scholars since the current available manuals and materials do not contain any information on their structure and architecture. Prof. Kapil Kapoor examines the Indian Society in the context of gender with a fresh perspective.

Sanskrit literature has been an important area for the people at all times and in all contexts. We have an important contribution by K.T. Pandurangi on Emotions and Values in Sanskrit Literature. The article by Wagish Shukla examines a reading of *Śakuntalā*.

Prof. Shashiprabha Kumar, Chairperson of the Special Centre for Sanskrit, Jawaharlal Nehru University, Delhi, deserves my special thanks. It is indeed due to her efforts that the volume finally took shape in its contents and printing. Prof. Kapil Kapoor, the Guest Editor of the first volume of

Sanskrit Studies, helped immensely and gave very valuable advice. The academic and the non-academic staff of the Special Centre for Sanskrit Studies very kindly helped at various stages, while the JNU administration was invariably helpful and encouraging. I owe my sincere thanks to them.

Finally, D.K. Printworld have done an admirable job of production against many odds in record time. The cooperation received from all these people is gratefully recognized. It is hoped that the readers will find the contents intellectually satisfying. Any deficiencies, of course, are to be credited to the account of the Editor.

Wagish Shukla

Key to Transliteration

VOWELS

अ *a* (but)	आ *ā* (palm)	इ *i* (it)	ई *ī* (beet)	उ *u* (put)	ऊ *ū* (pool)
ऋ *ṛ* (rhythm)	ए *e* (play)	ऐ *ai* (air)	ओ *o* (toe)	औ *au* (loud)	

CONSONANTS

Guttural	क *ka* (skate)	ख* *kha* (blockhead)	ग *ga* (gate)	घ *gha* (ghost)	ङ *ṅa* (sing)
Palatal	च *ca* (chunk)	छ* *cha* (catch him)	ज *ja* (john)	झ *jha* (hedgehog)	ञ *ña* (bunch)
Lingual	ट *ṭa* (start)	ठ* *ṭha* (anthill)	ड *ḍa* (dart)	ढ* *ḍha* (godhead)	ण* *ṇa* (under)
Dental	त *ta* (path)	थ *tha* (thunder)	द *da* (that)	ध* *dha* (breathe)	न *na* (numb)
Labial	प *pa* (spin)	फ* *pha* (philosophy)	ब *ba* (bin)	भ *bha* (abhor)	म *ma* (much)
Others	य *ya* (young)	र *ra* (drama)	ल *la* (luck)	व *va* (vile)	
	श *śa* (shove)	ष *ṣa* (bushel)	स *sa* (so)	ह *ha* (hum)	
	क्ष *kṣa* (*kṣatriya*)	त्र *tra* (*trishūl*)	ज्ञ *jña* (*jñāni*)	ळ* ḷ (*play*)	ॠ* ṝ

अं (ं) *ṁ anusvāra* (nasalization of preceding vowel) like *saṁskṛti*

अः *ḥ* (*prātaḥ*) *ḥ visarga* (aspiration of preceding vowel)

ऽ 'Avagraha' = consonant #'consonant (like:- *ime 'vasthitā*)

ꣳ (*guṁ*) = ꣳ

Anusvāra at the end of line is presented by म् = m (not ṁ)

* No exact English equivalents for these letters.

Contents

1

Ṛgveda is Pre-Haṛappan*

N. Kazanas

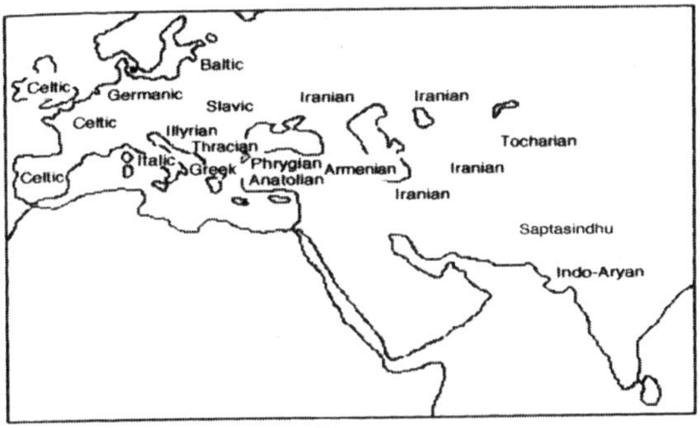

fig. 1.1

Argument: This paper presents the evidences and arguments for a *Ṛgveda* (*ṚV*) composed in bulk in the fourth millennium BCE. A basic consideration (but not the only one) is that the *ṚV* has no knowledge at all of many features that characterize the Haṛappan culture which began to emerge solidly *c.* 3000. Since the bulk of the *ṚV* must be assigned to a period before 3000 and since this is by general consensus stated to have been composed in Saptasindhu, then the Indo-Āryans or Vedic

---

* This is a revised version of a talk delivered at a Conference at the Center of Indic Studies, University of Massachusets in June 2006, and a paper included in Kazanas' *Vedic and Indo-European Studies* published by the Archaeological Society of India.

people were present in that location before 3000 and must therefore be regarded as indigenous by 1500, when, they are alleged to move in by the Āryan Invasion/Immigration Theory.

Horses and Chariots: Arriving *c.* 1500 BCE in Saptasindhu, the land of the seven rivers in what is today north-west India and Pakistan, constitute the main argument/evidence whereby many scholars hold the AIT (= Āryan Invasion/Immigration/ Ingress Theory).[1] The AIT has been the mainstream doctrine regarding Indian proto-history since the latter part of the nineteenth century. It teaches that the I-As (= Indo-Āryans) came to Saptasindhu from the Pontic Steppes or the Urals *c.* 1700–1500 and, although non-literate, they composed the *R̥V* (= *R̥gveda*) *c.* 1200–1000, the other Saṁhitās down to 800, the Brāhmaṇas and (early) Upaniṣads *c.* 800–600, then the Sūtra literature after 600 and then *c.* 300 BCE–CE 300 the two Epics, *Rāmāyaṇa* and *Mahābhārata*: all dates are approximate. The map shows the location of languages broadly, not peoples or races: it is a modification of the map used by J.V. Day, 2001, p. xiii.

Several linguistic arguments have been adduced to prop up this fanciful scenario one of them being the (loan-) words in the *R̥V* language which were allegedly borrowed from other languages met by the I-As on their way to and at Saptasindhu. A closely-related argument is the alleged common Indo-Iranian period during this journey to Saptasindhu.[2] Good examples of a combination of these two arguments are found in M.

1. Following others, I use the name 'Saptasindhu' simply as a *bahuvrīhi* adjective. The seven rivers are frequently mentioned in the *R̥V* (1.32.12; 34.8; 35.8; etc.), but not the name itself.

2. A common Indo-Iranian period there definitely was but this is to be found in Saptasindhu whence later the Iranians left (see n. 6 and § 13).

Witzel, (2005) and F. Kuiper (1991). But that 4 per cent of the Ṛgvedic vocabulary might consist of loan-words, or even 6 per cent or more, surely should not be surprising since the I-As did not live in a vacuum and there must have been people with different languages around them. However, this pet linguistic subject of Witzel's has been attacked by R.P. Das (1995 general critique), by Krishnamurti (2003: 37-38 mainly against Dravidian cognations) and Kazanas (2002a). In any case, no amount of arguing along these lines gives of itself any actual dates even approximately and the direction of movement can more reasonably be the reverse. There is B. Sergent who, although not at all an indigenist, argued in favour of a movement from Central Asia north-westward (1997). Also, Johanna Nichols, an eminent Indo-European (I-E) linguist, found on purely linguistic grounds that "the locus of the I-E spread was . . . somewhere in the vicinity of ancient Bactria"(1997: 113) — which is only a stone's throw away from Saptasindhu. Linguists will continue to disagree violently among themselves about the original locus, about the direction of the movement and about the date: some give a late period somewhere *c.* 3000 BCE, others an early one, in the seventh millennium (Misra, 1992). I ignore all such arguments and conclusions since they are so contradictory. The situation is in no way improving by claims that "I am right" and allegations that "the others are wrong." We must bear in mind also that all such arguments involve "reconstructed" proto-languages which are sheer conjectural affairs and therefore inadmissible in any impartial court of law.

Common Era Period and Ṛgveda

One of the best known comparative linguists of our times, Hans Hock, pointed out repeatedly (1996, 1999) that several dialects spoken in north-west India travelled north-westward at different times in the Common Era (= CE), the most notable one being that of the Gypsies in the early centuries CE (see also Fraser, 1995). Hock stated that Indo-Āryan indigenism and even the out-of-India theory could theoretically be possible, provided the distribution of the I-E isoglosses was accepted and the Vedic language was seen to be a devolved form of Proto-Indo-European (= PIE). But he opted for the mainstream doctrine (= the AIT out of the Pontic Steppe) because of the archaeological evidence of horses and chariots arriving in 'Saptasindhu in bulk after 1700 BCE (1999: 13). Thus he supports the spread of the Kurgan culture (as do also Allchin B. and R., Gimbutas, Kuzmina, Mallory, Parpola, Witzel et al.), even though the evidence for this diffusion is very limited according to J. Day (2001). Hock also mentions that it is simpler to have one movement into India rather than many out of it to account for the diversity and chronologies of the spread of the various I-E branches. But this is rather self-contradictory since, as he wrote (1996, 1999), the Indo-Āryan language left India north-westwards three times in the Common Era and generated new dialects and the Gypsies did reach the north-west extremity of Europe into England; so Indo-Āryan could have done the same in the misty past BCE. Besides, the ancient I-As could, in the out-of-India scenario, have left in a sizeable mass, stayed in a location in Baluchistan/Afghanistan (or even the Steppe).

For some time they successively moved in groups, in diverse directions. We need not make a problem out of this rather simple affair.

	Kazanas	2003 (§ 10, pp. 196-97)
		2002 (p. 305)
	Kochar	2000 (pp. 186, 192).
	Chakrabarti	1999
	Lal	1997
	Sharma	1996 (p. 17)
	Thomas et al.	1995
	Dhavalikar	1995 (pp. 116-17)
	Allchin & Joshi	1995 (p. 95)
	Rao	1991
necessarily	Sharma	1980 (p. 110 ff).

Fig. 2

For figurines of the horse: Thapar & Mungal, 1994; Lal, 2002

On the matter of horses and chariots, Hock was misinformed, I like to think. The evidence of horses and chariots proves the very opposite if examined with a modicum of attention. As one authority put it, "the horse was widely domesticated and used in India during the third millennium BCE over most of the areas covered by the Indus-Sarasvatī (or Haṛappan) Civilization" (Pande, 1999: 344; the square brackets original). I myself collected much evidence for horse-finds in different ISC (= Indus-Sarasvatī Civilization/Culture) sites in two papers in 2003, § 10 (pp. 196-97) and 2002 (p. 305): thus one may further consult, Kochhar, 2000 (pp. 186, 192); Chakrabarti, 1999; Lal, 1997; Sharma, 1996 (p. 17); Thomas et al., 1995; Dhavalikar, 1995 (pp. 116-17); Allchin & Joshi, 1995 (p. 95); Rao, 1991 and, necessarily, Sharma, 1980 (p. 110ff.). These publications show abundantly that the true horse, *Equus ferus* and *Equus cabalus,* was present in its wild state in India from *c.* 17000 BCE and there is much evidence now for the domesticated horse in the Mature Haṛappan period. Moreover, there are several terracotta figurines of this animal from different ISC sites as reported by Lal, 2002 and Thapar & Mungal, 1994.

As for the chariot, S. Piggott established the presence of a sophisticated type of vehicle with "one or two pairs of wheels with their axles . . . from the Rhine to the Indus by around 3000" (1992: 18).

Archaeological evidence does not consist only of the actual remains of buildings, weapons, tools, chariots, etc. Pictures, reliefs, toys and figurines of these things are also evidence. Many years ago H.K. Sankalia had pointed out that the six-spoked wheel appears on seals and signs of the alphabet (1974: 363). S.R. Rao found at Lothal "terracotta wheels . . . with diagonal lines suggesting spokes" (1973: 124). This representational practice seems to have been widespread, for S. Piggott mentions similarly marked wheels found in the Karpathian Basin from the Earlier Bronze Age (1983: 91-92). In his recent study, Lal presents four terracotta wheels (from Mature Haṛappan sites Banawali, Kalibangan, Rakhigarhi) with spokes painted on (2002: 74, *fig.*, 3.28 ff.). The Haṛappans had the technology for making spoke-wheels (Kazanas, 1999: 33; Basham, 1954: 21).

Finally, it was A. Parpola, an inveterate adherent of the AIT, who identified the figure on Haṛappan seal No. 3357 as representing simplistically a man with outstretched arms standing on two six-spoked wheels (of a chariot) realizing that this was "a later invention of the Āryans" (1969: 24). The later notion that it is a potter on two wheels is obviously far-fetched and, in any case, the wheel is spoked (Sethna, 1992)! L.S. Rao has recently presented many more finds of models of terracotta toy wheels with spokes from Haṛappan locations in *Purātattva*, vol. 36 (pp. 59-66), 2006.

Spoked Wheel Controversy and R̥gveda

The question of course is whether there were spoked wheels before 3000 since the *R̥V* uses the word *ara* which is usually

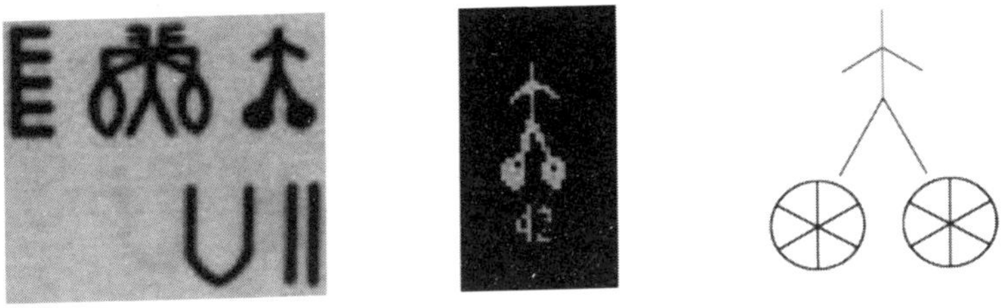

Fig. 3

translated as "spoke" (1.32.15; 5.58.5; etc). We don't know. Some Indian scholars approach the issue strategically and say that R̥gvedic hymns with *ara* are later intrusions from the second millennium when the spoked wheel was quite common. This is possible of course, since we know that some hymns are later interpolations. There could have been spoked wheels as we know them even at *c.* 3200 BCE and before. But then again, *ara* need not mean "spoke." It could mean a section of the (solid) wheel. After all, different I-E branches have a different stem for spoke (Gk *aktis, knēmē*; L *radius*; Gmc *speca/ speihha*, etc.) which suggests that spokes were developed after the dispersal (in the sixth or eighth millennium, or whichever). So *ara* could well have meant something other than spoke and only later acquired the meaning of "spoke," as we know it now. The spoked wheel poses, in fact, no problem for dating the *R̥V*. There are other more clearcut types of evidences.

The usual objection is that there are no chariot remains from that period. Here, there is the double assumption that *R̥V* chariots are necessarily like near-eastern ones of, say, 1500, or the Androvo, *c.* 1900 BCE, and that there should be remains. But why assume that the *R̥V* chariots are like the near-eastern ones? The only real-life vehicle in a race that we know is in 10.102 and this is pulled by oxen not horses (Kazanas, 2002) while 1.123.1 alludes to a "broad chariot" *pr̥thū rathaḥ*!

Elsewhere in the *R̥V* the chariot *ratha* is described as being *br̥hat* "tall," "big" (6.61.13) also *variṣṭha . . . vandhura*, widest . . . seated (6,9,47), *trivandhura* "three seated" (1.41.2; 118.2; 7.71.4; 8.22.5; etc.) and once even *aṣṭavandhura* "eight-seated" (10.53.7)! These are all *rathas* and hardly like the near-eastern battle-chariots. Then again, there are no remains of chariots in India from 1500 or 1000 or 700 BCE. So we shall say no chariots were brought in by the alleged I-E entrants either.

Haṛappan Features Absent in the R̥gveda

The Haṛappan or Indus-Sarasvatī Culture has certain characteristics which help to define its uniqueness. A number of these features are absent from the *R̥V* and this absence indicates that the *R̥V* is pre-Haṛappan. Arguments *e silentio* are not decisive since absence of evidence is not always evidence of real absence. But in this case the features are far too many. (Some of these were noted by Sethna, 1992.)

HAṚAPPAN FEATURES ABSENT IN THE R̥V

1. *iṣṭakā* — "brick," in *R̥V* metal, mud, stone, wood.
2. *karpāsa* — "cotton," in *R̥V* skins, tree-bark, wool.
3. *vrīhi* — "rice," in *R̥V* *yava* "barely"
4. *rajata* — "silver," in *R̥V* copper, gold. (once in *R̥V*, 8.25.22, it denotes a steed or chariot 'shining white').

See *Vedic Index* 2: 196-97.

NO MENTION IN R̥V OF:

5. *urbanization* — the word *pur* invariably means an occult, magical, psychological defence, stronghold, but never "fort(ress), town," cons-

			tructed/destroyed by humans.
6.	*ruins*	—	present in late Haṛappan.
7.	*fixed hearths/altars,*		
8.	*literacy*	—	possibly in *AV* 19.72.
9.	*iconography*	—	paintings,relief representations, statue (ttes), seals.

All these are attested in post-Ṛgvedic texts and are found in different phases of the ISC.

Fig. 4

(a) *iṣṭakā,* a brick — The *ṚV* mentions as building materials metal, stone, mud and wood but not "brick," which was the basic material in Haṛappan constructions. This is found in post-Ṛgvedic texts: the word *iṣṭakā* is not in the *ṚV.*

(b) Urbanization is wholly absent in the *ṚV*. There certainly was "nomad pastoralism" as mainstreamers emphasize repeatedly but there were also agricultural settlements (a fact which mainstreamers underplay or do not mention). The hymn to *kṣetrapati* "Lord of the Field/Soil" (4.57) alone should suffice but also the girl Apālā refers to her father's *urvarā* "fertile field" (8.91.5); then there are many cultivation implements *khanitra* "shovel," *lāṅgala/sīra* "plough," *sṛṇī* "sickle," etc. Moreover, there is weaving with loom, shuttle, warp and woof (*ṚV*, 1.134.4; 1.3.6; etc.) and metallurgy with smithies of sorts (4.2.17; 5.9.5; etc.). Such activities imply settlement.

Some writers think the Ṛgvedic and Haṛappan cultures converge (Gupta, 2005; Bisht, 1999; Lal, 1998; Singh,

1995). As evidence is cited the word *pur* — which denotes "city, citadel, fort, town" as its Greek and Baltic cognates *polis* and *pil(i)s* do. This is a very general misconception. In the *R̥V*, *pur* never means anything other than an occult, magical, esoteric defence or stronghold which is not created nor ever destroyed by humans (Kazanas, 2003: 224-25 and 2002b passim).[3] The ISC cities had regular blocks, large buildings, also domestic and urban water-supply (McIntosh, 2001: 100-101): the *R̥V* knows nothing of all these.

---

3. Bisht, for example, cites the numerous occurences of *pur* as evidence that the *R̥V* knew of towns and fortifications (p. 410 ff.). So does D. Frawley (2002: 13). This is wrong, of course; *pur* in the *R̥V* never means "fort" or "town" but a magical, esoteric defence. Merely citing verses in the *R̥V* but not analysing and exploring their meaning is not very sound scholarship. Here are some examples merely cited by both writers. In II, 35 the Offspring-of-Waters *Apā́ṁ Nápāt* is protected in *āmā́supūrṣú* (usually translated as "forts of unbaked bricks" even though bricks are nowhere mentioned!); the phrase means "non-artificial natural defences" (in this case obviously "divine"). In I.166, 8 Agastya prays to the Maruts to protect (*rakṣ-*) from evil *agha* and injury *abhihr̥ti* the man they favour (*av-*) with "hundredfold defences" *śatábhujibhiḥ pūrbhíḥ:* no such many-walled structure existed allowing for the hyperbole) and, moreover, it is difficult to see how people can be protected from evil by 100 fold forts/towns! VI.48, 8 is a similar prayer to Agni to protect (*pā-*) from anxiety *aṁhas* the fire-kindler with "100 *purs*": clearly one cannot be protected from anxiety with 100 forts/cities (again allowing for a hyperbole) but only with internal occult defences. A final example: X.101, 8 is a prayer to Viśvedevas "to fashion inviolable metal *purs*" to protect the rite of *soma*-pouring; obviously no forts or towns are meant to be built around the sacrificial locus but magical other-wordly defences against demons. Not one *pur* is built and not one is destroyed by human beings! See Kazanas, 2003, pp. 224-25 and n. 12; also <http://www.omilosmelton.gr/english/en_index.html> '*R̥gvedic pur*'; also Kazanas, 2006.

The words for "council" *sabhā* and *samiti* are also cited but, surely, any community can have a council of elders without urbanization. Allusions in the *ṚV* to chiefs/ kings *rājā* and overlords/emperors *samrāṭ* also do not show urbanization since such offices can just as easily exist in rural communities. (The Red Indians in North America, nomadic and rural tribes, had local chiefs and overlords.)

(c) Fixed altars or hearths are unknown in the *ṚV* but common in the ISC cities. The Ṛgvedic altar is a shallow bed dug in the ground and covered with grass (e.g. *ṚV*, 5.11.2, 7.43.2-3; Parpola, 1988: 225). Fixed brick-altars are very common in post-Ṛgvedic texts.

(d) Many cities were abandoned and fell to ruination after 1900 BCE when the Haṛappans began to move eastward because of the drying up of the Sarasvatī and of the more general desiccation due to tectonic disturbances and climatic changes. The *ṚV* knows nothing of such ruins even though, according to the AIT, the I-As moved through these regions *c.* 1700-1500 BCE (in small waves, settled there, in the midst of deserts, and wrote the hymns which praise the mighty Sarasvatī!). Some attempts have been made to read hymn, 1.133 with its *arma-ka* (= of unknown meaning, really) as a description of a ruined city (e.g. Burrow, 1963; Rao, 1991: 32) but, in fact, the hymn mentions no ruined buildings, no fallen walls and no materials such as wood, stone or bricks! It is a ghostly scene of frightful desolation, peopled only with unfriendly she-fiends and demons (*yātumati, piśācī* and *rākṣasa*). In sharp contrast the Old

English poem *The Ruin* contains such persuasive details of the ancient remains (from Roman times?) that some scholars think it refers to the town of Bath (Mitchell & Robinson, 1996: 252-55).

(e) No cotton (*karpāsa*) appears in the *R̥V* although this plant was extensively cultivated in the ISC and the fabric was exported as far as Egypt in the middle of the third millennium while the Mesopotamians adopted the name as *kapazum* (? from Prakrit *kapāsa*). The *R̥V* has "skin" *eta* (1.166.10; *ajina* in *AV* 5.21.7, etc.), "wool" *avi* (*R̥V*, 9.78.1) and *śāmulya* (*R̥V* 10.85.29) and numerous terms for clothing and weaving but no mention of cotton. Be it noted that *karpāsa* is the only word for cotton in Sanskrit.

(f) Silver *rajata* also makes no appearance in the *R̥V* though gold and copper are well attested and silver is plentiful in the ISC. The word *rajata* occurs in *R̥V* (8.25.22) and it denotes a steed or a chariot "shining white." Only in later texts is it used singly (*AV*, 5.28.1) or with *hiraṇya* to denote "silver" or "white gold" = "silver." (see *Vedic Index* 2: 196-97 and Lubotsky, 2: 1169).

(g) Rice *vrīhi* too is absent from the *R̥V* although it appears in various sites of the ISC from at least 2300 BCE (and in the Ganges Valley from the sixth millennium).[4] The *R̥V* knows only *yava* "barley." Rice becomes important in post-R̥gvedic ritual and the more general diet.

---

4. Private communication from S.P. Gupta, Chairman of Indian Archaelogical Society (June 2006). See also Sharma 1980 for rice in the Ganges basin in the fifth millennium and R. Tewari et al. in *Purātattva*, 2006 (vol. 36, pp. 68-75) for rice, again in the Gaṅgā basin, north-east, in the district Sant Kabir Nagar (UP) in seventh millennium.

(h) Literacy is not known in the *ṚV*. D. Frawley thought that a passage in *AV* (19.72) may refer to writing: "From whichever receptacle *kośāt* we have taken the Veda, into that we put it down." Books in ancient India comprised collections of palm-leaves or strips of birch-bark and were kept in boxes (1991: 249). Whether this is enough to establish knowledge of writing is doubtful. But in any event, writing was known in the ISC but not in the *ṚV*.

(i) The *ṚV* has no allusions to artistic iconography — paintings, relief representations, statue(-ttes) or seals, all so common in the ISC. (The *ṚV*, 4.24.10 asks "Who will buy this my Indra" and this is thought by some to refer to a statuette, but this could be a transfer of favour and it is the only reference in the whole *ṚV* without the use of any word for statue or icon.)

Post-Ṛgvedic Texts and the Haṛappan Culture

Now all the fore-mentioned features are found in post-Ṛgvedic texts — the Saṁhitās, the Brāhmaṇas and fully in the Sūtra literature. For instance, brick altars are mentioned in *Śatapatha Brāhmaṇa* (7.1.1.37 or 10.2.3.1), etc. Rice (*vrīhi*) is found in *AV* (6.140.2; 7.1.20); etc. Cotton (*karpāsa*) appears first in *Gautama Dharma-Sūtra* (1.18) and in *Baudhāyana Dharma-Sūtra* (14.13.10). The fact of the convergence of the post-Ṛgvedic texts and the Haṛappan culture was noted long ago by archaeologists B. and R. Allchin stated unequivocally that these features are of the kind "described in detail in the later Vedic literature" (1982: 203).

If we had a case of 2 or 3 items we could bypass them saying indeed that absence of evidence is no evidence of absence; but the items are many and the absence of the building material *iṣṭakā* in the *ṚV* (against the presence of wood, stone, mud and metal) seems to me quite decisive.

We must also take into account that many iconographic motifs, Haṛappan artefacts, decorations or seals, show affinity with elements found in post-Ṛgvedic texts. Thus P.K. Agrawala (2005) draws attention to round-bottomed perforated pots from Haṛappan sites and a vessel (*kumbha*) with nine holes (*navavitṛṇṇa*) or 100 holes (*śatavitṛṇṇa*) mentioned in *Śatapatha Brāhmaṇa* (5.5.4.27) and *śatatṛṇṇā kumbhī* (a pitcher with 100 perforations) in 12.7.2.13. These and other similar descriptions echo the White *Yajurveda* (*Vājasaneyī Saṁhitā*) verse 19: 87 "a pitcher with 100 streams." Such vessels were used for ritual sprinkling. A second parallel is furnished by the two-horned bovine-like animal, duplicated and facing itself, on a Mohen-jo-Dāṛo seal with long necks and the *pīpal* tree growing out of their juncture. This corresponds (writes Agrawala) to the two-headed cattle *dvāyā* in *AV* (5.19.7). Agrawala mentions other parallels of a two-headed tiger and a two-headed bird (2005: 10-13). Thus it is indeed the later Vedic texts that have parallels with the Haṛappan arts and crafts, not the *ṚV*.

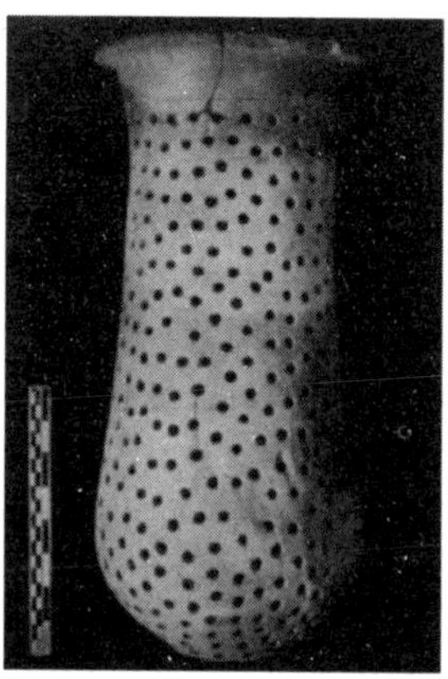

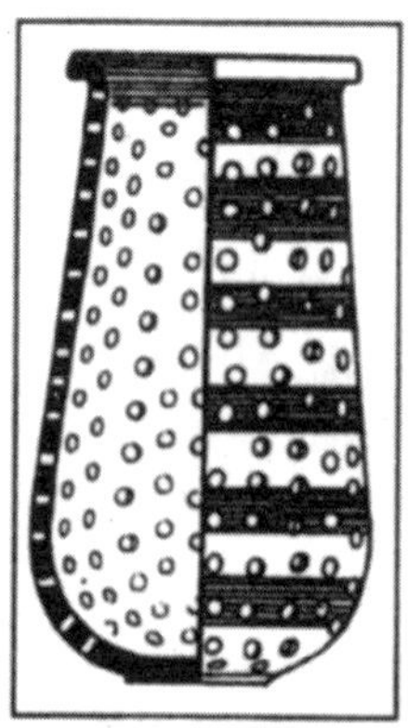

fig. 5

dvāyā in *Artharvadeda* 5.19.7; symbol of OM?
fig. 6

N. Rajaram follows a similiar line of investigation (2005) and adduces iconographic motifs from Haṛappan seals but does not distinguish between Ṛgvedic (or early Vedic) and post- Ṛgvedic (or later Vedic) periods and cultures. Thus he cites the *aśvattha*-tree foliage and the horse and links them to the *ṚV* disregarding the fact that these are not exclusively Ṛgvedic and therefore could be simply from a post-Ṛgvedic period. Moreover he cites the *svastika* and the sign of sound *OṀ*, both of which are, as he states, from post-Ṛgvedic texts. It is also doubtful that the seal-sign which is horizontal, depicts the symbol for *OṀ*, which should be upright, anyway. (But, of course, the seal could be seen as upright since we don't know what the symbols indicate.)

On this score, then, the bulk of the *ṚV*, is pre-Haṛappan, or 3000+.

Brāhmaṇas and the Ṛgvedic Hymns

Some Brāhmaṇas comment on or give explanations of incidents in the Ṛgvedic hymns. For example, the *Aitareya Br.* (7.13.33) narrates extensively the story of Śunaḥśepa, alluded to briefly in *ṚV* (1.24.12-13 and 5.2.7), while the *Śatapatha Br.* (11.5.1) comments on the Pururavās and Urvaśī love story given elliptically in dialogue form in *ṚV* (10.95). Another point to note. Some legends in the *ṚV* remain unexplained. For instance, who was Bhujyu whom the Aśvins saved from a tempest (1.116.3-4; etc.) and how did he find himself in that predicament? The later texts say nothing more. Or, take the birth of Indra; was he an unwelcome child to Aditi and did he commit parricide (4.18.1ff., etc.)? Again, the Brāhmaṇas tell us nothing. Obviously such exegetical texts would not be composed until the understanding regarding the older texts has lapsed: this implies many centuries.

What is the date of the Brāhmaṇas? Well, S. Kak ascribes the *Śatapatha* to the early third millennium (1994, 1997) saying that the Pleiades/Kṛttikas not swerving from the east, as is stated in this Brāhmaṇa (2.1.2.3), could only occur *c.* 2950 BCE. Narahari Achar (Prof. Astrophysics, Memphis, USA) using computer and planetarium apparatus arrived at a date *c.* 3000 BCE pointing out that S.B. Dikshit had arrived at similar conclusions 100 years earlier but was ignored by Western scholars (1999); these scholars really had no knowledge of astronomy. B.B. Lal too thought that "astronomical calculations (re *Aitareya Br.*) would place the *ṚV* in the fourth millennium" but did not then adopt such a date only because he could not judge the evidence (1997: 286).

So we could again place the *ṚV* easily before 3000.

The Bṛhadāraṇyaka Upaniṣad and Ṛgveda

The *Bṛhadāraṇyaka Upaniṣad* has three *vaṁśa*s, i.e. list of teachers, each comprising 65-70 names. The first four or five are names of gods in the normal Indic way which ascribes the beginning of every human activity to some deity. Let us take the mainstream date of early sixth century for this text (say 550) according to the AIT premises and let us take 60 teachers giving to each one an average of 15 years, though 20 and 30 would be more realistic. These calculations (60 × 15 = 900 plus 550) give us a date *c.* 1450 for the inception of the doctrines in this Upaniṣad. The chief doctrine is that the self of man (*ātman*) is the same in all beings and the same as the Self of the universe (*Brahman* "Mystic Spirit" or "Absolute") as in *Bṛh Up* 2.5.19. We should also bear in mind that the teachers' names are quite different from those of the seers of the *ṚV* hymns as given by the native tradition. Following others, M. Witzel thinks these lists "rest on typically weak foundations" (2001, § 19) but this is a typically weak subterfuge because the results of calculating the number of years prove how unrealistic the AIT chronologies are! Let us see, then.

The Upaniṣadic doctrine of the identity of the individual self and the universal self, in the formulations *ayam ātma brahman* and *aham brahmāsmi* "the Self is the Absolute" and "I am the Absolute," should be known, then, *c.* 1500 or 1300 or 1200 BCE, when, according to the AIT, the *ṚV* was composed. Yet, for undetermined reasons, quite surprisingly, this doctrine is totally unknown in the *ṚV* in these terms (although enunciated differently) and begins hesitantly to appear in the *AV* (e.g. 10.2.32-33; 11.4.23; etc.). Consequently, the *AV* should be placed at least *c.* 1600 BCE and the *ṚV c.* 1800 always following the AIT assumptions. But the *ṚV* is composed, even according to Witzel (2005: 90), in Saptasindhu, yet the I-As do not appear in this area before, at the very earliest, 1700 BCE, and the *ṚV* gets composed after several centuries!

This is one of the comical paradoxes that the mainstream chronology refuses obdurately to resolve. Yet, on the grounds given in § 4-6 above, we saw that the *ṚV* should be assigned to the fourth millennium, say around 3500 BCE. Now subtracting 900 or 1000 years (for the teachers), we should place the early Upaniṣads at the start of the period of the mature Haṛappan, i.e. 2600-2500 BCE (with the *ātma-brahman* doctrine having come down orally) and the Sūtra texts immediately after. These dates satisfy yet another requirement. The word for cotton *karpāsa* is first used in the Sūtra texts as we saw in § 5, above and the cultivation of the plant (although seeds of it were found in much earlier periods) gets well established *c.* 2500 BCE. All these dates are, of course, approximate.

Palaeoastronomical Research and Mahābhārata

Astrophysicist Achar pursued his palaeoastronomical research into the *Mahābhārata* (*Mbh*) epic also, examining astronomical references in books 3, 5 and 18. His sky map showed that all these converge in the year 3067 BCE (Achar, 2003; see also Kazanas, 2002: 295-97). Achar acknowledged that some 30 years earlier, in 1969, S. Raghavan had arrived at the same date. Now, it is obvious that the *Mbh* had acquired many accretions over many centuries and that it was streamlined stylistically at about the start of the Common Era. It is obvious that it contains much late material like 2.28.48-49, which mentions Rome and Antiochia (*roma* and *antakhī*): this could not be earlier than 300 BCE since Antioch was founded in 301 BCE. On the other hand, the frequent use of the bow and, moreso, the use by Bhīma of a (tree trunk as a) club show much more primitive conditions.

Thus the war took place in 3067 BCE and the core of the *Mbh* in poems and songs was laid down in that year. This and the native traditional view that the Kaliyuga came at 3102 are both correct, according to Achar. He pointed out that the Kaliyuga had no full force until the death of Kṛṣṇa which occurred 35 years after 3067 BCE, in 3032 BCE (private communication, June 2006); but immorality had set in already, as is shown by the unjust behaviour of the Kauravas and some reprehensible acts during the war itself. Surely no bards (compilers or redactors) in the third century CE or the third century BCE could possibly know the star and planet positions relative to the *nakṣatras* or the zodiac signs of the year 3067. The astronomical references examined by Achar (and Raghavan) are so numerous that chance coincidence has to be discarded (Achar, 2003). However, that the war took place in 3137 and bards began to sing of these events two generations later should not be precluded. Personally, I still tend towards the traditional view of the war taking place in 3137 BCE. The Megasthenes report (from *c.* 300 BCE) of the ancient kings from 6000+, surviving in Arrian and other classical writers, supports these long periods of the past. Then, deterioration in behaviour would have started in the *sandhyā* transitional period before the onset of the Kaliyuga — when also the kṣatriyas passed away. Here a question remains: how did the astronomers (and Āryabhaṭṭa especially) determine the date for Kaliyuga as 3102 BCE?

The River Sarasvatī and Ṛgveda

The Sarasvatī river furnishes useful literary and archaeological evidence for dating the *ṚV*. It is a mighty river extolled in all books of the *ṚV* except the fourth. It is *nadītamā, ambitamā, devītamā* "best river, best mother, best goddess" (2.41.16); it is swollen and fed by three or more rivers *pinvamānā sindhubhiḥ* (6.52.6); it is endless, swift moving, roaring, most dear among her sister rivers; together with her divine aspect, it nourishes the Indo-Āryan tribes (6.61.8-13). In 7.95.2 the river is said to flow pure in her course "from the mountains to the ocean" *giribhyaḥ ā samudrāt.* Then 7.96.2 and 10.177 pray to the river goddess for sustenance and good fortune while 10.64.9 calls upon her (and Sarayū and Indus) as "great" and "nourishing." Clearly then, we have here, even in the late Bk 10, a great river flowing from the Himalayas to the ocean in the south, fed and swollen by other rivers and sustaining the tribes of the I-As on its banks — not a river known in the past or in some other region, or a river now considerably shrunk (Witzel, 2001).[5]

Some scholars claim that here *samudra* does not mean "ocean" but confluence and especially the place where a tributary flowed into the Indus. The last point can be discarded since there is not the slightest hint elsewhere that the Sarasvatī flowed into the Indus — in which case the Indus and not Sarasvatī would have been lauded as the best river (2.41.16). The meaning "terminal lake(s)" adopted by Witzel is entirely fanciful. In his dictionary, M. Mayrhofer gives for *samudra* only "confluence" and "ocean/sea" (1996, *EWA*). And the Vedic poet would certainly have used (not *ā samudrāt* but) *ā sarobhyaḥ* "to the terminal lakes" maintaining his -U-- cadence. This phrase would then have indicated clearly the alleged fanciful etymological connection of the name *Saras-vatī* "she who has (terminal) lakes." The name means rather "she who has swirls and currents," since the primary sense of *sṛ* (>*saras*) is "movement" (*gatau*) or "flowing, leaping, rushing."

The river is thought to have dried up almost completely by 1900 (Allchins, 1997: 117; Rao, 1991: 77-79). In previous years it had lost tributaries to the Indus in the West and the Ganges in the East. Is there any evidence that it flowed down to the Indian (or Arabian) ocean at any earlier period?

G. Possehl examined (1998) all the palaeoenvironmental and geological data relevant to the Sarasvatī river and concluded that the river could have flowed down to the ocean

5. The mainstream view (Witzel's really) that the Vedic river is merely a memory of the Iranian Haraxvaiti which belongs to the common Indo-Iranian period, when the Irano-Āryans lived together in Iran before the I-As moved further south-east (according to the AIT), is no more than modern myth-making.

only before 3200 at the very latest and, more probably, before 3800 BCE! He re-stated his finds in his study of 2003 (pp. 8-9). P.H. Francfort has been just as certain of a date 3600-3800 in his survey of 1992.

All this helps us place the passages ascribing the grandeur of river Sarasvatī at a date before 3200 BCE at least. (For a detailed examination of this entire issue see Kazanas, 2004a; for more recent scientific investigations through satellite showing the course of the old Sarasvatī reaching the ocean, see J.R. Sharma et al., 2006.)

Ancient Mesopotamian Religion and Ṛgveda

In a recent publication Dr S. Levitt (of New York), who is by no means an indigenist, examined the development of the "early Indic tradition" and the development of religion in ancient Mesopotamia.

After comparing several elements in the Vedic and Mesopotamian religions, Levitt concluded: "We can date the early Indic tradition in the basis of comparable points in ancient Mesopotamia. By this, the *Ṛgveda* would date back to the beginning of the third millennium BCE, with some of the earliest hymns perhaps even dating to the end of the fourth millennium BCE" (2003: 356).

However, unaware of Levitt's paper, I myself made at about that time a very detailed comparative study of Vedic and Mesopotamian religions (mythological) motifs, published in *Migration and Diffusion*, vol. 24, 2005.[6] In this I showed that since more than 20 motifs in the Vedic texts had close parallels

6. This was badly printed and the Sanskrit transliterations are unreadable! A revised version will be published in *Adyar Library Bulletin*, 2006. See also <http://www.omilosmeleton.gr/english/en_index.html>

in other I-E branches (e.g. the horse mythology, the skyboat of the Sungod, the Flood, the elixir from heaven, the creation of cosmic parts from the dismemberment of a divine being, etc.) and were therefore of Proto-Indo-European (= PIE) provenance, they could not have been borrowed by the Vedics from the Mesopotamians as is usually alleged (McEvilley, 2002; Dalley, 1998) but must be inherited and therefore older than the Mesopotamian (Sumerian, Babylonian, etc.) parallels. Since the Mesopotamian culture (starting with old Sumerian) surfaces *c.* 3000 BCE, the Vedic motifs must be earlier. Most of these have no parallels in Uggarite, Hebrew and other intermediate Near-Eastern cultures.

Thus, again we arrive at a date before 3000 for the bulk of the *R̥V*.

R̥gveda Composed in Saptasindhu

Since, according to the preceding discussion we must now assign the (bulk of the) *R̥V* to *c.* 3200 BCE at the latest and since the *R̥V* by general consent was composed in Saptasindhu, then it follows that the I-As were ensconced in Saptasindhu by 3200 and that the ISC was a material manifestation of the early oral Vedic tradition expressed in the *R̥V*. This issue was treated by me extensively in many other papers and no more need be said now. I should only add that, in fact, more and more scholars in the West have re-examined the issue and rejected wholly or in part the mainstream view advocating a movement Out of India into Europe (Schildmann, 1998; Klostermaier, 1998 and 2000; Friedrich, 2004; Hasenpflug, 2006). Thus the mainstream strident cries of warning about "fundamentalists, nationalists, revisionists" in India and their colleagues in the West (Witzel, 2003; Huld, 2002; Kuzmina, 2002) are those slogans; for neither the indigenist scholars mentioned above nor the archaeologists (Shaffer 1994, Kenoyer 1998, McIntosh

2001, Possehl 2000, et al.) specializing in the ISC and insisting on its unbroken continuity down to the sixth century belong to this (non-existent) band of bogies.

To all this I should add the increasing evidence from Genetics which declares that no substantial flow of genes occurred from Europe or the north-western adjacent areas into India before 600 BCE. On the contrary recent genetic studies show an outflow from India into countries west and north and Europe (Sahoo et al. 2006; Oppenheimer, 2003). M. Danino has made a useful overview of the evidence produced by studies over the last ten years in his paper "Genetics and the Āryan Debate," published in *Purātattva* 2006. Thus the Indo-Āryans are now shown to be indigenous to Saptasindhu and there is nothing to undermine my contention that the *ṚV* in its bulk is pre-Haṛappan. However, I should make it plain that I do have some doubts about the out of India proposition even though I find it, on the whole, much more probable than the AIT. What I am arguing for is the proposition that, since the only biological change is in the skeletal record of the area and occurs *c.* 6000-4500 BCE (Kazanas, 2002a with references), if the Indo-Āryans made an entry it would have happened at that period; but by 1700 BCE they certainly were indigenous.

ṚV Composed in Fourth Millennium

Does it matter whether the *ṚV* was composed in the fourth millennium or *c.* 1000 BCE? whether the Indo-Āryans are indigenous or came to India *c.* 1500 BCE? After all life goes on irrespective of such ancient events. So from one point of view, no, it doesn't matter. But from another, it does matter. First, it is the function of scholarship to establish and promote true knowledge so that our life be regulated by this — not prejudices, partisan views (even patriotic but false) or pet theories. Second Indian (proto-) history must be restored and revalued in a correct time-frame. It is sad, indeed, as Frawley wrote (*The Hindu*, 18 June 2002), "to note how intellectuals in India are quick to denigrate the extent and antiquity of their history." Third, the *R̥V* contains ideas that are of great value to mankind and reveal, as other recent discoveries in prehistoric cultures (Rudgley, 1998, passim), that so-called "primitive" people had much important knowledge that held them at a fairly high level of civilization enabling them to live in harmony with the natural processes (*r̥ta*) of their environment. The *R̥V*, e.g. preserves for us, from that so ancient period, the idea of a Primal Unity that is the First Cause of the universe and all its phenomena: not only in the *Nāsadīya-Sūkta* and the *Puruṣa-Sūkta* (10.129 and 90) but also in 1.164, 6; 3.55 refrain; 6.75.9; 8.58; 10.114.5 and less obviously in others. This concept is absent from all other I-E traditions (Hittite, Greek, Roman, etc.) and may well have been an essential constituent of PIE culture lost in the other branches. Thus the R̥gvedic IA culture (and perhaps PIE) consisted not so much of material artefacts but of inner knowledge and spiritual strength — *bráhma várma mamā́ntaram* "the holy-power is my inner defence" (*R̥V* 6.75.19).

Let us hope that the noxious AIT and all notions rooted in it will sooner rather than later end up in the only place they should be — the dustbin of history. Let us also hope that the will be re-examined not only for its historical information but its cultural ideas that will illuminate many other studies and disciplines in ancient history, anthropology, civilization, linguistics, religion, sociology, etc.

Abbreviations

AIT	—	Āryan Invasion/Immigration/Ingress Theory
AV	—	*Atharvaveda*
CE	—	Common Era

I-A	—	Indo-Āryan
I-E	—	Indo-European
ISC	—	Indus-Sarasvatī Civilization/Culture
Mbh	—	*Mahābhārata*
PIE	—	Proto-Indo-European
ṚV	—	*Ṛgveda*

Bibliography

Achar, B.N.N., 2003, "Date of the Mahābhārata War . . ." in *Quarterly Journal of the Mythic Society*, vol. XCIV and issue nos. 1-2.

———, 2001, "Planetarium software and the date of the Mahābhārata war" paper read in Montreal, sent to N. Kazanas privately.

———, 1999, "On exploring the Vedic sky. . . ." *Electronic Journal of Vedic Studies*, 5-2 (3-9).

Agrawal, V., 2006, "Is there evidence for the Indo-Āryan Immigration to India?" talk at WAVES Conference August, see <http://www.omilosmeleton.gr/english en_index.html>.

Agrawal, A., 2005, *In Search of Vedic Haṛappan Relationship*, New Delhi: Aryan Books Intern.

Agrawal, D.P., 2002, Comments on "Indigenous Indo-Āryans" in *Journal of I-E Studies*, vol. 30, pp. 129-35.

Agrawala, P.K., 2005, "Two Haṛappan Motifs & their Vedic Affinity," in A. Agrawal, ed., pp. 10-13.

Allchin, B. & R., 1997, *Origins of a Civilization*, Delhi, Viking Penguin.

———, 1982, *The Rise of Civilization in India & Pakistan*, Cambridge: Cambridge University Press.

Allchin, F. & J. Joshi, 1995 (eds.), *Excavations at Malvan*, Delhi, Archaeological Survey of India (Memoir No. 92).

Aurobindo, Sri, 1914-1920, "On the Veda and the Secret of the Veda," articles in *Arya*, India (1956, reprinted in book form, Pondicherry).

Bisht, R.S., 1999, "Haṛappan and Ṛgveda: Points of Convergence" in G. Pande, ed. (1999) pp. 393-442.

Bryant, E., 2001, *The Quest of the Origins of Vedic Culture*, Oxford: Oxford University Press.

Burrow, T., 1963, "On the Significance of the Terms *arma-, armaka-,*" *Journal of Indian History,* vol. 41, pp. 159-68.

Cavalli-Sforza et al. 2003, "The Genetic Heritage of the Earliest Settlers . . . " *American Journal of Human Genetics,* 72, pp. 313-32.

Chakrabarti, D.K., 1999, *India: An Archaeological History,* Cambridge: Cambridge University Press.

Dalley, S., 1998, ed., *The Legacy of Mesopotamia,* Oxford: Oxford University Press.

Danino, M., 2006, "Genetics and the Āryan Debate," in *Purātattva,* vol. 36.

Darmesteter, J., 1965, *The Zend-Avesta* (1883), Sacred Books of the East 4, 23, Delhi: Motilal Banarsidass.

Das, R.P., 1995, "Hunt for Foreign Words in R̥V," *Indo-Iranian Journal* 38, pp. 207-38.

Day, J. V. 2001, *Indo-European Origins,* Washington: Institute for the study of Man.

Dhavalikar, M.K., 1995, "Cultural Imperialism . . ." Delhi: Books & Books.

Dhar, L., 1930, *The Home of the Āryans,* Delhi: Delhi University Press.

Elst, K., 1993, *Indigenous Indians,* Delhi: Voice of India.

———, 1999, *Update on the Āryan Invasion Debate,* Delhi: Aditya Prakashan.

Erdosy, G., ed., 1995, *The Indo-Āryans of Ancient South Asia,* Berlin/NY, Guyter.

Feuerstein, D. Frawley and S. Kak, 1995, *In search of the Cradle of Civilization,* Wheaton/Madras: Quest Books.

Francfort, P.H., 1992, "Evidence for Haṛappan irrigation system," in *Eastern Anthropologist,* vol. 45, pp. 87-103.

Frawley, D., 2002, "Witzel's vanishing ocean . . ." http://voice of dharma.com/indology/Reply to Witzel.html.

———, 1994, *The Myth of the Āryan Invasion,* Delhi: Voice of India (reprint 2000).

———, 1991, *Gods, Sages & Kings,* Salt Lake City: Passage Press.

Frawley, D. & N. Rajaram, 1997, *Vedic Āryans & Origins of Civilization,* Delhi: Voice of India.

Frazer, 1995, *The Gypsies,* Oxford: Blackwell.

Friedrich, H., 2004, "A Diffusionist's view on the concept of 'Language Families' ", *Migration & Diffusion*, vol. 5, no. 19, July-September, pp. 6-14.

Gnoli, G., 1980, *Zoroaster's Time and Homeland*, Naples: Instituto Universitario Orientale, Series & Minores, VII.

Gupta, S.P., 2005, "The Saraswatī and the Homeland of Early Ṛgvedic Ṛṣis" in A. Agrawal, ed., pp. 55-73.

Hock, H.H., 1999, "Out of India? The Linguistic Evidence" in J. Bronkhorst & M. Deshpande (eds.), *Āryan and Non-Āryan in South Asia*, Camb. Mass, HOS, pp. 1-18.

———, 1996, "Pre-Ṛgvedic Convergence' in E.M. Houben, *Ideology and Status of Sanskrit*, Leiden: E.J. Brill.

———, 1991, *Principles of Historical Linguistics* (2nd edn.), Berlin/NY: de Gruyter.

Huld, M.E., 2002, "Linguistic Science, Truth and the Indocentric Hypothesis," *Journal of I-E Studies*, vol. 30, pp. 149-60.

Jarrige, J.F. & R. Meadow, 1980, "Antecedents of Civilization in the Indus Valley," in *Scientific American*, August issue.

Kak, S., 1997, "Archaeoastronomy & Literature," *Current Science*, October issue.

———, 1994, *The Astronomical Code of the Ṛgveda* (rev. edn. 2000), Delhi: Munshiram.

Kazanas, N., 2006a, "Diffusion of I-E Theonyms," in *Quarterly Journal of the Mythic Society* (Bangalore, India) vol. 97, no. 1, pp. 1-29.

———, 2006b, "Ṛgvedic pur," in *Man and Environment*, vol. XXXI (1), pp. 121-25.

———, 2005, "Vedic and Mesopotamian Cross-influences," in *Migration & Diffusion* (Vienna), vol. 24, pp. 96-129.

———, 2004a, "Samudra & Sarasvatī in the *ṚV*," in *QJMS*, vol. 95, pp. 90-104.

———, 2004b, "Sanskrit & Proto-Indo-European," *Indian Linguistics*, vol. 65, pp. 75-100.

———, 2003, "Final Reply," *Journal of I-E Studies*, vol. 31, 1 & 2, pp. 187-240.

———, 2002a, "Indigenous Indo-Āryans & the Ṛgveda," *Journal of I-E Studies*, vol. 30, pp. 275-334.

———, 2002b, "Ṛgvedic pur" in *Brahmavidyā: Adyar Library Bulletin,"* vol. 66, pp. 1-14.

———, 1999, "The Ṛgveda and Indo-Europeans," ABORI, vol. 80, pp. 15-42.

Kenoyer, J. M., 1998, *Ancient Cities of the Indus Valley Civilization,* Karachi/ Oxford: Oxford University Press

Klostermaier, K., 2000, *Hinduism,* Oxford: Oneworld Books.

———, 1998, "Questioning the Āryan Invasion Theory . . ." *Iskcon Communications Journal,* 6: 1 (pp. 5-16). Republished in *International Quarterly of Indian Philosophy,* June 2001, pp. 63-78.

Kochhar, R., 2000, *The Vedic People,* Hyderabad: Orient Longman.

Kuiper, F.B.J., 1991, *Āryans in the Ṛgveda,* Amsterdam Atlanta, Rodopi Publisher.

Kuzmina, E.E., 2002, "Comments on Kazanas," *Journal of I-E Studies,* vol. 30, pp. 161-69.

Lal, B.B., 2005, *The Homeland of the Āryans,* New Delhi: Aryan Books International.

———, 2002, *The Sarasvatī Flows On,* Delhi: Aryan Books International.

———, 1998, *India 1947-1997: New light on the Indus Civilization,* Delhi: Aryan Books International.

———, 1997, *The Earliest Civilization,* Delhi: Aryan Books International.

Lal, B.B. & S.P. Gupta, eds., 1984, *Frontiers of the Indus Civilization,* Delhi: Indian Archaeological Society.

Leach, E., 1990, "Āryan Invasions over four millennia," in E. Ohnuki-Tierney (ed.), *Culture Through Time,* Stanford: Stanford University Press, pp. 227-45.

Levitt, S. H., 2003, "The Dating of the Indian Tradition," *Anthropos,* vol. 98, pp. 341-59.

Lockwood, W.B., 1969, *Indo-European Philology,* London: Hutchinson University Press.

Lubotsky, A., 1997, *A Ṛgvedic Word Concordance,* New Haven: American Oriental Society.

Mallory, J., 1997, "The Homeland of the Indo-Europeans," in R. Bleach and M. Sprigg (eds.), *Archaeology & Language,* London/NY, Routledge, vol. 1, pp. 93-121.

MacDonnell, A. & A. Keith, 1995, *Vedic Index* (1912), Delhi: Motilal Banarsidass.

———, 1989, *In Search of the Indo-Europeans,* London: Thames & Hudson.

Mayrhofer, M., 1996, *Etymologisches Wörterbuches des Altindischen,* Heidelberg: Carl Winter.

———, 1956, *KEWA (Kurtzgefasstes...),* Heidelberg: Carl Winter.

McEvilley, Th., 2002, *The Shape of Ancient Thought,* New York: Allworth Press.

McIntosh, J.R., 2001, *A Peaceful Realm,* Boulder (Colorado): Westview.

Misra, S.S., 1992, *The Āryan Problem: A Linguistic Approach,* Delhi: Munshiram Manoharlal.

Mitchel, B. & F. Robinson, 1996, *A Guide to Old English,* Oxford: Blackwell.

Nichols, J., 1997-98, "The Epicentre of the I-E Linguistic Spread" and "The Eurasian Spread Zone . . ." in R. Blench & M. Spriggs (eds.) *Archaeology & Language,* NY/London: Routledge, vol. 1, pp. 122-48 & vol. 2, pp. 220-66.

Oppenheimer, S., 2003, *The Real Eve: Modern Man's Journey Out of Africa,* NY: Carroll & Graf.

Pande, G.C. (ed.), 1999, *The Dawn of Indian Civilization up to 600* BCE, New Delhi: PHISPC, Centre for Studies in Civilization.

Parpola, A. et al. 1969, *Decipherment of Proto-Dravidian Inscriptions . . .* Copenhagen: Scandinavian Institute of Asian Studies.

———, 1988, *The Coming of the Āryans to Iran and India,* Helsinki: Studia Orientalia.

Piggott, S., 1992, *Wagon, Chariot and Carriage,* London: Thames & Hudson.

———, 1983, *The Earliest Wheeled Transport,* London: Thames & Hudson.

Possehl, G.L., 2003, *The Indus Civilization,* New Delhi, Vistaar Publication.

———, 1998, "Did the Sarasvatī ever flow to the Sea?" in G.S. Phillips et al. (eds.), *Arabia & its Neighbours* (in *Honour of Beatrice de Cardi*), Turnhout: Brepols, pp. 339-54.

Rajaram, N., 2005, "Connections between Haṛappan Seals and the Vedic Literature" in Agrawal, A., 2005, pp. 135-41.

Rao, L.S., 2006, "The Haṛappan spokedwheels . . ." in *Purātattva,* vol. 36, pp. 59-67.

Rao, R., 1980, "Puzzles for the Philologists," *Theosophist*, 1, pp. 305-08.

———, 1973, *Lothal & the Indus Civilization*, Bombay: Asia Publications.

Rao, S.R., 1991, *Dawn & Devolution of the Indus Civilization*, Delhi: Aditya Prakashan.

Renfrew, C., 1989, *Archaeology & Language*, Hammondsworth: Penguin.

Rix, H., 1998, *Lexicon der indogermanischen verben . . .*, Wiesbaden: Reichert.

Rudgley, R., 1998, *Lost Civilizations of the Stone Age*, London: Century.

Sahoo, S., Singh, A., Kivisild, T . . . et al. 2006, "A Prehistory of Indian Y-chromosomes," *Proceedings of the National Academy of Sciences*, (USA), vol. 103, no. 4, pp. 843-48.

Sankalia, H.D., 1974, *Prehistory & Protohistory of India & Pakistan*, Poona: Deccan College.

Schildmann, K., 1998, *Indus/ Burrows Cave USA — Deciphering*, Bonn: Studia Orientalia et Indo-Attentica, Fascicle 1.

Sergent, B., 1997, *La Genése de l' Inde*, Paris: Payot & Rivages.

Sethna, D.K., 1992, *The Problem of Āryan Origins*, 2nd edn., Delhi: Aditya Prakashan.

Shaffer, J.G., 1984, "The Indo-Āryan Invasions: Cultural Myth and Archaeological Reality" in J.R. Lucaks, (ed.), *The People of South Asia: the Biological Anthropology of India, Pakistan & Nepal*, New York: Phenum.

Shaffer, J.G. & D.A. Lichtenstein, 1999, "Migration, philology & South Asian archaeology," in J. Bronktorst & M. Deshpande (eds.), *Āryans and Non-Āryan in South Asia*, Cambridge, Mass: HOS.

Sharma, G.R., 1980, *History to Protohistory: Archaeology of the Vindhyas and the Ganga Valley*, Allahabad: Allahabad University.

Sharma, J.R., A.K. Gupta and B.K. Bhadra, 2006, "Course of Vedic river Sarasvatī . . ." in *Purātattva*, vol. 36, pp. 187-95.

Sharma, R.S., 1999, *Advent of the Āryans in India*, New Delhi: Orient Longman.

———, 1996, *Looking for the Āryans*, Hyderabad: Orient Longman.

Singh, Bh., 1995, *The Vedic Haṛappans*, Delhi: Aditya Prakashan.

Swadesh, M., 1955, "Towards greater accuracy in lexico statistical dating," *International Journal of American Linguists*, vol. 21, pp. 121-37.

———, 1953, "Archaeological and Linguistic Chronology . . .," *American Anthropologist*, vol. 55, pp. 349-52.

Talageri, S., 2000, *The Ṛgveda*, New Delhi: Aditya Prakashan.

Tewari, R., R.K. Srivastava, K.K. Singh and K.S. Saraswat, 2006, "Further Excavations at Lahuradeva, District Sant Kabir Nagar. . . .," *Purātattva*, vol. 36, pp. 68-75.

Thapar, B. & R. Mungal, 1994, "The Indus Valley (3000-1500 BCE) in A. Dani & J.P. Mohen (eds.), *History of Humanity*, vol. 2, London/Unesco, Routledge, pp. 246-65.

Thapar, R., 1999, *The Āryan Question Revisited*. <http://members.tripod.com/ascjnu/aryan.html>.

Thomas, P. et al. 1995, "Haṛappan Subsistence Patterns . . ." *Man & Environment* (India), vol. 20, 2, pp. 33-41.

Watkins, C., 2001 (1995), *How to Kill a Dragon: Aspects of I-E Poetics*, Oxford: Oxford University Press.

Winternitz, M., 1981, *History of Indian Literature* (tr. V.S. Sarma), 3 vols., Delhi: Motilal Banarsidass.

Witzel, M., 2005, "Central Asian Roots and Acculturation in South Asia," in *Linguistics, Archaeology and the Human Past*, ed. Osada Tosiki, Indus Project, Research Institute for Humanity and Nature, Kyoto.

———, 2003, "Ein Fremdling in Ṛgveda," *JIES*, vol. 31.

———, 2001, "Autochthonous Āryans," *Electronic Journal of Vedic Studies*, pp. 7-3, 1-93.

———, 1995, "Early Indian History" and "Ṛgvedic History" in G. Erdosy (ed).

2

About the Charms of Atharvaveda

Tatiana Elizarenkova

Introduction

As it is well known, *Atharvaveda* (*AV*) is the most ancient collection of old Indian charms which took form approximately in the beginning of first millennium BC. It is a large text, very heterogeneous (the Śaunaka recension which is regarded as a vulgate consists of 20 books, *kāṇḍa*s, including, 374 hymns or 6000 verses, but also prosaic parts). Various parts of this collection were created at different times; most ancient is the Śaunaka recensions or the first seven books, which consist mainly of charms and spells, and also some speculative hymns). The analysis of this paper is based just on the material of this Saṁhitā.

Charms and spells of the *AV* have reached us in a brāhminized form — Brahmins are not only editors, but sometimes authors too. At the same time, there are some charms which have rather close parallels in other ancient Indo-European traditions, and therefore can be attributed to the common Indo-European epoch.

AV, in its content, is the most independent of the Vedas (Veda — "sacred knowledge"). There are four Vedas and *Ṛgveda* (*ṚV*, Veda of the hymns) is the oldest among them (middle of the second millennium BCE). It is addressed to the gods, being a classic example of elevated religious poetry. *Sāmaveda* (Veda of melodies) and *Yajurveda* (Veda of sacrificial formulae) completely depend on the *ṚV* each in its manner. This cannot be said about the *AV* which in its ancient basis is opposed to the *ṚV*. Charms and spells of the *AV* have no aim to eulogize the heroic deeds of the gods. Mythological plots are not worked out in these texts. The gods are often mentioned in groups, the functions of one god can be ascribed to another — in short, the gods were needed as an instrument to frighten the demons so that the conjurer could manipulate with their help. The most archaic core of the *AV* is based on magic folk's rites, and it is just in this sense that this Saṁhitā is the most popular of all Vedas.

Magic Rites and Religion

Mutual relation between magic and religion were usually rather complicated in ancient cultures. A part of magic rites was included into religious practice (charms for strengthening the king's power, for gaining victory over an enemy, for getting a good harvest, etc.). Another part was reduced to the state of prohibited sorcery (such as bewitching, spoiling, etc.). Just for this reason the *AV* was not included among the Vedas even once. There existed from the beginning threefold knowledge — *trayī vidyā*, that is three variants of the same sacred knowledge.

The *AV* remained beyond, and the word Veda did more a part of its name. It was *Atharva* or *Atharvāṅgiras*, according to the names of two mythical tribes. White magic was connected with the *Atharvans*, the fire priests, and black magic with the *Aṅgiras*es, the half-divine *ṛṣis*. Connection between pure religion and magic is a well-known problem discussed by the scientists. Both religion and magic agree that human existence is conditioned by supernatural powers (Schayer, 1925). The difference lies in the fact how this conditioning is interpreted. Religion means dependence on the divine will, while magic tries to govern these supernatural powers by means of magical techniques.

AV as a Different Veda

The ritual background of the *AV* is also different from that of other Vedas. The *ṚV, SV* and *YV* are connected with the high Śrauta-ritual which is concentrated on the *soma*-sacrifice. As to the *AV*, these were *gṛhya*-rituals (home-rituals), simple rites connected with the domestic sacrificial fire. There existed correspondingly the opposition of kinds of priests, who took part in these rituals. It is the Hotar in the *ṚV*, who performs sacrificial oblations, Udgātṛ in the *SV*, who sings the melodies and the Adhvaryu in the *YV*, who did everything that was necessary with his hands. As in the *AV*, it was the domestic priest of the king, i.e. *purohita*, and connoisseur of charms — Brahman.

It is evident that the *AV* is opposed to the remaining three Vedas on all levels. But the matter is that there are numerous borrowings in the text of the *AV* from the *ṚV*. Verses and parts of verses are borrowed literally or with variants, those of the *AV* being usually distorted, which is clear from the violation of sense and metrical schemes. At last, hymns as a whole, can also be borrowed — they function as charms, and are connected in the ancillary literature — *Kauśika-* and *Vaitāna-Sūtra*s, with various magic rituals.

Now, there arises a general question in connection with the described situation. What is so fascinating about *AV* that makes it a hymn? To answer this question one should see what differences of structure, style and contents between a hymn and a charm are. First, attention should be drawn to the names by which a hymn and a spell are called in Vedic.

Hymn as Explained in ṚV

Hymn in the *ṚV* is called *ṛc* (feminine) and *sūkta* (neuter). the substantive *ṛc* (from the verb *arc* to shine, to glorify) has the following meanings according to Böhtlingk's dictionary. 1. Glanz; 2. heiliges Lied-vers; insbes. in Unterschied vom gesungenen (*Sāman* and von der Opferformel, *yajus*); 3. der Vers, so der Text, auf welchem eine Handlung beruht oder auf welchen uine Erklärung sch beruht; 4. die Sammlung der *ṛc*, der *Ṛgveda*, gewöhnlich Tl. (Böhtlingk 1, p. 261). This definition stresses the opposition *ṛc-sāman-yajus-*, but it has no relation to the concept of charms. The substantive *sūkta* is a compound word: *su-ukta* "well said," (from *vac-* "to say, speak"), which means according to Böhtlingk: 1. eine schöne Recitation; 2. ein guter Spruch, ein schönes-gutes Wort; 3. bei den Commentatoren das vedische Lied, Hymne (Böhtlingk, 7, p. 175). This name is not connected with the meaning "charm" either.

The meaning "spell" is expressed by the words *Brahman*(*n.*). *mantra*(m). Böhtlingk gives such a definition of their meanings. The substantive Brahman — 1. die aus Drang und Fülle des Gemüths auftretende und den Gottern zustrebende Andacht, über.jede fromme Aeusserung beim Gottesdienst, 2. ein helizer Spruch, namentlich Zauberspruch, 3. das heilige Wort, Gotteswort, der Veda etc. (Böhtlingk, X, 4, 236-37). The substantive *mantra* is explained as 1. Spruch Gebet, Lied alps Erzeugnis des Geistes; 2. ein vedisches Lied, ein heliger Spruch; 3. magische Besprechung, Zauberspruch, 4. Verabredung, Berathung, Entschliessung; Rat, Plan, geheimer Plan. . . ."/(Böhtlingk, 5, 25). This way, there is no special word in the Vedic language which would express "charm" specially in contrast to "prayer" and "hymn." The meaning "charm" is regarded as a development of the meaning "hymn." The conclusion that follows is that a hymn can function as a charm, but not vice versa; a charm cannot function as a hymn.

Some time ago "average models" of a laudatory hymn of the *R̥V* and that of the charm of the *AV* were suggested.

Hymns for Various Usages

The laudatory hymn (and they were the majority of hymns in this monument) can be found as consisting of the two parts: an "explicative" description and an appellative part, that calls and appeals to the gods (Elizarenkova, 1968, pp. 255-68).

The explicative part is made by the hierarchy of oppositions of distinctive features of different levels, characteristic actions of the deity; his constant epithets; his attributes — that is objects and qualities that belong to this deity; his external connections.

Constant switching over of the levels and changing of codes take place in the model of a laudatory hymn.

For instance, the explicative part of laudatory hymns to Indra consists of following oppositions of distinctive features. The actions are: Indra killed Vr̥tra, set the rivers free, killed the demons, generated the sun, the sky, the morning dawn; let the cows free from the *Vala* cave, he drinks *soma,* etc. The epithets are: murderer of Vr̥tra, victorious, manly, master of cows, generous, etc. The attributes are: the thunderbolt *vajra, soma,* the chariot, etc. and his external connection are first of all the Maruts. The appellative part: kill Vr̥tra, kill the demons drink *soma,* give victory, give riches! The switching of levels is evident: Indra kills Vr̥tra — murderer of Vr̥tra — kill Vr̥tra.

Now the average model of charm of the *AV* follows the contents of the charm which can be described as transition from the initial state to the desired one carried out by the conjurer with the help of magic procedure (Gerasimov, 1964, pp. 95-104).

Expressing the Hymn's Desired State

The desired state is always expressed. There are various requests: to get longevity, good health, riches, love of a women or a man, etc. to drive away illness, sorcery; to make free from sin, from bad omens; to kill ones enemies and so on. The initial state is expressed not always, in some cases one can guess it from the contents of the requests.

It is advisable to describe the desired state comparing it with the initial one. Three types of relation are possible here (Elizarenkova, 1976, 24 following).

The first type: the desired state is opposed to the initial one (e.g., spell for the rain, for driving away the diseases, etc.)

The second type: the desired state is equal to the initial one (e.g. for preserving king's power).

The third type: the desired state contains a greater degree of some quality (e.g., for longevity lasting a hundreds of autumns).

Each charm has a subject. It is not obligatory that the conjurer who pronounces the charm and who therefore always exists would be the subject of the desired state. In this case he pronounces the charm on behalf of the client (*yajamāna*). The subject of the desired state cannot coincide with that of the initial (if it is an enemy or a rival).

The magical procedure is an important element of the charm. It is obligatory and can be accompanied by magical actions: real or symbolic.

Some peculiarities of the recitation of a charm are explained by the belief that the word possesses magical power. For instance, an enemy should be called by his name and it should be said that the conjurer knows everything about his kinship and origin. It was supposed that this would give more power over him. For instance, the verse of charm against the disease called *jāyānya* — VII, 81, 1: "We know, indeed, O *jāyānya*, our origin, whence, O *jāyānya*, you are born: how should you slay us, in whose house should we perform oblation?"[1]

It was believed that the pronunciation of truth had also magical power, e.g. VII, 117, 1: "Beautiful are heaven and earth, pleasant nearby of great vows; seven divine waters have flown; let them free us from distress."

The desirable state is often depicted as if it was already acquired. The motivation of it is magical: it was enough to pronounce aloud: "I did it," that the act was really done, e.g. in the charm IV, 18 against sorcery with an amulet made of grass we find in verse 5:1, I with this herb "have spoilt all witchcraft" while in verse 7 the conjurer asks the herb again to wipe out the disease, the curse, the witches.

The magical power of word is also revealed in such a method used in the charms as enumerations. When a disease is driven away, all the parts of the body where it had its seat are enumerated in strict sequence (e.g. *yakṣma* in II, 33), and if it is sorcery, all the places, where it has been created are named (V, 31).

Role of a Mediator

Often a mediator is used in the magical procedure carried out by the conjurer, and then it is him who plays the part of the

1. Usually W.D. Whitney's translations are used and expressed in modern English.

subject and causes the transition from the initial state to the desirable one. Mediators can be objects with which direct contact is possible — various amulets (herbs, plants, leads, pearls, etc.) and also gods and powers of nature.

If it is a charm with a mediator, it is just him who is lauded, his mythological past is mentioned, and his relatives are called by their names. The conjurer appeals with his request to the mediator, and his qualities that can help to attain the transition to the desired state are eulogized. For instance, the charm V, 4 addressed to the *kuṣṭha*-plant against the *takman*-fever begins with the following verse: "You that were born on the mountains, strongest of plants, come, O *kuṣṭha*, effacer of *takman*, effacing the fever from here."

The first verse of the I, 2 against damage and disease, where the reed is mediator is addressed to the reed: "We know the reed's father, Parjanya the much-nourishing; and we know well its mother, the earth of many aspects."

If the charm is directed against enemies, the conjurer (himself or with the help of the mediator) tries to turn the actions of the enemy against the enemy himself, the curse against the one who curses, sorcery against the sorcerers, poison against the snake, etc.

This is the description of the structure of the charm of the *AV* in general outline. A laudatory hymn of the *R̥V* and charm of the *AV* are clearly opposed to each other in their stylistic peculiarities. A lot has been written about the style of the laudatory hymn of the *R̥V*, beginning with the "anagrams" of de Saussure (Starobinsci, 1971).

In my short characteristic of this subject I am basing on my book *Language and Style of the Vedic R̥ṣis* (Albany, 1995). Much less is written about the style of the *AV* — here first of all the works of J. Gonda should be mentioned (Gonda, 1938, 1939, 1959, etc.).

The aim of the laudatory hymn of the *R̥V* is to establish communication with the god, from whom they are awaiting various gifts, and to reach this aim the hymn should be built according to the truth as it was many times expressed in the *R̥V*. That is its structure should be of such a kind that the deity would be forced "to hear" the poet. The most important means for it is the pronunciation of the eulogized gods name. As it was shown by de Saussure, the hymns are built according to the principle of anagrams (R.O. Jakabson calls it "expressive grammar"), when each verse or each *pāda* begins with some case-form of this name, that is it occupies a metrically strong position. All the hymn sounds in the musical key of the god's name which rings in the echo-words. De Saussure illustrated it by the first hymn of the *R̥V* dedicated to *agni*. It is a typical trait of the R̥gvedic style, and one can give many examples of this kind. Such, for instance, is the hymn to Bhaga (and other gods) VII, 41. The laudation of Bhaga begins in verse 3:

> *bhaga praṇetar bhaga satyarādho,*
> *bhagemām dheyam ud avā dadan naḥ;*
> *bhaga pra ṇo janya gobhir aśvair,*
> *bhaga pra nr̥bkir nr̥vantaḥ syāma.*

This shown by a formal play, hinting at this gods name: *bhagam bhakṣi* "I want to participate in Bhaga!" The next verses go on with this play and the whole hymn echoes the name of Bhaga: verse 4: *bhaga . . . bhagvān . . . ! bhagvantaḥ syāma! bhaga . . . bhava*, etc.

Ambiguous use of Words and Phrases

Hymns of the *R̥V* are characterized by a suggestive style, for which ambiguous reference of words and phraseological combinations is typical, e.g. *samudra* "confluence of waters," "the sea on the earth," "the sea vessel"; or *amṛtasya nābhiḥ* lit. "naval of immortality — 1. the alter, 2. the centre of the sky, 3. the drink of *soma*. The plion with the denotatay is going on all the time, and the choice of the meaning of the word or of a combination of words can sometimes be determined by the reference of fragment of a hymn or a whole hymn.

The words are polysemantic and have often symbolic meanings, e.g. *adri* — "rock," "mountain"and at the same time "missile," "a stone for pressing *soma*," but also "a storm-cloud" (the semantic motivation being the *Vala*-myth — see Grassmann, 1955, pp. 39-40). A certain part of the vocabulary is ambivalent, and the choice of the meaning of word depends on its appurtenance to the "favourable" or "unfavourable" sphere (Renou, 1939, pp. 161-235), e.g. *aprati* "meeting no resistance/a god) — putting up resistance" (an enemy or demon).

A considerable part of the vocabulary (both nouns and verbs) has conversive meanings. The difference of meaning depends on the fact whether the word is connected with the god or with the worshipper (Elizarenkova, 1995), e.g. *bhaj* "to provide" (the subject being a god), "to partake of" (the subject being a worshipper); *dhī* "attention" (of the god) "poetic language," "prayer"(of the worshipper).

In syntax these are first of all the very frequently used chains of adjectival epithets or substantives to the name of god, with an unclear predictivity. For instance, the characteristics of the deified horse Dadhikravan in IV, 40, 5:

haṁsaḥ śuciṣad vasur antarikṣasad,
dhotā vediṣad atithir duroṇasat;
nṛṣad varasad ṛtasad vyomasad,
abja gojā ṛtaja adṛjia ṛtam.

A swan, being in the bright sky,
a Vasu, being in air,
a *hotar*, being on the altar,
a guest being in the house,
(a god) being among men, on a best (place),
being in the cosmic order
being on the firmament,
born from the water
born from the cow,
born from cosmic order from the rock
— the cosmic order.

At last, semantization of form of the hymn conditioned by its contents is also typical of the Ṛgvedic style. The last hymn of the *Ṛgveda Saṁhitā*, calling the Aryans to unite (*sam* "together") and to achieve conformity of ideas (man "to think"), is based on that principle X,191, 3:

samāno mantraḥ samitiḥ samanī,
samānam manaḥ saha cittam eṣām,
samānam mantram abhī mantraye vaḥ,
samānena vo haviṣā juhomi.
A single counsel,
a single assembly,
a single thought and mind have they,
a single advice I advise to you;
With a single libation do I sacrifice to you"

These are the main characteristics of style of the laudatory hymns of the *ṚV*.

The language of the *AV* is less archaic than that of the *ṚV* (Renou, 1956: 32), but more important than that is the difference in style. The style of the *AV* is so to say socially conditioned; the charms are intended for other strata of society, than the hymns of the *ṚV*. The suggestive style of the Ṛgvedic hymns is alien to the charms of the *AV*.

The most important differences concern the vocabulary and phraseology. The charms of the *AV* are not characterized by such a developed lexical polysemy and symbolic use of words, as it is in the *ṚV*. The vocabulary whose denotata belong to the sphere of things in the *AV* is much simpler and richer, than in the *ṚV*. This concerns first of all the words which designate things and notion of everyday life; the man, parts of his body, various animals, insects, snakes, plants, herbs, names of domestic utensils, parts of a hut, etc. It is for the first time in old Indian science that special terminology is met in such fields of knowledge as medicine, botany, astronomy that one finds in the *AV*.

Many new words are testified in the *AV* as compared with the *ṚV*, for instance, *astra* "weapon," *kapāla* "skull," *deśa* "region," *puccha* "tail," *puṣpa* "flower," *śilā* "stone," *suṣ* "to dry," *sūtra* "thread." (Renou, 1956: 33-34). According to Renou, this speaks for the new requirements, and does not mean that these words were not known in the time of the *ṚV*.

Repetitions are very frequent in the *AV* on all levels, but they function in different ways than in the *ṚV*. In certain cases isomorphic syntactic structures are repeated, and a whole charm is based on them, e.g. III, 27, 1: "Eastern quarter; Agni overlord; black serpent defender; the Ādityas arrows, homage to those overlords."

III, 27, 2: "Southern quarter; Indra overlord; cross lined [serpent] defender; the fathers arrows; homage to those"; etc.

All the six verses of this charm have such a structure. The ritual application of it (as well as of the preceding charm which has the same structure) is to gain victory over the enemy in the battle, to kill snakes and scorpions, to worship the quarters. A whole group of charms in the *AV* has a similar structure based on repetitions (beside III, 26 and 27, also II, 24; II, 33; IV,

39 and 40; V, 10; V, 15 and 16; V, 24, etc.). There are also a numerical charm with an amulet of herb. This is its first verse: "Both one of me and ten of me [are] the exorcisers, O herb; you born of right, you rich in right, may you, honeyed, make honey for me" (an appeal to the herb). In the next eleven verses the number in *pāda* increases according to the natural numerical series. Verse 2 runs: "Both two of me and twenty of me . . ." and so up to the last verse: "Both a hundred of me and thousand. . . ." The last remaining *pāda*s are common refrain. Its ritual application prescribed by the *Kauśika-Sūtra* is the medical treatment of cattle. The next charm V, 16 is also numerical. Phraseological combinations and separate words can also be repeated in charms. Typical of it is the repetition of a "magical word," because it was believed that pronunciation and repetition of it might help the attainment of the desired state. The "magical word" in a bewitching charm with sweet herb I, 34 is honey (*madhu*), for example, verse 4:

madhor asmi madhutaro
madhughan madhumattaraḥ,
mām it kila tvaṃ vanāḥ;
śākhāṃ madhumatīm iva.

Then honey am I sweeter,
than the honey-plant more honeyed;
of me verily shall you be fond,
as of honeyed branch.

The hostile power is usually sent back in the *AV* to the person who had sent it. This formula represented by some variants is typical of the charms, e.g. in a charm against a snake's poison — *V*, 13, 4 . . . *ahe mriyasva mā jīvīḥ, pratyag abhyatu tvā viṣam.* ". . . die, O snake, do not live; let your poison go back against you," in a charm against witchcraft with a plant — V, 14, 4: "Lead you away the witchcraft back to the witchcraft-maker, grasping his hand; set it straight before him, that it may smite the witchcraft-maker"; against the Kimidins — II, 24, 1: "O *śerabhaśca, śerabha* . . . whose you are, him eat you; who has sent you forth, him eat you . . ."

Usage of Pronouns in AV

The structure of charms of the *AV* is reflected in the usage of pronouns in these charms. It is often a conscious play with the pronouns which creates uncertainty (Elizarenkova, 2004, pp. 155-65), e.g. the charm against Nirṛti-Perdition — VI, 63, 2 "Homage be to you, O Nirṛti, you of keen keenness. Unfasten the bond-fetters of iron, Yama verily gives you back to me; to that Yama, to death be homage." "You" in the first half-verse refers to Nirṛti, while in second half-verse to the person on whose behalf the spell is uttered (noticed by Lanman).

There exists in the charms of the *AV* the opposition of reference between the demonstrative pronouns of the close and distant plan: *ayam* "this one (which is here)" and *asau* is usually referred to an enemy, who is mentioned for the first time, e.g. in a charm for victory, addressed to a war drum — VI, 126, 3: *prāmūm jayābhīme jayantu* (after the emendation *amūn* for *amūṃ*) the translation is: "Conquer you those yonder; let these here conquer (themselves)."

One more peculiarity in the usage of pronouns in the charms should be mentioned. In love charms the man or the woman who is to be bewitched are referred to by the demonstrative pronoun of a distant plan, e.g. in the refrain in the charm VI, 130, 1-4: *asau mām anu śocatu* . . . Let that [man] burn for me."

Attention should also be drawn to such a peculiarity in the usage of grammatical tense of the verb: present and past, in contradiction to reality, that is to the moment of speech. This syntactical peculiarity reflects the semantic structure of the charm, when the conjurer claims the desired state to be real (see above), e.g. verse 2 in the charm against enemies III, 2 runs as follows: Agni here has confounded the intents that are in your heart "(*amūmahat- aor* of *muh-*). And in the next verse 3 Indra is asked to do it, as if nothing had been done already: "O Indra! Confounding [their] intents, move hitherward with [their] design" (part *pr.caus.* of *muh-*).

Negative personages that are most dangerous such as Death, Perdition (*nirṛti*), sometimes also venomous snakes are driven away by means of laudations, which can be alternated with the formulae of banishment, e.g. the charm against death VI, 13 looks like laudation and worship. Verse 2: "Homage to your benediction; homage to your malediction; homage to your favour, O death; this homage to your disfavour."

Worship of Snakes

Another variant is found in the charm against snakes VI, 56, where verse 2 expresses the worship of snakes: "Homage be to the Black [snake], homage to the crosslined, . . . homage to the divine people." But the tone of the conjurer changes completely in the next verse 3: "I smile your teeth together with tooth, your (two) jaws together with jaw, your tongue together with tongue, your mouth, O snake, together with mouth."

At last, the style of the charms of the *AV* is characterized by parallelism between the spheres of nature and that of man — this trait that is typical not only of charms, but of other genres of folklore as well. It is believed that phenomena of nature influence human life and govern it. It can be two parallel pictures as, for instance, in a spell against the *kṣetrīya* disease — II, 8, 1: "Arison are the (two) blessed stars called the unfasteners; let them unfasten of the *kṣetrīya* the lowest, the highest fetter." Even more often this parallelism has the, first verse of the bewitching charm in the form of comparisons, e.g. VII, 30, 1: "As the wind here shakes the gross of the earth, so do I shake your mind that you may be the one loving me, that you may be the one not going away from me." These are in short the peculiarities of style of the *AV*.

Conclusion

It is clear from the above-said that the difference between a hymn of the *ṚV* and charm of the *AV* in their aims; structure, contents and style are great. However, there are a number of hymns in *AV* addressed to the gods which have no features of a classical laudatory hymn. Besides, there are hymns addressed not to god/gods, but to various elements of nature: to the waters, to the earth, to healing herbs. They do not possess the structure of a charm, but are treated by the *Kauśika-Sūtra* as such, and a magical ritual application is also prescribed to them. In short, there are many hymns of indistinct structure, functioning as charms.

Now it is time to come back to the question that was put in the beginning. What makes a text in the *AV* a charm: its contents, structure, style or ritual application?

1. If a text has the structure of an average charm (especially if it is addressed to a mediator), it is always a charm, and cannot be a hymn.
2. If the addressee of a text is deity, but the text itself is not characterized by the structural distinctive features of laudatory hymn, while stylistic peculiarities of charm exist, it is charm, e.g. III, 26 "Homage to the gods of quarters" is a prosaic text addressed to the gods and consisting of 6 isomorphic verses."

(i) "You gods that are in this eastern quarter, missiles by name — of you there, the arrows are fire, do you be gracious to us."

(ii) "You gods that are in this southern quarter, impetuous by name — of there the arrows are love."

3. If the text has the structure of laudatory hymn, but it is connected by the *Kauśika-* and *Vaitāna-Sūtra* with a certain magical practice, this is only a functional charm. The hymn to Bhaga (VII, 41 that was already mentioned) can serve an example of it. It has the classical structure of laudatory hymn, but the *Kauśika-Sūtra* connects it with the ritual for generating wisdom; when a person awakes and washes his face; in a number of rituals for acquiring splendour. Such a "charm" can be regarded only as a functional one.

As to the testimony of ancillary ritual literature, it is far from being always persuasive. A part of the text is not at all commented, e.g. the *paryāya-sūkta*s of books XV and XVI, the speculative hymns (e.g. to X, 2 and XV, 8) the hymns that were included in *AV* only at late time. Sometimes the *sūtra*s prescribe such a ritual application that seems to have nothing to do with the contents of the text (e.g. VI, 33; VI, 80). It should be said, drawing the conclusion, that one has to discern to a greater or lesser degree of certainty the proper texts functioning as charms.

Bibliography

Atharvaveda anthology translation, commentary and introduction by T.Y., Elizarenkova (in Russian).

Böhtlingk, O., Sanskrit, *Worterbuch in Kürzerer Fassung*, 1-7, Theil, St. Petersburg, 1879-89.

Elizarenkova, T.Y., *An approach to the description of the contents of the Ṛgveda-Mélanges d indianisme a la mémorie de Louis Renou*, Paris, 1968, pp. 255-68.

———, *Languagè and Style of the Vedic Ṛṣis*, Albony, 1995.

———, "On the function of pronoun in some old Indian texts," *Bulletin of the Deccan College Post-Graduate and Research Institute, Professor Ashok R. Kelkar, Felicitation Volume*, vols. 62-63 (2002 and 2003), Pune, 2004, pp. 155-65.

(Gerasimov, A. V., an attempt of an analysist of contents of hymns of the Atharvaveda — in "*India v drevnosti*," 1964, pp. 95-104 in Russian).

Gonda, J., *Stilistische studie over Atharvaveda I-VII*, Wageningen, 1938 in Russian.

———, "alliteration und Reim im Satzbau des Athavaveda," *Acta Orientalia*, 18, Leiden, 1939.

———, *Stylistic Repetition in Veda*, Amsterdem, 1959.

Grassmann, H., *Wörterbuch zum Rig-Veda*, 3, A., Wiesbaden, 1955 (1. Aufl., 1872).

Renou, L., "L ambiguité du vocabulaire du Ṛgveda," *Ja.*, 231, 1939, pp. 161-235.

———, *Histoire de la langue sansrite*, Layon-Paris, 1956.

Schayer, S., *Die Structure der magischen Weltanschauung nauh dem Atharva-Veda und den Brāhmaṇa-Texten*, München-Neubiberg, 1925.

Starobinski, J., *Les mot sous les mots*. Paris, 1971.

Whiteny, W.D., *Atharvaveda Saṁhitā*, trans. into English, with critical and exegetical commentary by W.D. Whitney. Revised and edited by Ch. R. Lanman, vol. I, II, Delhi, 1996 (1st edn. 1905).

3

Schools of Vedic Interpretation

G.U. Thite

Meaning of Veda

DUE to the antiquity of Vedic literature and due to many archaisms in the language and style, the difficulty in understanding the meaning of the Veda was recognized at a very early date. Naturally attempts were also made towards the understanding of the Veda. Collection and edition of the scattered *mantras* (*saṁhitīkaraṇa*) can be considered a very primary attempt towards the interpretation of the *Ṛgveda*. The hymns are classified and arranged on the basis of their authorship (*ṛṣi*) and their subject matter (*devatā*). These two principles form an important role in the process of *saṁhitīkaraṇa*. *Padapāṭha,* i.e. analysis of the words on the basis of dissolution of *sandhi*s is also an important next step towards the interpretation of *Ṛgveda* and other Saṁhitās. Unless one understands the meaning and form of *avasāya,* one will not be able to split the word. Thus if the word is a gerund of *ava-so* there will be an *avagraha* in-between *ava* and *sāya*. But if it is a dative singular of the word *avasa,* there will be no *avagraha* in the *padapāṭha*. Thus the author of *padapāṭha* also must have tried to understand the meaning of the Veda at least to a certain extent. The Brāhmaṇa-texts also try to interpret some formulae which they prescribe to be used in ritual with intention to justify their use. This can be called ritualistic (*yājñika*) type of explanation. The Vedāṅgas, particularly *Nirukta* and Vyākaraṇa (*Aṣṭādhyāyī* of Pāṇini) are directly or indirectly connected with the interpretation of the Veda.

Nirukta and Veda

In *Nirukta* there is an important discussion on the "meaningfulness" of the Veda. While Kautsa was of the opinion that the *mantras* are meaningless, Yāska, the author of the *Nirukta* strongly opposed this view. It, however, seems that Kautsa has not been properly understood by Yāska as well as by the students of *Nirukta*. Yāska ridicules Kautsa by saying that it is not the fault of a post if a blind man does not see it. This ridicule is also not correct. For Kautsa does not mean that the *mantras* are literally "meaningless" as would appear from his expression *anarthakāḥ*. What he means is that not the *mantras*, but the "meanings" of the *mantras* are meaningless. Thus when Kautsa argues that there are some contradictions in the meanings of the *mantras* or when he points out that there are some verses which are difficult to understand, he accepts that there is some meaning of the *mantras*. The meaning however is not worth understanding and therefore the view of Yāska that one should try to understand the meaning of Veda with the help of *Nirukta* methodology does not deserve any serious attention. In the course of history, Kautsa's view seems to have been successful, for the priests used to study the *mantras* by heart without ever paying attention to the meaning of the Veda. Kautsa thus appears to be the "Ur-priest."

Yāska has mentioned some schools of Vedic interpretations: the most important among them are the Nairuktas and the Aitihāsikas. While the Nairuktas are more interested in the etymologies, the Aitihāsikas consider everything mentioned in the *Ṛgveda* to be real. Thus according to the Nairuktas, Vṛtra stands for a cloud because the word is connected with the root√*vṛ* to cover and a cloud covers the sun, etc. The Aitihāsikas considered Vṛtra to be son of Tvaṣṭṛ and thus a demon. According to the Aitihāsikas, the proper names refer to the real personalities. Thus it seems that they do not make any difference between the imaginary characters and the real ones. In other words for them the stories and history are not different from each other. The *Nirukta* is mainly interested in the etymologies of the words and therefore it has given the principles of etymology. The most important principles among them are as follows:

(i) One should never say no to give an etymology.

(ii) One should try to give an etymology remaining firm to the meaning.

(iii) One need not pay attention to the rules of formation and the accent.

In the very early stage of the science these principles are indeed very helpful. But they are rather too simplistic and not very scientific at the advanced level. It is possible to have some preconceived notion first and then a root suitable to that meaning may be found out. The etymologies based on these principles may at times lead to any desirable meanings and these would not remain trustworthy. Yāska himself has said that one should give prominence to the meaning and the grammatical rules may be neglected. This has given rise to fanciful etymologies. Thus for example it is obvious that the word *ṛṣi* contains the root √*ṛṣ*. So the meaning of word *ṛṣi* is "leader" because the root √*ṛṣ* means to go forward. But because Yāska has assumed the meaning "seer" of this word, he artificially connects it with the root √*dṛś*. This is a result of the principles of etymology given by Yāska himself.

The mediaeval commentators like Sāyaṇa are the faithful followers of Yāska. In the commentary of Sāyaṇa whatever meaning is convenient at a particular place, has been given. This has resulted into two facts: multiplicity of the meaning of the same word at different places and anachronism. Sāyaṇa interprets the *Ṛgveda* as if it were produced in his time. So all the philosophical and ritual progress in the time of Sāyaṇa has been reflected in the commentary of Sāyaṇa. Since the followers of Sāyaṇa also think anachronistically, they do not notice this peculiarity of him.

Streams of Vedic Interpretations

In the modern period, i.e. approximately for the last two centuries, we find that there are two streams of Vedic interpretations simultaneously: Indian as well as Western. These two ways of interpretations can be described in two words: fruit-oriented and root-oriented. The Indian way of Vedic interpretation has remained fruit-oriented and this is in conformity with the Yāska's guiding principle: *arthanityaḥ parīkṣeta.* The Indian interpreters have always used the Veda to solve their problems in their periods. While up to the first half of the twentieth century, Indian interpreters gave more importance to philosophy, during the last five decades they are giving more stress on science and technology on one hand and "relevance" of Veda from the point of view of social and political life on the other. The scholars of the first half of the twentieth century used to say that in the Western World there has been some material progress based on science and technology, but still the people there are not happy; they do not have mental peace. For this mental peace they have to turn to India and read Upaniṣads, *Gītā,* etc. During the last forty years, Indian Vedalogists seem to have forgotten "mental peace." They are trying to find out modern science and technology in the Veda. Moreover they are also trying to find out "ecology" in the Veda. It is very noteworthy that as and when new information comes forward through newspapers, Indian Vedalogists find it in the Veda. In the nineteenth century, they could find railways in the Veda; in the first half of the twentieth century they could find aeroplanes and atom bombs in the Veda. In the last quarter of the twentieth century they started finding out computer and ecological awareness in the Veda. Recently in the twenty-first century they are finding mobile phones in Veda. So the science and technology in the Veda according to the Vedic scholars have two limitations: firstly, science and technology should first be developed in the West, and secondly, this science and technology should have some news-value. Further this science and technology should be childish, i.e. even children should be able to use it. The complicated details of science and technology cannot be found in the Veda, for these Vedic scholars do not know them. Moreover only those things which are "relevant" even today are found in the Veda. Thus during the British period Vedic scholars in India found out nationalism in the Veda. Frankly speaking the concept of nation and nationalism are foreign to India. The word *rāṣṭra* in the Veda does not mean "nation" but rather "state." Indian authors on political science in ancient India do not make any difference between "state" and "nation" as the Western authors do. Since in modern days we accepted the word *rāṣṭra* in Sanskrit for nation, this does not mean that the word existed in that sense in ancient days. To see the concept of nation in *rāṣṭra* will thus be anachronistic. Similarly the concept of ecology, pollution, etc. are modern. They have no history of more than fifty years even in the Western way of thinking. Therefore to find these things in Sanskrit or in the Veda is anachronistic. Just as a healthy man is not aware of the fact that he has heart or brain,

Vedic men were not aware of ecology because there was no pollution, no ecological problems. Even though there are descriptions of rivers, mountains, trees, birds, etc. in Sanskrit literature, there is no word for "Nature" in Sanskrit. There was no concept of nature in Sanskrit literature. Western critics praise Kālidāsa for his descriptions of nature. But no Indian critic of earlier days has ever praised Kālidāsa for this, for there was no concept of nature at all in ancient days. There is a "relevance-mania" among the Indian thinkers and leaders. In order to show that everything in ancient days is "relevant even today," they anachronistically find modern problems and solutions to them in Vedic or classical Sanskrit literature. This is not logical. The "fruit-oriented" Indian Interpretation on Veda or any other ancient literature therefore is not scientific; it reflects a primitive mentality on the part of the scholars.

Western Interpretation on Vedas

With this background in mind we may compare the Western point of view towards Vedic interpretation. It can be summarized in the word: "root-oriented." The Western interpreters always try to seek the "original" meaning of the Vedic texts irrespective of the fact that it may or may not be relevant today. Incidentally it may be noted that in Sanskrit there is no concept like "original." No Indian scholar tries to claim that he is original (even when he is original). He only claims to be a faithful interpreter of something what has been already said in earlier texts or taught by his teacher. In the absence of awareness of any history for an Indian thinker, Veda is *nitya*. It was as it is today and will be as it is today. From the Western point of view the way of thinking in the R̥gvedic period may be different from that of the Yajurvedic period. Similarly the Brāhmaṇa-texts, Upaniṣads, Vedāṅga-literature, epics and Purāṇas, classical literature may be different in their viewpoints. The Ṛgvedic scholars in the West try to find out what the Ṛgvedic poets might have thought. Rosen, the first translator of some Ṛgvedic hymns in Latin, immediately recognized that Sāyaṇa's interpretations are anachronistic and therefore not very reliable. The same was the position of scholars like Roth, or Grassmann.

Ṛgveda translated in Various European Languages

ṚGVEDA TRANSLATED INTO ENGLISH

Meanwhile there was a long discussion among the Western scholars on the place of Sāyaṇa in the Vedic interpretation. Scholars like Wilson were strong supporters of Sāyaṇa and they believed that Sāyaṇa was in the line of continuous interpretations of Veda in India and therefore he is in a better position to understand the Veda than a European scholar of nineteenth century. Wilson translated the whole of the *Ṛgveda* into English and in India his translation is very much used because it is in English (and not in German or French — the languages not within the reach of most of the Indian Vedists). Wilson's translation was highly criticized in the West. It was pointed out that his translation is not that of the *Ṛgveda* but that of the Sāyaṇa's commentary.

Although Roth and Grassmann tried to understand the *Ṛgveda* independently, their interpretations are also not free from objections. These two scholars also are not free from the objection "multiplicity of meanings" of the same words. Moreover they changed the available texts by suggesting numerous emendations. This point was also not appreciated by other scholars in the West.

ṚGVEDA TRANSLATED INTO GERMAN ETC.

Ludwig and Bergaigne represent two different directions of Vedic interpretation. Ludwig used the entire Vedic literature for the understanding of the *Ṛgveda*. He completely translated the *Ṛgveda* into German and added a detailed commentary. He, however, tried to find out the "real history" in the *Ṛgveda* and in that sense he belongs to the school of "Aitihāsikas" mentioned in the *Nirukta*. Bergaigne wrote a very big book on the Ṛgvedic religion in French. In this book consisting of three volumes, Bergaigne used the method of "rapprochement." Thus he tried to bring all the relevant passages together, compared them with each other and tried to decide the meaning of the Ṛgvedic words. Thus he has indirectly translated a large part of the *Ṛgveda* into French. His work remained rather neglected. V.G. Paranjape has translated the work of Bergaigne from French into English almost forty years ago. Still his work has remained unknown in India.

Pischel and Geldner wrote numerous essays on the Vedic words. They were strong supporters of Indian tradition while understanding the Veda. Pischel was a great scholar in the field of classical Sanskrit and Prakrit. So these scholars used the entire later literature for understanding the *Ṛgveda*. Geldner, however, slightly changed his position later on. When he translated the entire *Ṛgveda* into German, he has simply referred to Sāyaṇa, but not followed him.

Oldenberg has a unique place in the history of Vedic interpretation. He wrote detailed notes on the *Ṛgveda*. In these notes he criticized all the earlier attempts of Vedic interpretations. He has also followed the method of "internal comparison (rapprochement)" while understanding the *Ṛgveda*. Unfortunately, he did not translate the *Ṛgveda*. His notes, however, are very important and deal with many problematic text places in the *Ṛgveda*.

Renou continued the work of Oldenberg in a different way. He has translated almost sixty per cent of the *Ṛgveda* in French along with up to date notes. He has used all the literature published up to the time of his translation. He has also used the method of internal comparison. For the time being, his translation is the best. Unfortunately, his translation does not follow the order of hymns in the *Ṛgveda* and is scattered in seventeen volumes. Moreover he also could not complete the translation of *Ṛgveda*.

Contributions of scholars like Gonda are very significant. He has written numerous books and essays on the various aspects of Vedic studies. He has discussed the views of earlier scholars and tried to give systematic translation of numerous passages from the *Ṛgveda*. Unfortunately again, he also has not translated the *Ṛgveda* in the order of the hymns in the *Ṛgveda* and his views are also scattered in numerous books and articles. It is very much desired that a complete index of all the text places discussed by him is prepared in future.

It may be added here that Max Müller was the editor of the *Ṛgveda* with Sāyaṇa's commentary. His contributions are important from the point of view of history of religion but for the interpretation of the *Ṛgveda*, he has not contributed much.

H.D. Velankar from Mumbai has also translated almost 70 per cent of the *Ṛgveda* into English. Though Indian, his translations are in the Western traditions. He also uses the method of "internal comparison" while translating the *Ṛgveda*. His translations are also philologically root-oriented and therefore deserve to be mentioned among the Western contributions. He is quite different from other Indian interpreters.

Obstacles in Vedic Studies

It may be observed that in India Dayananda Saraswati, Sri Aurobindo and Madhusudan Ojha seem to have influenced most of the Vedic scholars. Moreover, in India most of Vedicists are followers and worshippers of Veda. Their main motive is the glorification of Veda and not the study of Veda. It seems that many Indian Vedicists have strong bias against Western scholars, although they do not even know the names of Vedic scholars in the West. The same is the case with the Western scholars who do not take into consideration the writings of Indian scholars on the Veda. There are mainly two reasons for the absence of any rapport between Vedic and Indian scholars. The first is the absence of knowledge of the languages. Indian scholars have hardly any acquaintance with languages other than English. Secondly, it is almost impossible for majority of the Indian scholars to get the literature published in the West, due to the high prices as also due to the ignorance. Late R.N. Dandekar published six volumes of *Vedic Bibliography* in which he has exhaustively recorded all the literature in the field of Veda. His efforts, however, have remained unnoticed. The absence of critical attitude and of pure philological approach towards the Vedic studies is a great obstacle in the Vedic studies in India. There seems to be thus anarchy in the field of Vedic studies in India. To promote the philological approach to the Vedic studies is a desideratum in India. This can be achieved by means of following ways:

(1) Revival of the old attitude of Indian scholars of *niṣkāraṇa* Vedic studies. Veda is not to be studied for any practical purpose but for the sake of Veda.

(2) The books of the Vedic scholars written in German and French should be translated into English or other Indian languages.

(3) Research papers on the Vedic subjects written in German and French also should be translated into English and other Indian languages.

(4) It should be made compulsory on the part of Vedic students to study German and French.

(5) Academic, philological studies by Vedic scholars and popular, propagatory writings of the devotees of Veda should not be confounded with each other.

(6) Objective philological studies of Veda deserve to be encouraged.

(7) Resources of the Maharshi Sandeepani Rashtriya Veda Vidya Pratisthana should be used for such types of Vedic studies.

(8) Lectures, classes by Vedic scholars following philological methodology be encouraged.

It may be noted that in India there is the concept of *Veda-prāmāṇya,* i.e. the authoritativeness of the Veda. This concept has religious and philosophical significance. I also notice that in India there is another concept unknowingly accepted by the people, viz. *pramāṇa-vedatva.* This means "Vedaness of the authoritative." Thus whatever is regarded authoritative by Indian people is also considered by them to be Veda. In ancient days the *Bhagavad-Gītā* was accepted by the tradition as an "Upaniṣad" (see the colophons of this text). In modern days people considered the writing of Śaṅkarācārya or of some other scholars respected by them to be Vedic texts. Thus for Indians the Veda is not only eternal, it is also an open book. On the other hand, Veda is a historical document for the Western scholars. This difference of outlook also creates a great difference of opinion among the Indian and Western scholars of Veda. The Indian scholars have forgotten the ancient principle: *brāhmaṇena niskāraṇo dharmaḥ ṣaḍaṅgo vedo 'dhyeyo jñeyaśca.* Thus Veda is to be studied without any practical purpose. But the present-day Vedic scholars, trying to show the relevance of Veda, have neglected this principle. This principle, however, needs to be revived.

4

Dharmaśāstra — A Natural Science?

M. Krzysztof Byrski

Last year upon the invitation of Professor Shashiprabha Kumar, I spent three months lecturing at the Special Centre for Sanskrit Studies of Jawaharlal Nehru University. It has been there in the atmosphere of that Centre — the atmosphere of dedication to the rationalist spirit of ancient Sanskrit heritage that as the result of my interaction with the students and staff of the Centre some of the thoughts, which I am presenting in my paper, got clarified. I should like to dedicate this presentation to all my friends of the Centre.

Plight of Dharma

THE present plight of *dharma* in India has quite obvious sources. But let me first explain what I mean by "plight"? A simple question addressed to any one in India or from India as to what is the equivalent of the term "religion" in any of the Indian languages, will meet with the answer that it is *dharma*. This fact has ominous consequences not only for the proper understanding of the term by foreigners, but also for the way the original, English-educated users perceive it. The encounter of the two civilizations did not begin on equal terms. The superiority of Europeans in military terms was not the main reason. What happened was not only a simple conquest, but in a way similar to that performed of yore by Alexander the Great or later on by the Muslims — it has been the aftermath of it in terms of civilization impact, which counts foremost in all these cases.

Extensive Use of Dharma

The last conquest of India by Europeans signified a confrontation between the civilization of sustainability and containment and that of development and expansion. While in political terms Europeans had to leave India forced out by powerful mass movement headed by Mahatma Gandhi, in terms of civilization impact their presence proved not only to be lasting but also to be outright victorious. India has accepted the gospel of development and expansion for her own with dire consequences for some of her traditional values — *dharma* being the main victim.

Let me clarify at this moment, that I do not think any other course of events has been possible. The spirit of development and expansion evolved a tool without which further existence of mankind seems to be impossible. It is technology! Thus — paradoxically — I believe that it is now only with the help of the technological mind that the traditional values may be reactivated — *dharma* included. But meanwhile it is on the defensive, while efforts go on to lock it in a temple in the way similar to that in Europe, where religion is being not all too unsuccessfully relegated to a church alone.

By putting an equation mark between religion and *dharma*, the latter has become a victim of similar discrimination. While from what we have said earlier it follows that *dharma* being an equivalent of sustainability and containment should be rather equated with culture or civilization model than with religion.

Analysing Dharma

If so it is now time to analyse minutely the term in question. During my tenure as the Ambassador of Poland to India I received a xerox-copy of a letter sent over to all embassies. Let me quote what I wrote about it in one of my papers to be published soon in India:

> In it the author gave vent to his exasperation over the idea of religion-less conduct (*dharma nirapekṣatā*),[1] obviously prompted by the well-known election slogan of the Congress Party about separation of religion from politics. It will come as a surprise to the reader that the problem was not of ideological nature but of purely semantic one. The author insisted that if we accept such mode of conduct, then nature also may start functioning likewise and series of catastrophic events such as earthquakes may occur. Since each and every aspect of perceptive reality has its proper *dharma*, how can one separate one's conduct from one's *dharma*? Certainly the author of the said letter, traditionally educated, must have understood the term *dharma* in the way the *Kārttikeyānupreksā* — a Jaina treatise formulates its definition: *dharmaḥ vastusvabhāvaḥ*.[2]

In order to understand the attitude of the highly perplexed author of the letter in question, we have to refer to the etymology of the word *dharma*. It is derived from the verbal root $\sqrt{dh\d{r}}$. According to Apte, it means among others "to be," "to exist," "to live," "to hold," "to bear up," "to maintain," "to support," "**to sustain.**" It is significant that the same

---

1. "*. . . jab samvidhān aur vicārdhārāeṅ dharma nirapekṣa hone lagatī hai to prakṛti bhī apne dharma se nirapekṣa hokara vikarāla rūpa dhāraṇa karane lagatī hai.*" — From a letter of Mukesh Suman of Nazibabad dated 17.10.1995.

2. Svāmi-Kumāra, *Kārttikeyānupreksā*, Śrī Parama-Śruta Prabhāvaka Maṇḍal, Agās, 1997, p. 364 (XII.478).

authority does not list as the primary meaning of its derivative *dharma* — "being," "existence," "way of life," "holding," "bearing up," "maintenance," "support," and **"sustenance"** or "**sustainability**." The only explanation would be the selective approach to the word which otherwise has a very broad semantic value.

On the whole dictionaries betray an axiological bias concentrating on the moral, ethical, legal and ritualistic dimensions of the term while ignoring its ontic and epistemic import. So far as the first aspect is concerned no doubt the most fundamental is the definition mentioned above, to be found in the Jaina treatise *Kārttikeyānuprekṣā*. *Dharma* is the nature of things. It is the principle that bestows upon all aspects of perceptive reality their characteristic features. It is the principle, which maintains (sic!) them in their unique separateness. Finally, it is the support of the world; it is sustenance of **the proper nature** of it, in accordance with the other definition such as *dhārayate lokam iti dharmaḥ*, or *dhārati lokam iti vā dharmaḥ* — *dharma*.[3] As it is evident, there is nothing religious — in the common understanding of the term "religion" — about the notion of *dharma* in its ontological dimension.

Dharma Linked to Religion

Now, the question arises, why is it so when axiology is concerned? Most obviously in each and every civilization value systems are usually closely interrelated with eschatology. Now, since science in the actual sense of the word, has little or nothing at all to say in this respect, the idea of god or gods is naturally referred to and He or they are invoked and thus

3. P.V. Tripathi, *Puruṣārthacatuṣṭya*, Rājavidyā Granthamālā, Vārāṇasī, 1970, p. 42.

this sphere of human behaviour acquires religious hue. Yet, we should remember that with reference to *dharma* only — so to say — one-third of it could be called religion *par excellence.*

For let us note that one of the descriptions of the character of *dharma* speaks about it as consisting of three debts (*ṛṇāni triṇi*), which have to be reimbursed during one's lifetime.[4] It is the debt towards gods and that towards sages and towards ancestors. The first is repaid by offering sacrifices to gods; the second — by studies; and the last — by begetting progeny. Neither the second, nor the third aspect carries with itself any uniquely religious import. Only the first may be treated as a religious act but only at the level of popular beliefs. Because, if one understands the proper meaning of the sacrificial act then even this aspect loses a lot of its religious tint. The crux of any sacrificial act is feeding fire with oblation. No doubt man is the only creature capable of igniting and feeding fire. If so, then we could possibly treat the ritualistic form of the same act as a sort of tribute paid to the very essence of human nature understood as the microcosmic epitome of the entire universe.

Revaluing the Dharma Theory

Such an approach requires a revaluation of our comprehension of what *sanātana dharma* is — both in its meaning and in its ritualistic embodiment. **To our mind it is a particular communication system in which the nature of the world as perceived by Indian thinkers is encoded so that man may regulate his conduct accordingly**. It is a rationalistic system down to its very core and the only requirement is to decode properly the particular language used and the ritual acts, which

4. *Manusmṛti,* ed. J.H. Dave, Bharatiya Vidya Bhavan, Bombay, 1978, vol. III, pp. 205-06 (*Adh,* VI, *śl.* 35, 36 & 37).

follow the language. Certainly, the equation of the notion of *dharma* with that of religion alone does not serve the purpose well.

Having hopefully clarified the ontological and axiological aspects of *dharma*, let us turn finally to the third one, which consists of its epistemic dimension. The nature of the world that *dharma* is — in order to become the reference point of human conduct — has to be known. In short, we may say that the notion of *dharma* embraces the nature of things itself, knowledge of this nature and suitable conduct that follows. To repeat — it is obvious that whatever is supposed to guide human behaviour first has to be known. Thus knowledge of *dharma* is inseparable from *dharma* itself or better is inherent in it.

Conclusion

This aspect of *dharma* has become to be known as *Dharmaśāstra*, literally "the science of *dharma*." But if we follow the definition of *dharma* to be found in the *Kārttīkeyānuprekṣā* then it should be *Vāstu-Svabhāvaśāstra* "the science of the nature of things" — **the natural science!**

In the light of the above conclusion we have to reinterpret our understanding of the title of the best-known treatise on the subject, i.e. *Mānava-Dharmaśāstra*. The term *mānava* commonly is understood as ascribing the text to Manu Svāyambhuva, its mythical author from whom it comes. Yet, the same term means according to Apte "human" and "mankind." Consequently, the title of the best-known treatise on *dharma* could be read as *The science of the nature of mankind*. If we peruse carefully the content of the entire text we shall find there precious little of purely religious character. Thus a question may be asked why not only the text in question but the entire concept of *dharma* has been forced into the straitjacket of religion understood very much the European way?

Only too often modernity, rationality, scientific approach and secularism in India has been identified with the technological civilization, which is the product of different environment — that of Europe. Consequently, Indian traditional thought "lock stock and barrel" has been perceived as its opposite notwithstanding its rationality. Most of Europeans and many an Indian intellectual consider rational only what is technologically viable. Furtheron they identify it as secular in contradistinction to what is irrational, i.e. religious and in the Indian context what is termed as *dharma.* It is in such a way that a distinction of human attitudes into secular and religious — never ever known to the Indian tradition has been espoused by considerable section of Indian intellectual elite. *Dharma* became the victim of this process and Dharmaśāstra has been practically identified with theology and ritualism.

Modern science in Europe in its development has been relaying heavily on the achievement of ancient Greek and Roman thinking and on the terminology evolved then. Consequently our language in order to be scientific has to be saturated with such terminology (currently though more and more Anglo-Saxon than Greek and Roman). Had the modern technological development originated in the context of Indian civilization we would not speak today about natural sciences but about Dharmaśāstra and not about humanities but about *Mānava-Dharmaśāstra.*

This conclusion by no means should be construed as an expression of a sort of disappointment that the development of modern technical sciences did not take place in the context of the Indian civilization. I only hope that it will facilitate its joining the mainstream of modern scientific thought enriching it with its peculiar sensitivity to sustainability, the importance of which is signalled when sustainable development is talked about as the goal of the mankind in the current century.

5

Sanskrit in China

Lokesh Chandra

Advent of Sanskrit into China

INDIAN press has reported the discovery of a Sanskrit inscription of the fifth century from the Hunan province of China. The advent of Sanskrit into China is as early as the third century BCE, when Indians were at the Imperial court during the Tsin dynasty and named the country from this dynasty as China and propagated this name throughout Central Asia, India and South-East Asia. Sanskrit has been known in China as *Fanyu* — the language of *Brahman*, the language of Cosmic dimensions, the language that gave the Chinese access to the immensity (*Brahman*) of the "Barbarian" world and opened up their vision to the several universes of culture and civilizations. The Sinocentric frontiers became ever-expanding horizons.

The Buddhist kingdoms of Central Asia brought Sanskrit books, sculptures and paintings, as well as ideas that ushered new perceptions in the Chinese mind. Sanskrit entered China on Serindian horses sought after by Chinese emperors. It was the Parthian prince An Shih-kao turned Buddhist monk, who initiated a school of transcreations of Sanskrit works into Chinese, which became the most impressive achievement of

Chinese culture. Sanskrit was accompanied by *moho sabo* (Chinese transcription of *mahā-sārthavāha*) or transnational merchants who brought prosperity to China. An Shih-kao who had translated 176 Sanskrit works into Chinese was also a Commandant of the Cavalry. Among his translations, that of the *Sukhāvatī-vyūha* of Amitābha gained great popularity. The glories of the Sukhāvatī Paradise became vivid as Iranian beauties of Parthia danced in the joyous tenderness of their vibrant movements. The sensuous elegance of their bare bodies bade the onlooker into worlds of the luminous beauties of Sukhāvatī. Sanskrit came to be associated with fiery steeds of conquest, with caravans laden with affluence, with the passionate beauty of life, and with enlightenment of the mind.

Sanskrit Greatly Influenced Chinese

During my visit to the Marble Buddha Monastery in Shanghai, which escaped desecration during the cultural revolution, the monks recited their prayers in a loud and sonorous voice. At times, a word or two would sound Sanskrit. They handed over their book of recitations and lo and behold, it was a Sanskrit hymn to Nīlakaṇṭha which had been transcribed into Chinese ideograms by *Bhagavad-dharma* of western India in the seventh century. During researches in Beijing, I came across coins from Sinkiang which were in Sanskrit on one side and in Chinese on the other, and could be dated to the second century BCE by their Chinese inscriptions. At the Shanghai monastery I glanced through a seventeenth century edition of the Buddhist Canon in about 800 cases, neatly arranged in the large Sūtra Hall. Therein I came across a glossary of a thousand words by the famous pilgrim I-tsing's (Sanskrit–Chinese glossary) which had interesting words like *prasāra* in Sanskrit for bazaar, and even *kurtā* for a shirt. It is a valuable source for the spoken Sanskrit of the seventh century.

In the seventh and eighth centuries, the Chinese were fascinated by the new sciences of astronomy, calendrical know-how and mathematics in Sanskrit texts which were known as the "Pho-lo-men or Brahmin Books." Indians were appointed Presidents of the Imperial Board of Astronomy, for instance, Kāśyapa headed it around CE 650. It is a paradox that we owe to Gautama Siddha the greatest collection of ancient Chinese astronomical fragments. He introduced from India the zero symbol, an early form of trigonometry and other innovations. To the Chinese, Sanskrit was the language of Exact Sciences, of statecraft, of military tactics, and of surveying the sidereal locations of cities from Tashkent to Vietnam. An emperor of the Thang dynasty sent a military mission against the king of Campā (on the coastal region of modern Vietnam) to bring his library of 1350 Sanskrit manuscripts as war booty to China.

In CE 1057 Pao-chang the great Chinese master of Dhyāna (Zen) was commissioned by the emperor to go to India and acquire texts for Imperial victories. On return he conducted Imperial rites centered on the deity *Trailokyākṣepa* "Conqueror of the Three Worlds." The original Sanskrit manuscript was preserved in the Phu-an monastery in the 1920s. Its end folio gave the initial stanzas of the three *mahākāvya*s of Kālidāsa. This was the earliest known manuscript with quotations from the great Indian poet.

Sanskrit Mantras Widely Used

The origins of printing in China also goes back to Sanskrit. The first printed sheet has the goddess Pratisarā in the centre with *mantra*s in Sanskrit letters written concentrically around her. It is dated CE 757 and was excavated in 1944 from a grave near Beijing.

Sanskrit inscriptions and the use of sheets with *mantras* was widespread in Yunnan. Even the family deity of the royal house was Ajeya "The Invincible." The Victory Pillar of Kunming with Sanskrit inscriptions is a splendid example of an architectural sculpture with about three hundred images of all sizes, and recalls the monument at Chittor.

Sanskrit Inscriptions on the Imperial Arch

Ever since the Han dynasty in the first century BCE the gate at the Chu-yung-kuan pass has been one of the nine important gateways to China. This gate was constructed as a protection against barbarians from the north. In Imperial times, more than ten thousand troops were stationed here. An Imperial Arch was constructed in CE 1333 and a 36 ft long inscription was inscribed in Sanskrit for the protection of the capital Beijing. The use of Sanskrit *sūtras* for National Defence in China goes back to ancient times. When Hiuen Tsang returned to China, the Emperor invited him to stay in the palace. The Emperor was delighted to know that the six hundred scrolls the pilgrim had translated contributed to the protection of the State. Imperial admiration and awe wanted to ascertain: "everything must be exactly as in the Sanskrit original." The pilgrim-scholar assured the Emperor that he had brought three copies of the texts from India for clearing doubts: "when clouds open the sun appears."

Christie's sold a blue and white Chinese bowl of the fourteenth century for £ 209,000. Its lid has since been located at the Palace Museum, Beijing. It was used by Emperor Xuande. It has eight auspicious emblems (*aṣṭa-maṅgala*) including the *śrīvatsa* of Viṣṇu, interspersed with sacred hierograms. It has a Sanskrit inscription running around its body which is a benediction to grant well-being and luck for all times of the day. During this period, a twelve-member Indian mission had gone to China for the stability of the Emperor and the Empire. The Museum at Taipeh has quite a few cups and saucers sanctified by Sanskrit *mantras* around their rims.

Buddhist Influence in China

As we have the Litany of the Thousand Names of Viṣṇu (*Viṣṇu-sahasranāma*) so does China have the thousand names of the Buddha, which go back to the third century. Emperor Chien-lung of the seventeenth century, who had the longest reign as well as the most extensive territories China ever had, used to recite the Sanskrit names of the thousand Buddhas. My father Prof. Raghu Vira, brought the original xylograph from Beijing. Emperor Chien-lung had studied Sanskrit as a young prince and was devoted to its promotion. He got Sanskrit *mantras* collected from all over and had them published in a hundred volumes.

On his final journey a Chinese Buddhist was enshrouded in silk that had Sanskrit *mantras* woven with golden threads, specific for each part of the body. This silken shroud with Sanskrit prayers ensured him the Heavenly Fields of Sukhāvatī.

Sixty years ago, my father received six huge cases of Buddhist *sūtras* and scrolls from the Buddhist Book Store on the Ashoka Road in Shanghai. No Indian road in those days had the honour of being named after Emperor Aśoka. Among them were large-size woodcuts of Buddhist deities that bore Sanskrit inscriptions. On next page is a specimen of Sanskrit from among them, in the ornamental script of seventh century India, transmitting rhythms of serenity.

The Divine symbolized above in the simple flow of lines is Amitābha, flanked by Vajrapāṇi to the left and Padmapāṇi to the right. Amitābha is boundless light, immeasurable splendour. Vajrapāṇi is the adamantine essence, the *vajra* of Indra, smashing evil designs and impediments. Padmapāṇi with aiding hands holds green foliage and he is the indomitable overflow of Nature, an obeisance to Life, threaded in one string with the Divine phenomena of the Cosmos. The *mantra* is written in the Celestial Empire of China in the ornamental Siddham script of seventh-century India. In the harmony of a circle, it transmits rhythms of purity and joy, silent, liquid and serene.

6

Emotion and Value in Sanskrit Literature

K.T. Pandurangi

WHETHER literature is an art or criticism of life is an old dispute among critics. If it is an art, its objective would be to produce joy. To produce joy it has to delineate emotion and describe beauty. If literature is a criticism of life, then, its objective would be to delineate value. To achieve this objective literature has to elucidate human nature and human conduct. Therefore, one has to first examine whether literature is an art or a criticism of life, or both.

It would be better if we take a look at the views of Sanskrit writers on poetics in this respect. A majority of the writers on Sanskrit poetics mention both joy and instruction as the aim of literature.

Bhāmaha, the earliest writer on Sanskrit poetics, says:

धर्मार्थकाममोक्षेषु वैचक्षण्यं कलासु च। करोति कीर्तिं प्रीतिं च साधुकाव्य निषेवणम्।

dharmārtha kāma mokṣeṣu vaicakṣaṇyaṁ kalāsu ca ।
karoti kīrtiṁ prītiṁ ca sādhukāvya niveṣaṇam ॥

— *KS* I-2

Good literature helps to achieve success by pursuing values of life in the arts. It gives joy and fame. Here we may note that the source of *prīti,* i.e. joy, is personal and *kīrti,* i.e. fame, is social. *Kīrti* is the appreciation and admiration by the society to an individual on achievements. Success in pursuing values of life is both personal and social. The values are aimed at the development of the individual and the society. Thus the aim of literature is both personal and social. It is both joy and value.

This twofold approach with respect to the objectives of literature is maintained by all major writers on Sanskrit poetics. Ānandavardhana who declares *rasa* or the delineation of emotion as the essence of poetry at the close of his *Dhvanyāloka* states that

> रसस्य पुरुषार्थस्य च स्वप्राधान्येन चारुत्वमविरुद्धम् ।
> *rasaśya pusuṣārthasya ca svapradhānyena cārutvavi ruddham* ।
> There is no contradiction in delineating both emotion and value in literature in their respective areas.

Mammaṭa, an outstanding representative of the Rasa School sets the aim of literature as:

> काव्यं यशसेऽर्थकृते व्यवहारविदे शिवेतरक्षतये ।
> सद्यः परनिर्वृतये कान्तासम्मिततयोपदेशयुजे ॥
> *kāvyaṁ yaśase 'rthakṛte vyavahāravide śivetarakṣataye* ।
> *sadyaḥ paranirvṛtaye kāntāsammitatayopadeśayuje* ॥

परनिर्वृति (*paranirvṛti*), "highest joy," and कान्तासम्मिततया उपदेश (*kāntāsammitatayā upadeśa*), "instructions in the manner of a beloved's advice," are the two major objectives of literature. The latter aims to necessitate the delineation of values.

Kuntaka who opposed the idea that emotion alone was the essence of literature, states the need for the delineation of values more specifically.

धर्मादिसाधनोपायः सुकुमारक्रमोदितः ।
काव्यबन्धोऽभिजातानां हृदयाह्लादकारकः ॥
dharmādisadhanopāyaḥ sukumārakramoditaḥ ।
kāvyabandho 'bhijātānāṁ hṛdayāhlādakārakaḥ ॥

हृदयाह्लादकत्व (*hṛdayāhlādakatva*) and धर्मादिसाधनोपायत्व (*dharmādisādhanopāyatva*), that is to say, joy and value are clearly stated as the objectives of literature. He further says that mere आह्लादकत्व (*hṛdayāhlādakatva*) will make it a mere pastime. सत्यपि तदाह्लादकत्वे काव्यबन्धस्य क्रीडनकादि प्रख्याता प्राप्नोति *satyapi tadāhlādakatve kāvyabandhasya krīḍanakādi prakhyātā prāpnoti* ।

If it is mere emotion, then, it is only a pastime. If it is mere value, then, it is not literature. It will be a book of moral preaching. Therefore, both emotion and value have to be harmonized in literature. The depiction of emotion, the description of beauty, and the depiction of values through the elucidation of human nature and human conduct have to be properly balanced in literature.

In Sanskrit literature the above-mentioned aspects are found in different degrees in different forms of compositions. It goes by the temperament of the poet, the theme selected by him, and the purpose he has in mind. An attempt is made to group the poets as: *Rasakavi, Śāstrakavi* and *Ubhayakavi*.

The propounders of the Rasa School naturally consider the *Rasakavi* and *Rasakāvya* as superior. But Rājaśekhara feels that each one is great if he excels in his own field. He remarks:

स्वविषये सर्वो गरीयान्। नहि राजहंसः चन्द्रिकापानाय प्रभवति नापि चकोरः अद्भ्यः क्षीरोद्धरणाय।

svaviṣaye sarvo garīyān । *nahi rājahaṁsaḥ candrikāpānāya prabhavati nāpi cakoraḥ adbhayaḥ kṣīroddharaṇāya* ।

The swan is not able to suck the moonlight and the *cakora* bird is not able to distinguish between the milk and the water.

II

In the long history of Sanskrit literature, we find that the beauty of nature is described in the Vedas. In the epics the elucidation of human nature and human conduct is found in-depth. Probably, in no other literature in the world, there is such a detailed elucidation of human nature and human conduct as in the *Mahābhārata* and the *Rāmāyaṇa*. In the *Rāmāyaṇa, rāsa,* i.e. emotion is also delineated in-depth. That is why it is called *Ādikāvya*. In *Mahākāvya*s — dramas, prose romances and *Campū*s — both emotion and human conduct are delineated. In fables, didactic poetry, *Anyokti* poems and *Subhāṣita*s, there is more stress on human conduct and values. Thus Sanskrit literature has been serving human interest both by providing joy and instruction by delineating beauty, emotion and value. It would be difficult to illustrate this. Therefore, I propose to illustrate with reference to drama supplementing some points from other forms of literature wherever necessary.

A majority of Sanskrit plays depict the emotion of love or *śṛṅgāra*. The value depicted in these differ from play to play, depending upon the theme.

Svapnavāsavadattā of Bhāśa, the three plays of Kālidāsa, *Mṛcchakaṭika* of Śūdraka, *Mālatīmādhava* of Bhavabhūti, *Ratnāvalī* and *Priyadarśikā* of Śrī Harṣa are prominent among the Sanskrit plays that delineate the emotion of love. The *Uttararāmacaritam* of Bhavabhūti delineates both love and pathos, i.e. *śṛṅgāra* and *karuṇa*.

The love depicted in Sanskrit drama ranges from the sensuous to the sublime, from a delicate expression of passion to the vulgar display of lust. It reveals an aesthetic sensitivity of a very high order as well as the tendencies of indulgence.

In no other literature the physical beauty, the love gestures, love dodgnings, love psyche, and the fulfilment of love are described in such minute detail as in the Sanskrit. Indian mind is supposed to be philosophical and reflective. But if one reads this *śṛṅgāra* literature in Sanskrit, one will see the other side of the Indian mind, i.e. the emotional and the aesthetic sides. One is apt to think that the Indian mind entertains contradictory values. But the Indian mind knows how to balance them.

Each one of these plays with a love theme develops a value also. Values like sacrifice, magnanimity, morality, responsibility to the public are depicted in some of the major ones. To detail some of them, I may mention that *Svapnavāsavadattam* delineates love and sacrifice, *Mṛcchakaṭikam* delineates love and magnanimity, *Śākuntalam* delineates love and morality and *Uttararāmacaritam* delineates love and responsibility to the public. These plays have left a deep impact on the Indian mind because of this double achievement. Mere delineation of love would not have made such an impact.

Love is purely a personal matter. If Udayana and Vāsavadattā have loved each other intensely it is none of our concern. It is the sacrifice made by Vāsavadattā in allowing Udayana to marry Padmāvatī in the interest of her husband and the kingdom, that makes the play very appealing.

Similary, the love of Duṣyanta and Śakuntalā that had a smooth run until Dūrvāsā's curse, becomes problematic when Duṣyanta is unable to recognize her as his wife which raises a moral issue — whether one should accept somebody else's wife as his own and be immoral or reject one's own wife and be cruel.

Only the lifting of the effect of the curse could solve this moral problem.

III

In *Svapnavāsavadattam*, the hero Udayana and the heroine Vāsavadattā are a happily married couple. Udayana is a handsome and lively person intensely loving towards his beloved wife Vāsavadattā. He teaches her *vīṇā*. As a king he is liked by his subjects, ministers and all others. Hunting is his hobby. This young king falls on bad days. He loses his kingdom and has to live in a village called Lavāṇaka. His wife and minister Yaugandharāyaṇa are with him. A soothsayer tells his minister that if Udayana marries Padmāvatī, the daughter of the Magadha king, he will get back his kingdom. The soothsayer's episode is merely an excuse. In the olden days political alliances were made through matrimonial relations.

Udayana's marriage with Padmāvatī is planned by his minister Yaugandharāyaṇa for such a political alliance. Vāsavadattā is advised by the minister to sacrifice her personal interest for the sake of her husband and for getting the kingdom restored. She agrees. But it is difficult to convince Udayana. When Udayana is away hunting, a rumour is floated that Vāsavadattā has been burnt in a fire. Yaugandharāyaṇa also jumps into the fire. They escape to the forest. Then Yaugandharāyaṇa manages to deposit Vāsavadattā with Padmāvatī at the place of the Magadha king. He then engineers a marriage between Padmāvatī and Udayana. The events from the introduction of Vāsavadattā in the guise of the maid Avantikā till the marriage of Padmāvatī and Udayana, and the reunion of Vāsavadattā with Udayana, form the story of this play.

While depicting these events, Bhāsa delineates the emotion of love and the value of sacrifice. To illustrate this love, I will quote only one or two events. When Udayana returns from the hunt and learns that Vāsavadattā has been consumed by fire, he laments:

> तस्याः शरीरोपभुक्तानि दग्धशेषाणि आभरणानि परिष्वज्य राजा मोहमुपगतः। महीतलपरिसर्पणपांसुपाटलशरीरः सहसा उत्थाय किमपि किमपि बहुप्रलपितवान् "इह तया सह हसितम्" " इह तया सह कथितम्" "इह तया सह कुपितम्" "इह तया सह शयितम्" इत्येवं विलपन्तं तं राजानममात्यौ महता यत्नेन तस्माद् ग्रामाद् अपक्रान्तम्।
>
> *tasyāḥ śarīropabhuktāni dagdhaśeṣāṇi ābharaṇāni pariṣvajya rājā mohamupagataḥ mahītalaparisarpaṇapāṁsupāṭalaśarīraḥ sahasā uttāya kimapi kimapi bahupralapitavān "iha tayā saha hasitam" "iha tayā saha kathitam" "iha tayā saha kupitam" "iha tayā saha śayitam" ityevaṁ vilapauntaṁ taṁ rājānammātyau mahatā yatnena tasmād grāmād apakrāntam* ।

When this is narrated to Vāsavadattā in the forest, she feels like shouting: अलीकं अलीकं जीवामि मन्दभागा (*alīkaṁ alīkaṁ jīvāmi mandabhāgā*)

Starting from this, throughout the plays there are dialogues and events that indicate their deep love. Even after marriage with Padmāvatī, Udayana's mind belongs to Vāsavadattā.

> पद्मावती बहुमता यद्यपि रूपशीलमाधुर्यैः।
> वासवदत्ताबद्धं न तु तावन्मनो हरति॥
> *padmāvatī bahumatā yadyapi rūpaśīlamādhuryaḥ* ।
> *vāsavadattābaddhaṁ na tu tāvanmano harati* ॥

While this is the depth of love, the depth of sacrifice is even greater. When the news of Udayana agreeing to marry Padmāvatī reaches Vāsavadattā, she spontaneously exclaims "अत्याहितम् (*atyāhitam*)" a tragedy has befallen. But she has to soon conceal her feelings and say she only expressed her wonder as to how Udayana could now marry another woman having lamented so much for his first wife. All the same she feels that: आयुपुत्रोपि परकीयः संवृत्तः (*āyuputropi parakīyaḥ saṁvṛttaḥ*).

My husband is no longer mine now. It is her misfortune that she has to prepare the wedding garland for her co-wife. She refuses to put the leaves meant for सपत्नीमर्दन (*sapatnīmardana*). It is in the dream scene that we really realize the depth of her sacrifice. Her husband Udayana feels her presence in the dream and asks her किं कुपितासी? (*kiṁ kupitāsī?*). Are you angry with me? Her reply is नहि नहि दुःखितास्ति (*nahi nahi duḥkhıtasti*). No, no I am only hurt.

She has sacrificed her personal interest of exclusively possessing her husband for the sake of his getting back the kingdom by allowing this new matrimonial alliance. It is the delineation of this value of sacrifice that makes *Svapnavāsavadattam* a great play.

IV

In *Uttarāmacaritam,* the emotion of love makes room for the emotion of pathos by creating a problem of responsibility to the public. Rāma deeply loves Sītā, he has no doubts whatsoever about Sītā's chastity.

उत्पत्तिपरिपूतायाः किमस्याः पावनान्तरैः ।
तीर्थोदकं च वह्निश्च नान्यतः शुद्धिमर्हतः ॥
utpattiparipūtāyāḥ kimasyāḥ pāvanāntaraiḥ ।
tīrthodakaṁ ca vahniśca nānyataḥ śuddhirmahataḥ ॥

However, people carry a wrong impression and start a bad whisper campaign.

चत्वरापणरथ्यासु वनेषूपवनेषु च ।
catvarāpaṇarathyāsu vaneṣūpavaneṣu ca ।

Rāma knows and believes the truth though people do not. From the people's point of view, it is a choice between personal interest and public interest for Rāma. From Rāma's point of view it is a choice between truth and responsibility to the public.

> स्नेहं दयां च सौख्यं च यदि वा जानकीमपि।
> आराधनाय लोकानां मुञ्चतो नास्ति ये व्यथा॥
> *sneharh dayāṁ ca saukhyaṁ ca yadi vā jānakīmapi* ।
> *ārādhnāya lokānāṁ nuñcato nāsti ye vyathā* ॥

So the problem remains until people are made to realize the truth. Once the people realize their mistake and accept the truth, the problem is solved. It is the delineation of this value, i.e. responsibility to the public and the sacrifice made by Rāma and Sītā to uphold that value, that has made *Uttararāmacaritam* a great play. What ended tragically in the *Rāmāyaṇa* is made to end happily in order to delineate this value here.

In *Mṛcchakaṭikam* the value upheld is magnanimity. The two lovers are magnanimous to each other. Vasantasenā is prepared to sacrifice a luxurious life for the sake of her love and Cārudatta is prepared to accept a courtesan as his wife. Not only the hero and the heroine, but every other character in the play, i.e. the thief, the dice player, the cart-driver, the Buddhist monk, and even Vasantasenā's old mother, are magnanimous. The title of the play is *Mṛcchakaṭikam* or the earthen cart but the value depicted is about a heart of gold.

V

The problem in *Mṛcchakaṭika* is that a courtesan is raised to the status of a housewife, of a *veśyā* becoming a *kulavadhu*.

The society in which Cārudatta and Vasantasenā live is one that has accepted its courtesans. But this society has also allowed the courtesans to return to normal life and also live as housewives. In such circumstances, those who would like the courtesans to continue as such would oppose their becoming housewives. Śakāra represents such people. Throughout the play he argues with Vasantasenā that she is a courtesan and she must accept him for a sum of money and because he is a relative of the king.

On the other hand Cārudatta accepts her love and is willing to accept her as his wife. None of the characters depicted in the play consider it wrong. It is purely Vasantasenā's choice whether she should accept Śakāra's entreaties and remain a courtesan or go by her love for Cārudatta and become a housewife. Naturally, Vasantasenā chooses the latter course and suffers a good deal of harassment by Śakāra. The dramatist Śūdraka clearly favours the conversion of courtesans into housewives. Not only are the hero and the heroin depicted to lead this movement but even minor characters like Śarvilaka and Madanikā get married in this way. It may be noted that both Cārudatta and Śarvilaka who marry courtesan and raise their status to that of housewives are brāhmaṇas. Naturally one can expect such a social movement among all *varṇa*s of the time. Such a social reform is possible only if there is a noble and magnanimous attitude on the part of everyone concerned. This is found in this play except in Śakāra who provides a contrast.

VI

In *Mudrārākṣasa,* heroism is the emotion depicted. The values are loyalty, sacrifice, and the appreciation of merit. Amātyarākṣasa, heroically tries to rehabilitate Malayaketu in the place of Nandas, because of his loyalty to Nandas. His loyalty to Nandas is unshaken. He is prepared to make any sacrifice for that. So is the loyalty of Candanadāsa to his friend Amātyarākṣasa. The spies employed by Cāṇakya are very treacherous to Amātyarākṣasa, but they are very loyal to Cāṇakya. Thus, every character in the drama displays the quality of loyalty. Amātyarākṣasa displays the quality of sacrifice also to sustain his loyalty. It is Cāṇakya who displays the quality of appreciation of the merit of Amātyarākṣasa. He realises the depth of Amātyarākṣasa's quality of loyalty and shifts it to Candanadāsa.

From this brief sketch of Sanskrit dramas, it is clear that both emotion and value are deliniated in Sanskrit dramas which has made them to survive for centuries and make impact on Indian mind even today.

7

Sanskrit Sociology, Hindu Women, Traditions and Modernity*

Kapil Kapoor

Flawed Feminist Critiques

FEMINIST critiques of Indian social reality are flawed in that they assume an absolute, universalist Hindu code. They are also asymmetrical with given Indian reality in that they are derived from the reality of, for want of a better word, Western social system which in its history of unbridled sexuality and in its progressive weakening of the institutions of family and marriage and a general ethical collapse, in the nineteenth-twentieth century, is foundationally different. Again the Feminist Theory, like other Western sociological, economic, political and biological theories, is open to interrogation for its evolutionary imperative that constructs "modernity" as a "higher stage of development." Again, the Feminist critique is insufficiently argued because it is carried out in total disjunction with the long tradition of sustained sociological thinking in India. We therefore argue, that the question of Indian womanhood has to be discussed in the context of total

* An earlier version of this paper was presented at the national Seminar on "Women, Tradition and Modernity" at the Indian Institute of Advanced Study, Simla, 2002.

knowledge of thought and practice and it must come down to the contemporary legal and factual situation of Hindu women, a very progressive legal condition with progressively reducing disabilities, a state which is in continuity with and, in fact, enabled by Indian sociological thought and practice as enshrined in the Dharmaśāstras, Nibandhas and the Customary Law.

I

Use of Western Feminist Discourse

While there is a long textual history[1] of discussion of women-related issues in the Indian tradition, the contemporary urban-centered debate by English educated men and women originated as a response to Western Feminist discourse and concerns. There are two important dimensions of this Western Feminist theory — first, originating in a concern for social and political inequality of women, it has developed into an aggressive arm and ally of minority politics by using the logic of "constructedness" of female identity and roles devised for subjection of women, a logic that is claimed to be applicable to all the "others"; secondly, the theory though ostensibly concerned with gender, is in fact, fundamentally rooted in sexuality and how the societal ethics has handled or handles sexuality in the West. It has, therefore, spawned 1980s onwards, Gay and Lesbian criticism.

In both these dimensions, Feminist theory was found to be of immense political use in the Indian context. As an

1. Upaniṣads have stories/narratives that constitute and resolve women-related problems, the story for example of Jabala in *Chāndogya Upaniṣad*. Yaska (ninth c. BCE) discusses questions such as a daughter's right to property, her eligibility for performing death-rituals of her parents, and the participation of a woman in a complex social network that gives her a multiple identity.

articulation of minority politics, it has come in handy to subvert the mainstream Hindu traditions. Read all the papers and all the collection — the analyses are directed only at the Hindu society in what is a self-evident political act. And as a theory of the rights of sexuality, particularly of female sexuality, it enables a questioning of the two central institutions of family and marriage that are governed by the principles of restraint and norm (*saṁyama* and *niyama*), whole Hindu ethics in fact.

II

Limitations of Western Theory

As in other areas of knowledge, in women studies also, we have tried to fit the Indian reality to a borrowed Western framework. It is not that women in India have no problems — the issue is whether these can be rightly understood in an alien social framework without reference to our own history of social practice and ideas. In the process of applying every shifting framework, we unquestionably accept not only the constructs but also the assumptions that are always so definitely culture/history bound. The choice of the alien framework then constrains the discourse and the methodology — the analysts selectively choose and mine, Indian social phenomena/ practices and knowledge texts, specifically sociological texts (Dharmaśāstra), mythology (Purāṇa) and literary texts (Mahākāvya) to demonstrate the adequacy of the Western theory and to rubbish Indian life and traditions.

As the Indian reality and context are crucially different and as India has a strong tradition, continuous and cumulative, of sociological thinking that has always taken into account the internal multiplicity and diversity of Hindu social reality and thus has been sensitive to the intrinsic non-absoluteness of sociological constructs, it is not only advisable but imperative to look into the whole question of construction and status of women by locating oneself in this Indian paradigm.

There is a further limitation — we often get trapped at a particular point, while the Western thought, like any other dynamic thought, moves on. A case in point is the opposition of tradition and modernity — theme statement for this seminal — an opposition that assumes "tradition" and "modernity" as two stages in the evolution of culture. While some of us — "traditionalists," if you please — have always been questioning the validity of the basis of this opposition, voices have now begun to be heard from within the West. But the practitioners of Western theories have not yet woken up to the emerging critique of this whole thinking in general and of "modernity" in particular. In the precincts of Western universities, the ethnocentric and evolutionary prejudices embedded in structures such as "modernity" have begun to be questioned and the whole idea of progress is now seen as a myth, a myth rooted in "biological Darwinism" that bred at one point of time enthusiastic optimism in all thinking, including that in the social sciences, about the future of humanity.

Disllusionment with "Modernity"

Pessimism has replaced this enthusiasm and concepts such as "development" and "growth" are now suspect as they have begun to be seen as simply loaded valuations of "change." "Modernity," it is realized, is not an evolved state as it was made out to be but simply another culture, an alternative culture. Its evolutionary assumption of Darwinism, of time, is once again being revalued in relation to the non-Modern culture's cyclical concept of time. As Prof. Jorge Armand, apart from his views on "modernity" and Darwinism that we have reported above, puts it:

> It is much more scientific to think of modernity as a culture and not as a stage in the evolution of human race. . . . There is also the unfounded supposition that "progress" really exists, which . . . is one of the principal myths of modernity.[2]

The same evolutionary prejudices, Prof. Armand argues, are deeply embedded in the contemporary social theory, in the idea of social change and progress, a kind of "social Darwinism." However, the scholar goes on to note that "the idea that human kind had passed from a condition that was in every way inferior (ethically, economically, socially, etc.) to a superior one (with greater human fulfilment, freedom, decency and happiness) today seems native, considering the historical events of the twentieth century."[3]

In fact, there is a general disillusionment with what "modernity" has actually achieved. A Chilean scholar is quoted as saying:

> A rural lifestyle had been the norm until the eighteenth century. Western societies changed this and went for urban life, and now we have megalopolises, slums and all the problems of cities. Western societies went for industrialization and have achieved the alienation of man in a technocratic world run by computers. They went for hygiene and have ended up meddling with the natural biological order with all the unforeseen consequences that arise from this. But above all Western societies went for freedom as their essential goal and now face an excess of regulations, all kinds of pressures and consequently, a lack of freedom.[4]

---

2. Jorge Armand, *Beyond Modernity* (2000), Merida, Venezuela, Universidad de Los Andes, p. 8, Mimeod. It reached me, courtesy Prof. Asis Datta, Vice-Chancellor, JNU.
3. Ibid., p. 11.
4. Luciano Tomassini, in "EL into del desarrollo," Attali, Castoriadis, Domenach et al., ed. Kairos, Barcelona, 1987, p. 73, quoted by Prof. Jorge Armand in the tract cited above.

What the world faces is a "generalized crisis" — ecological disaster (hole in the ozone layer and global warming); population explosion; high consuming, much wasting human being; unequal food distribution; appearance of "pandemics" (AIDS, Acquired Immune Deficiency Syndrome); reappearance of infectious diseases; return to tribalism and ethnic wars, and generalized dependency on drugs — "culturally acceptable drug dependence."[5]

Problems of Western Society

More serious than all this with reference to the Western society, Jorge Armand says there is:

> this lack of an ethical frame of reference as we approach the new millenium. *The values and basic social conventions that have existed since time immemorial, that determined human relations, especially the family and gender roles, and which had fundamental role of giving coherence to society have lost their authority and force.* No alternative set of values has replaced them; quite the contrary. Traditional religious beliefs and socio-political ideologies that were valid until recently are continuously giving ground in the face of the silent advance of a shapeless and stultifying belief in economic power, money, consciousness and status . . .[6]

Two scenarios of the future of mankind, we are told, are being sketched — the apocalypse, a thermo-nuclear collapse of modern Western civilization and the dehumanized Cybernetic-genetically engineered world, a final triumph of Logic and

5. Eli Lily and Co. put Prozac on the market in 1988. According to *Newsweek* . . . worldwide sales of this anti-depressant are currently running at more than 1 billion dollars a year. Doctors, the majority of whom are not psychiatrists, are issuing 1 million prescriptions each month, mostly for healthy people who just want to feel "happy." (February 7, 1994). Cited by Prof. Jorge Armand.

6. Ibid., p. 6.

Science, where human beings would be robotic. Is there a third choice?

As the crisis deepens, it is said, "it cannot be overcome by simply putting filters in chimneys and water-treatment plants in factories . . . solutions . . . must come from a critical reappraisal of the modern world and the culture itself. . . ."[7]

The solution, it is suggested lies in "(1) ending the historic dichotomy of Science and Religion; (2) acknowledging the intrinsic oneness of man and the universe, and as a corollary to that unity, a universal ethic; (3) the acceptance of the cognitive value of centres of human energy other than intellectual/rational, such as the corporeal/emotional, and the possibility of communicating knowledge by means other than the conventional written or numerical systems."[8] Making a distinction between "man's *innate* or *natural* needs [that are] common [to all human beings] and *induced* or *created* needs, which vary in nature and complexity from culture to culture," they also argue that "the two principal psychological needs are security and membership of a group. Furthermore all human beings also need to feel that there is a significant purpose to their existence."[9] This is a sum up of what "traditions," "non-modern" societies have stood for, what the Indian intellectual tradition and the lived life have always stood for.

III

Arguing Tradition

Tradition, therefore, is being argued back, and pushed centre-stage by real life experience as an alternative culture. Strong, resilient cultures like ours have in any case withstood

7. Ibid., p. 7.
8. Ibid., p. 30.
9. Ibid., p. 21.

challenges, retained their basic character and yet at the same time modified themselves and evolved in response to changed contexts and needs. The Dharmaśāstra has always asserted that *dharma,* individual and social, has to be constantly renewed according to time, place, community, individual and extraordinary conditions (*kāla, deśa, jāti, vyakti, apāta*). But what is happening in the case of women-related discourse in India is a sustained attack on those very time-tested traditional Hindu practices by the English educated spokesmen of modernity. While modernity-spokesmen are uninformed about the foundational Indian sociological thought, those who know that thought have not joined the argument.

But a real debate is possible between Indian tradition and modernity with reference to feminism. We should take a look at the validity, applicability and efficacy of the Feminist theory, at what it would ultimately amount to in terms of Indian social structure and social goals. We should also examine the foundational sociological thinking, the Dharmaśāstras, to grasp the rationale of the existing social practices and also evaluate this thought in the context of changing social reality. Finally, we should look at the contemporary legal and societal position of women.

IV

Different Indian and Western Social Conditions

Western social condition has been and is very different from ours. Three facts stand out. First of all the societal attitude to sexuality, both male and female, has been different. Both homosexuality and lesbianism have some kind of legitimacy ever since Plato (Symposium) and Sappho, the poetess of Lesbos. Add to this the Old Testament narrative of the two cities of Sodom and Gomorrah and you have a picture of unbridled sexuality — a sexuality not governed by any societal institution or by an ethical framework. There is a sanction, in Genesis, in the roots of Western civilization, for self-indulgence and for the gratification of one's appetites and desires. No ethics of restraint governs these.

Secondly, as we have already noted, there is an ethical vacuum. There always was of a certain kind. The post-renaissance collapse of ethics following the death of God, is a story in itself. In any case, there never was anything analogous to the Indian system of *saṁyama* (restraint) and *niyama* (the right way). The closest you come to it is in the Greek ideal of moderation. In this frame of unbridled sexuality women are more vulnerable and pay a higher price. We see this unbridled sexuality in the high incidence of teenage abortions and unwed mothers and the concomitant trauma.

This unbridled sexuality is more harmful when the institutions of family and marriage are weak. We see in our times all kinds of non-conventional modes of living together designed for transient pleasures and satisfactions. In line with the inbuilt obsolescence of modern technology, human relationships also come with inbuilt transience. They are also in tune with consumer economics, the use and discard economy. Nothing endures about these relationships. And when the core family has dissolved, there is no question of any larger network of relationships or social roles. In this framework the woman loses her bio-social identity as a mother or as a wife and there is no question of any larger meaningful identities.

Add to this the paradigm image of the unwed mother and the complete absence of the sister role, in the Western tradition, after the one and only Antiqone, we can see the real problem of woman's identity in that society. What is the woman's identity? None. She ends up as "Baby-doll" with the Marilyn Monroe image.

The denial of bio-social roles, intrinsic to womanhood, in contemporary Western history, therefore, does not amount to much, for there is in fact no substance to these roles in the Western society. It is easy therefore to argue that these are just empty words — which is what the Feminist assertion of socialization through language amounts to.

V

Indian Social and Intellectual Context

It is easy to see how the Indian context is totally different. The Hindu family is recognized by sociologists the world over as a recognizably different and a vibrant institution, recent changes none the less — sociology texts devote separate chapters to this institution. The Hindu family structure extends in varying degrees, depending on the intensity of Western influence, to widening concentric circles of relationships. Both men and women therefore have complex identities in terms of these human relationships besides the identity they may have or claim in terms of their profession or personal achievement. As much honour attaches to achievement of excellence in these bio-social roles as to professional roles and there is individual, collective and psychiatric evidence that these bio-social roles well-performed yield deep satisfaction and are important, perhaps necessary, components of happiness. The whole structure or network is founded on the key concept of duty (as against rights in the Western society and in our Western inspired constitution) — a parameter that places equal disabilities on both men and women.

And this family-network is not a recent development — it is an ancient system and its survival over thousands of years is the proof of its value. Talking of the conceptual method of functional relationship or role definition, Yāska the ninth century BCE semanticists gives the example of the same lady being identified as mother, daughter, wife, sister, *bhābhī, mausī, cācī, nanad, māmī, buā*, so on and so forth. The existence of innumerable kinship terms in the Hindu social system — and their absence in the West — tells its own story of cultural density in the area of human relationships. For an average adult Indian, there are infinitely many answers to the question "Who am I?" And this applies to both men and women. This *over-identification*, if one may use the term, has a deeply useful psychic-moral effect of curbing your *ahaṁkāra*, of taking the focus away from your own self, and enabling you to seek satisfaction by doing things for others.

So the bio-social roles are very real and substantial and are not just linguistic constructs. Their reality is ensured by the concomitant conduct, acts and expectations and the deep sense of identity they provide.

Again, India has handled sexuality differently. Its reality and its power have been more explicitly recognized than in any other culture (no other *śāstra* has devoted to it) and no other culture has honoured sexual union as our culture has done (witness its place in temple sculpture). But from reality of the urge to an honoured fact of life, there is a movement through a rigorous ethical framework, both institutional and general. Sex is an appetite and its gratification, like that of other appetites such as hunger, has to be regulated as is required by the general Indian philosophy of self-imposed restraint and abstemiousness (*saṁyama*). Again, unlike other appetites, its gratification has social, beyond-the-individual consequences. Therefore apart from the personal, there is the need for social regulation. And the Indian sociological thought therefore restricts sex to marriage and procreation. "I am also the sexual desire attended by a desire to procreate," says Śrī Kṛṣṇa to Arjuna. These constructs are deep-rooted and immanent and provide the necessary strength and character to the institutions of marriage and family — violations notwithstanding.

And then the language and the paradigm images. *Śuddha Brahman* is gender-free; its expression in language is in all the three genders — *bhagavatī/citti; ātman/puruṣa; brahma-jñāna.* Both *duḥkha*, suffering and *mokṣa*, freedom from suffering, are gender-neutral. Modern Indian languages (Punjabi for example) are in fact woman-friendly. Consider for example, the grammatical gender of clothes — male and female.

VI

Feminist Critique of Hindu Society

We have to therefore examine the whole question of woman's identity and place in our society in the total context of knowledge that is available to us.

The feminist movement took shape in India in the 1970s. Rather than being the cause or instrument of a new-look and life conditions of the urban and of the educated/working women, *it in fact became possible because of the change that had already occurred due to the increasing education of women.* It is difficult to assess what contribution it has made. The three major women's movements that we saw in the last two decades in India, the Chipko Movement and the two anti-drinking movements in Andhra Pradesh and Haryana, mass movements that succeeded, albeit temporarily, were purely native movements inspired by traditional thought and had nothing to do with the urban, academic Feminist discourse which in terms of activism rarely proceeds beyond slogan-shouting, in a posh or politically important place, with media in attendance.

In fact, there is a clear divide between the speakers and audiences of this academic discourse and the mass of women struggling to change their life-conditions. Take for example the case of dowry — while the urban educated elite would want it to be eliminated, the rural woman, on account of the need to prevent fragmentation of land, would want to restore the strict concept of *strīdhana* — the daughter's share in the form of gold and silver (and not *consumer* items — computer, fridge, television, etc.) over which she had complete control by law. Theory must address the reality and at the same time accommodate change.

Therefore, uncritical acceptance and application of a Western theory we said would always be problematic. Consider for example the elements of Hindu society that have come in for criticism at the hands of the Feminists, elements that have a bearing on the status and treatment of women in Hindu society. We can examine these in four sets: (a) issues; (b) customs; (c) signifying instances; and (d) images representations in mythology and thought.

(a) The following *issues* have been raised:

1. Is fidelity (monogamy) an ideal only for women?
2. What rights of divorce and re-marriage obtain for them?
3. Do they have equal right to education?
4. Do they have equal right to parental property?
5. Can women/daughters perform rites, particularly death rites and rituals?
6. Do/Did women have access to knowledge texts?
7. Are they subject to father, husband and son in the three stages of their lives?
8. Why *kanyā-dāna*?

(b) Questionable customs and practices:

1. *satī*
2. dowry (*daheja*)
3. infanticide (aborting the girl child)
4. bride-burning
5. taking on husband's family name
6. not being able to be known by the mother's name

(c) The signifying instances are:

1. Sītā's *agni-parīkṣā*
2. Renunciation of Sītā by Śrī Rāma
3. Draupadī's disrobing

(d) Images and representations that are questioned are:

1. of goddesses representing powers and functions
2. icon of *ardha-nārīśvara*
3. philosophic opposition of *puruṣa-prakṛti* (Sāṁkhya), and of
4. *ratī-praṇa* (*Praśnopaniṣad*)

A thorough exposition of the facts and issues involved in all these is something that will need independent and extensive space. But before we respond briefly, we say that we are told about all these but much is left out. So this amounts to a half-truth and half-truth is a form of falsehood. We are not told that there is a balance of Śiva-Śakti that holds the cosmos and everything in the cosmos in place. We are not informed about the 51 *śakti-pīṭha*. We are not told that no family ritual or ceremony is complete or possible without the wife. We are not told that in our psychology, all the positive propensities (*daivī sampadā*) that are conducive to liberation from suffering are feminine (both in gender and in context) while the demonic properties (*āsurī*) are masculine. We are not told of the eight learned women named and honoured in the Vedas (Śaci, Gārgī, Mamatā, Viṣwavārā, Apālā, Ghoṣā, Suryā, Vāk), we are not told that Sarasvatī is the goddess of all Vedic learning. We are not told that some of the most beautiful images are female, such as Haṁsavāhīnī Sarasvatī and Makarvāhinī Gaṅgā. For those who have not fully assimilated these or lived with these images, for those who are unfamiliar, it is easy to dismiss these as "deification" designed to cover up. But, they are as real as and are certainly to be preferred to the images of demonization. We are not told that a wide variety of concepts and practices, often contradictory, are subsumed under the designation Hindu and that we cannot make general statements such as "Hindus practise *satī*" for that just is not true across the spectrum, or even true across time being a custom that once was localized and conditioned by the external factors."

We are not told that there is a history to the Hindu social practices, that they have been dropped, added to, changed and have evolved over time in response to real life situations and needs. "We are also not told that Hindu Society continues to be, as it always was, amenable to reform by law."

VII

The Vedic Position

Above all, we are not told about what the ancient intellectual texts have to say about the ideal of life. Upaniṣads speak neither of man nor of woman separately but of human beings. They speak of and suggest human problem solutions. The solutions are based on a tremendous principle, the principle of all of us evolving towards *mukti*, freedom. It is a movement from the physical to the spiritual, from the mundane to the divine, an effort at realizing oneself — "I am the body and the mind. But more than that I am the spiritual principle." This is the basic message of the Upaniṣads. Both men and women may identify themselves with this principle. Swami Vivekanandaji, nearer our times, stressed the same powerful idea of the freedom of the self for both men and women alike. Our psychology also says that both men and women are basically spiritual; the body and the mind are instruments — it is the *ātman*, the self, which is the *tattva*, the *kartā* which is seeking *mokṣa*. This is captured in that image in the *R̥gveda* — the body is the chariot, mind the reins, and *ātman* the driver.

The problem remains the same wherever the person is born and whether as a man or as a woman. The difference lies in the method — if one identifies with the body, the problem is physical; if with mind, it is intellectual, and if with spirit, it is spiritual.

There was thus absolute equality in Upaniṣadic times, *dharma* was the same for both men and women. During the epic period the demarcation began between men and women. Kr̥ṣṇa and Rāma seek *mokṣa*, liberation, in ways that are different from those of Draupadī and Sītā. Or, is it the same? The performance of one's *niyata karma*, duty? Why was the difference introduced in the first place? This merits research. And the fact that in spite of that there have been extraordinary women-intellectuals, sages, rulers, warriors in the long Indian history right down from Ahalyā Bāī Holkar of Indore to Indira Gandhi in our times.

VIII

Women in Hindu Law and Practice

The elements of Hindu society that come in for criticism and that have been listed in Section VI can be looked at from the point of view of contemporary Hindu law and practices and also from the point of view of the Dharmaśāstras. For example, there are mistaken notions about what the texts say about questions such as fidelity and the right of divorce, right to property, right to remarriage and the right to perform rites and rituals — in fact all the issues that we have listed under "(a)" above. It needs to be stated quite categorically that in the Dharmaśāstras fidelity is mutual — as much a man's duty as a woman's. Similarly, we should note that some Dharmaśāstras explicitly grant women the right of divorce under certain conditions as also the right to remarriage. We may also note that certain restrictions about ceremonies or rites applied only to the *gṛhastha* women and not to the class known as *brahmavādinī*, women who devoted themselves to a life of learning. Again there are discussions in these texts about the right of woman to perform ceremonies and rituals — Yāska for example describes this in his *Nirukta*. Again no one is debarred from study of knowledge texts — what is restricted is the right to *recite* those texts, an activity that needs years of *technical* training and is required to be performed with great precision. Given the socio-familial life of married woman, this activity was not considered fit for them as they could not be expected to give so many years to the training needed. However, as we are all aware now that things have changed, women have formed sorts of consortiums to perform rites and rituals and if Pune experience is a pointer then this fact is obviously welcomed by the larger society. The question of right to parental property is a tricky question. In the *dharma* texts, this has been debated and discussed at great length. The girls have a right to their father's property is not denied by anyone. The point at issue is the form that this girl's share should take. This is important for an agricultural society such as India's where fragmentation of land leads to unproductive holdings, a matter which has been agitating the Jāṭa peasantry of Punjab and Haryana even in recent times. The traditional solution to this problem was in the form of *strīdhana* — a share in the form of gold and silver. It is not surprising that giving the girl her due share in some form or the other is still the most widespread practice and has often taken odious forms. It has taken today the form of consumer goods — fridge, television, oven and a Maruti car. In a discussion on the television, the experienced rural women expressed themselves against this form of *strīdhana* or "dowry" because the consumer items are used and expended by the in-laws and at the end of it all the woman is left with no security against adverse circumstances. These ladies argued that *strīdhana* should be in the form of only gold and silver. This is one case where the progressive legislations (Prohibition of Dowry and Woman's Right to Property Act) have proved not only ineffective but also sometimes socially fissiparous, a case of law not in tune with the spirit and reality of the society.

If we look into the customs and practices that are evidently irrational, practices such as *satī*, bride burning, aborting the girl child, taking on the husband's family name and not being able to be known by one's mother, we find that there are misconceptions about what the *dharma*s lay down about these matters and also that there are competing practices and points of view. No text prescribes *satī* as a desirable practice and the first *satī* according to Purāṇas took place when the husband was in fact alive. There is no question of arguing for such a practice and no *dharma* lays it down as a social duty. Even when it was practised — during middle ages particularly — it was not a pan-Indian phenomenon restricted as it was to certain upper castes and classes in Rajasthan and Bengal. Today, not only the law but even the community looks askance at this. It is another matter that when such a thing takes place it becomes an object of curiosity mixed with reverence — but this is no confirmation of a social practice but only an expression of a sense of awe at such a supreme *tyāga*, sacrifice, which it is assumed to be. Practices like *satī* and bride burning or infanticide and its current form of aborting the girl child are legally and socially rejected and condemned as criminal acts. Both the law and the community are unforgiving towards a family in which bride burning takes place or in which both bride burning and infanticide takes place. The point is that these are criminal acts and are treated as such by the Hindu society. They are performed in secret — so the perpetrators know that they are committing a wrong. We have to judge the society by its attitude to such acts and not by the incidence of criminality.

In the other two matters again, there is not much substance. There are ancient tales such as one we have mentioned in the beginning of Satyakāma Jābāli which show that even in ancient India one could be known by one's mother. The contemporary practice takes care of this — now we are required to mention the father's name and the mother's name and girls are now free and often do, in fact, retain their maiden names even after getting married. These are now non-issues. Then why *kanyā-dāna*? Why not *putra-dāna*? In a civilization that puts greatest premium on renouncing, the giving away of the dearest and the most precious object, is the highest sacrifice. Hence *kanyā-dāna* as the highest sacrifice. But there is *putra-dāna* also — witness the Naciketā story in *Kaṭhopaniṣad*.

As for the signifying instances — Sītā's fire-ordeal, renunciation of Sītā by Śrī Rāma, Draupadī's disrobing — suffice it to say that these are matters of interpretation because they figure in *kāvya* texts where the meaning is constituted by several factors such as the composer's intention, the context, coherence between various parts of the text, the literary mode of communication and the theories of meaning. Just as "acid test" in English is not literally an *acid test*, in the same way *agni-parīkṣā* is not literally an ordeal by fire. As for the renunciation of Sītā, it is a very complex act in the ethical domain and would require much space to discuss. Here one can point out two things — one, Śrī Rāma after the renunciation lived the life of an ascetic and second, Śrī Rāma later had also to renounce his most beloved and devoted brother, Lakṣmaṇa. Both these acts of renunciation had disastrous consequences. The renunciation of Sītā is not thus a simple matter of a woman being ill-treated. As for Draupadī's disrobing, apart from the ambiguity about what this disrobing had actually meant in effect, it may be pointed out that this act was the turning point in the history of our civilization. And that for this single act of dishonouring a woman publicly, the country and the community waged a cataclysmic war with total devastation as the consequence. Therefore to treat this simply as an insult of a woman is to reduce the episode to the level of the trivial. As for images and representations of woman as goddesses and the objection to them as "deification" that is designed to hide the truth, one may respond in a number of ways — Hindu mythology evenly distributes primal energy in all creations between the male and the female; Hindu philosophy sees them as a unity and not as two opposing principles; Hindu iconography captures the philosophical assumptions as well as the attributes of those elemental forces that are given "forms," male or female. A political reading of this rich texture of thought can only be subordinate to the philosophic, the aesthetic and the physical readings. Above all, "demonization" can be as much motivated as "deification" and I am sure that, psychologically, demonization is worse than deification.

To sum up, in a discussion of matters such as these, there are three domains — private, public and conceptual. Sociological criticism will be inadequate if it restricts itself only to the public domain, if it restricts itself to the level of the phenomenon, without going into its conceptual foundations. Such superficial criticism, unrelated to the thought and the community, is not likely to have any socially significant effect. Most of the elements of Hindu society that have come in for criticism are now archaic and they have become archaic because the Hindu society is a very dynamic, self-reforming society, with its reforming spirit deeply embedded in a introspective, self-reflective process of intellection which manifest in the long traditions of texts, figures and commentators.

IX

Hindu woman is very vital today. As Sādhvī Vivekaprajñā of the Ramakrishna Order observed in her 1994 discourse:

> The only field in which some of Swamījī's [Swāmī Vivekānanda] vitality is visible is in the field of women. Women, modern Indian women, Hindu women, are very vital today. They have tremendous problems. I would rather call them challenges. All around, these challenges abound and women accept them and try their best to come to terms with them.[10]

Their success story is self-evident. There is no domain now which is an exclusively male domain. And whichever field they choose to work in, they distinguish themselves. They are getting educated at a fast rate — the rate of growth of schoolgoing girls is twice that of boys. The parents take pride in educating their daughters and the daughters are more

10. From notes taken in a lecture delivered by the speaker in JNU in 1999.

grateful. There is now a high level of public acceptance of women leaving the precincts of their homes and entering the public sphere.

And governed as she is by modern Hindu law, she suffers from no legal disability. Codified Hindu Law is the contemporary Dharmaśāstra and of course there is the Constitution — Article 15 (1-3) after excluding all disability on grounds of sex, goes on to say that:

> Nothing in this article shall prevent the State from making any special provision for women and children.

This progressive Hindu law did not arise in a vacuum. It is rooted in history and tradition, in customary law which is itself rooted in the large body of sociological thinking enshrined in the Dharmaśāstras and the Nibandhas. Its eclecticism, its acceptance of diversity and its dynamic spirit that provides room for change and reform are products of a tradition. It is therefore worthwhile to look at the traditional sociological thinking in relation to women.

X

Women and Hindu Dharmaśāstra Texts

There are two sources of the modern Hindu law — texts (grantha) and custom (*ācāra*). There are three kinds of texts — Śrutis, Smṛtis and Nibandhas. Smṛtis are of two kinds — Dharmasūtra and Dharmaśāstra — and span the period roughly from 800 BCE to CE 600. The Nibandhas, digests and commentaries, are glosses on important Dharmaśāstras and span the period roughly from seventh century to the end of the eighteenth century CE. These were written in different parts of India, in the local languages, and served as law in that area. Custom that becomes authentic basis for norms should be ancient, continuous, definite, not unreasonable, not immoral, not opposed to public policy, not opposed to given laws. The structure of texts looks like this:

Sources of Hindu Law

- Texts (*grantha*)
  - Śruti
  - Smṛti
    - Dharmasūtra
    - Dharmaśāstra
  - Nibandha
- Custom (*ācāra*)

Dharmasūtra	Dharmaśāstra
[Six major]	[Six major]
Gautama	*Manu*
Budhāyana	*Yājñavalkya*
Āpastamba	*Parāśara*
Vasiṣṭha	*Nārada*
Viṣṇu	*Bṛhaspati*
Hārīta	*Kātyāyana*

The Dharmaśāstras are not just prescriptive texts — they record widely varying practices and customs as well. So they differ from each other on crucial issues — thus attesting an acceptance of plurality and the principle of non-absoluteness in social practices. The important point is that in almost all important matters, there is not just *one* right way. In that sense, the social code is not rigid.

To take some examples —

The *Baudhāyana-* and *Āpastamba-Sūtra* differ on several points. Unlike Āpastamba, Baudhāyana approves of *niyoga* and *eight forms of marriage*[11] from strict śāstric to downright

11. Brāhma, Devatā, Ārsa, Prājāpatya, Āsura, Gandharva, Rākṣasa and Piśāca.

abduction. *Hārīta Dharmasūtra* also recognizes eight forms of marriage but two of these are different from the Baudhāyana, thus adding up to ten kinds of marriages in vogue in different parts of the country. *Hārītasūtra* also recognizes two classes of women — *sadyovadhu* (newly married) and *brahmavādinī* (devoted to knowledge). The second category is allowed *upanayana*, like men, and study of Vedas (knowledge texts). The *Vasiṣṭhasūtra* allows re-marriage of widows. *Śaṅkha* and *Likhitasūtras* allow even widows to have a child by *niyoga*. *Viṣṇudharmasūtra* allows inter-caste marriages. Kauṭilya allows widow re-marriage, also allows re-marriages of women the whereabouts of whose husbands are not known, allows desertion by a wife of a husband who is of bad character or a traitor or impotent. He also allows divorce on grounds of mutual hatred. The *Kātyāyana Smṛti* deals specifically with rights of women — the *strīdhana*.

Such conflicting views are a recognition of plurality of practices. At any given time in a vast society such as ours, all practices may co-exist at a given time. Is there a fixed norm in the face of this variation? What the *smṛtikāras* do is to establish a cline of acceptability, a valence among the competing practices. Then guided by a wider world-view and philosophy, a *niyama*, the preferred mode, is propounded. *Niyama* is just one of the many ways of doing something, the preferred way no doubt but not the norm — it will vary from place to place and time to time and community to community. This is the closest to the concept of something being ethically correct. The decision is not always easy. Confronted with contradictory practices or views, and the problem of individual and collective welfare, the decision is taken with the help of a set of meta-rules. Thus that is to be preferred which:

(i) is in consonance with equity, justice and reason,
(ii) has wide acceptance among people,
(iii) is applicable in the new age,
(iv) is in accord with *ācāra*, common practice,
(v) is not against the spirit of the age, if not in accord with *śāstra*.

There is a line of authority to decide the above:

(i) Śruti (Vedic texts), and where Śruti is silent,
(ii) Smṛti (philosophic/sociological texts), *śāstras*,
(iii) *śīla*,[12] where even the Smṛti is silent,
(iv) by *ācāra*, the common conduct, where there is no model,
(v) by *śiṣṭavyavahāra*, the conduct of the cultured, where common conduct is not available, and
(vi) by one's own conscience, if no other guiding principle is available.

Deciding Right and Wrong

So *dharma* as enjoined duty or as right conduct is not something absolutely given, but something to be constituted.

We have used the word *dharma* in the sense of "the enjoined duty." *Dharma* in this sense has the following characteristics. It is —

(i) what is approved by the conscience of the virtuous (Manu),
(ii) duty (Medhātithi),
(iii) what obtains widely and also what ought to,
(iv) a consolidated scheme in which widely divergent practices, none really obnoxious are accepted (Manu, I.108-10), and

---

12. The conduct of the virtuous who are free of hatred or in ordinate affection.

(v) practices restricted to peoples and places, time and emergency (Manu, I. 118).

Dharma, thus, being relative and variable, social criticism that assumes an absolute, universalist Hindu code is fundamentally flawed.

But there is another larger sense of *Dharma*, an overriding ethical principle or righteousness which finally determines the desirability of even the enjoined duty. *Dharma* in this second sense, as an over-arching parameter that decides desirability or righteousness of a course of action, has *niyama* or discipline as its basic function. In the absence of such a determining parameter, the society will descend into anarchy. As has been said —

> There is hardly any activity of man which is not prompted by desire (*kāma*)
> but to act solely on desire is not praiseworthy; so to enable him to act with
> propriety, *dharma* is promulgated. (Manu I.5)

Dharma controls *artha* (material pursuits) and *kāma* (worldly desires) and acts that are the results of that control are also *dharma*. It is not exclusive — there is a lower *dharma* in which a thing is permitted and a higher *dharma* in which refraining from it is considered more meritorious. It involves truth (*satya*) and non-violence (*ahiṁsā*) — what it sanctions must not cause trouble to any being, must not hurt people (M: IV, 238), must not end up unhappily and be derided by the people (M: IV, 176). The ethical correlates of *dharma* are: truth, non-violence, non-stealing, purity and control of one's senses. *Mahābhārata* gives the widely quoted definition:

> *Dharma* is that which is attended by the welfare of the world and by non-injury to beings. (XII, 109.10.15)

Dharmaśāstra thus are texts that go into the details of human life and seek to lay down rules of conduct that are governed by an overarching ethical principle — the welfare of all. The whole structure is centered on what we owe to others and is in sharp opposition to the self-oriented philosophy grounded in rights. This code of *niyama* governs all aspects of life. Patañjali in *Mahābhāṣya* explains this Mīmāṁsā construct — *niyama*; if there is more than one way of doing something, one of them is to be preferred over the rest. "The law-givers and the Mīmāṁsakas knew only too well that their laws had been changed or modified from time to time according to the needs of an expanding society, but the content of *dharma* in all its essential parts remains the same. Just as a person may grow and shed particles of his body and yet retain unchanged his individual identity, so does this body of Hindu *dharma* retain its unity and individuality across the ages from the time anterior to the *R̥gveda*. Its *sanātana* (timeless) character is not destroyed but maintained by its adaptability and adaptations. The institutions of today are founded on ideas that were active and alive in the R̥gvedic and pre-R̥gvedic times."

XI

This universal human ethics of *dharma* (*sāmānya dharma*) is the overall framework *applicable to all* both men and women. Within this global framework, there is specific *dharma* (*viśiṣṭa dharma*) for each constituent of the social order.

The specific *dharma*s are laid down with reference to the Hindu family — the husband/father's; the wife/mother's; the son/brother's; the daughter/sister's. And the *dharma* of each is progressively enjoined in relation to the immediate family, the larger family, the society and the country. The thinking is not governed by the welfare or the "identity" of the individual — it is governed by his happiness which *is only possible through the* *happiness of others*. As for woman, a commonly cited text says — "wife is home," a statement of the woman's centrality in the family. The *śāstra*s, therefore, lay down many injunctions how she is to be regarded/treated:

> everyone should honour her if they want to prosper
> — M. III. 55
>
> where they are not honoured, all good acts become futile
> — M. III. 56
>
> where she is dishonoured, the family perishes
> — M. III. 58
>
> where both husband and wife are happy, auspiciousness and general welfare resides. — M. III. 60

It is also noted that no rite can be performed without the wife and that as mother she takes precedence over the father and the teacher in receiving respect. It is also said that

> she should always be married to a worthy man — better she remain a spinster than she marry a worthless man.
> (M. IX. 89).

Marriage is a sacred, indissoluble bond and the marriage hymns stress the mutuality of both husband and wife.

In the *Atharvaveda* marriage hymns, it is said —

> May we have divine protection; may we live together, with all our differences; may we not hate each other; may what we acquire in the way of knowledge be strongly efficient in its results. (*Atharvaveda*, 14.1.42)

> I hold your hand for *saubhāgya* (good luck) that you may grow old with me. (*Atharvaveda*, 14.1.50)

While the *dharma* is tough both for the man and the woman, it is harder for woman. The *śāstra*s themselves recognize this:

> *yaga: para: puruṣo dharma*
> *tapa pradhāna nārī.*

Woman's life or role is seen as a *tapa* — a rigorous, a rigorous life — and it is no doubt dedicated to some object or cause, here the welfare of the family. This emanates partly from her being the mother and partly from the social structure at the time. It is important to note that the modern, successful Hindu women does not move away from this definition.

We must reiterate here the meta-rule for all *dharma* — it is subject to change and modification with change in time, place and community and with change in the general conditions of life. Thus while most of the injunctions listed above remain alive in the current social practice, sometimes in form and quite often in spirit as well, the changes in the economic pattern of life have created pressures on the social pattern as well — the most important being the need for a Woman to contribute to the family income. Added to this is the other important factor — the thought and example of the Western society with its ideals of freedom and identity, its individualism and its relaxed sexual mores. How has the Hindu society responded to these challenges?

XII

Response of Hindu Society

The Hindu society has been keeping pace with the changes in life conditions. Even a cursory examination of the recent history of Hindu law makes it amply clear that the Hindu society is completely amenable to reform by law — there is non-resistance to reform by law. The *dharma* of woman has been constantly redefined. Beginning with the 1856, Hindu Widows' Remarriage Act, there have been a series of legislations that have in effect altered the social, and individual, condition of Hindu[13] women: Special Marriages Act (1954), Hindu Marriage

13. Constitutionally, Hindu law applies to Hindus, Sikhs, Buddhists and Jains.

Act (1955), Hindu Marriage (Amendment) Act (1976), Hindu Succession Act (1956), Hindu Adoptions and Maintenance Act (1956), Dowry Prohibition Act (1961), Hindu Minority and Guardianship Act (1956) and Hindu Widows Property Act (1997). There have been, besides these and other enactments, about 2000 judicial decisions in suits concerning women's rights.

The effect has been tremendous. The Hindu women today are the most vibrant section of the Hindu society. Whichever field they enter and, none is barred to them, they excel men. The Hindu parents have pride and pleasure in the education of their daughters. Studies have shown that the rate of growth in the number of girls going to schools is twice that of the boys. Of course, the effect is uneven. The pattern of life of rural women remains broadly what it was but it is changing fast with rural girls going to schools in increasing numbers. The poor women and the women of other castes still suffer most of the disabilities. But then again it is not always or uniformly so.

In many respects women working as a part of labour force live a less constrained and socially more equal life which is not very different from that of the menfolk. The point is that the reform is definite though uneven and the pace of reform is increasing. This reform is matched by changes in the community attitudes and manners that are hard to define. The Hindu society is evidently resettling into modes that are required by the changed conditions. There is an interesting example. Till 1976, a husband could go to the court and force a working wife to give up the job in another town and return to restore his "conjugal rights" but after 1976 under Marriages Law (Amendment) Act, a woman cannot be forced to give up a job for this reason.

A purely legalistic view is insufficient in the context of our society. The law shows the direction of change and, on the other hand, the way the customs are modified or new customs come into being show how the society is assimilating a new injunction. With its traditional wisdom, the Hindu society would ultimately decide the value of everything by estimating how it contributes to and detracts from the individual and collective happiness. This wisdom is also a part of the individual psyche. Only this can explain why even in this increasingly materialistic environment, the Indians (both man and woman) continue to attach so much importance to human relationships. Only this can explain why a successful professional Indian young woman seeks to combine her familial duties with her professional duties, bearing in the process enormous strain and challenge. It is evident that in the process the Indian males are also going to change — they are going to share more and more of those domestic responsibilities that were earlier considered to be exclusive duties of woman alone.

XIII

Need for Right Perspective

Again and again in this essay we have been talking of the text and the practice. There is and there has been always, as is only to be expected, a dialectical relationship between the two. In fact, a large number of successive Dharmaśāstras, Nibandhas show that thinkers were constantly revising their systems in response to the changing needs and conditions. Also the number of conflicting practices incorporated in a given text show that just as there are divergent injunctions, there are also divergent practices coexisting at a given time in a populous society inhabiting a vast geographic area.

Therefore, a simplistic view is excluded for the reason that such a view would not achieve much. There can be no discussion on any one unit's rights or duties without a discussion of the principles or of the contexts. Also a wife's rights or duties, or for that matter of a husband cannot be discussed in isolation from the rights and duties of the respective partners, the parents, the parents-in-law and the children. Also, we cannot discuss practice in isolation from *śāstra* just as we cannot evaluate *śāstra* in isolation from practice. A holistic view is necessary if the discussion is to have some practical value.

However, while practice may diverge from the injunction, it is important to take note of the fact that the practice and the injunction also converge in another instance in the same society, at the same time and in the same context. The contemporary research attitude of focusing on deviations, on exceptions, on error and on difference, makes sense only in the current ethnographic mode of thought. No doubt ethnography and empiricism have gone hand in hand for a long time now in modern research but this does not negate the fact that there is an alternative point of view, that of the synthesis, of the norm and of commonness and unity. It is an interesting fact of intellectual history that Monistic, Hebraic systems tend to take to ethnography and empiricism while the pluralistic, Pagan systems (Indian/Greek) tend towards models of synthesis and convergence. Had it not been so in our intellectual history as well, India would not have survived as a cultural/intellectual identity.

A shift in the perspective would thus lead to a very different kind of investigation and results even in woman's studies.

XIV

The Philosophical Dimension

We come finally to the wider philosophical dimension. As we said earlier we all live at three levels — physical, mental and the spiritual. Depending on which level we are focusing on, the problem will take that particular hue. It has been a belief in India, a belief as old as the Upaniṣads, that this universe is a vast pulsating entity. There is an element of life immanent in every thing. Manifestation of this life is not all alike or of one grade. It is said that this life "sleeps in metal; is awake in plants; moves and grows in animals; knows and knows that it knows in man." Self-awareness is the attribute of being human. It is because of this self-awareness that human being is always striving to transcend his little self and approximate godhead. We all want to become more than ourselves, i.e. we want to grow beyond our physical self. It is clear that progress beyond being a man, i.e. being a human, is not in the physical domain. It is in the domain of the mind and spirit — *ādhyātmika*. It is in the realm of the culture and spirit that we become free of our body and its limitations, its *duḥkha*. Free of the body, we cease to be a man or a woman and of the goal of our endeavour as identical — *mokṣa* — which has been defined in Sāṁkhya as liberation from suffering here and now. In the Indian tradition the *puruṣārtha*s — *dharma, artha, kāma, mokṣa* — are common ends for man and woman alike, the ultimate being *mokṣa*. It is not a coincidence that the three key categories, *brahma, duḥkha, mokṣa* are gender-neutral. Śrī Kṛṣṇa, Rukmiṇī and Rādhā all achieved *mokṣa* — their paths, instrumentality, differed.

XV

Conclusion

We conclude by saying that it is necessary to relocate ourselves in the rich intellectual tradition to be able to analyse the specificities of the Indian woman's situation. Of course, we have to take into account the other traditions and also contemporary thought. We also have to take into account the living practices, the competing practices and juxtapose them with theory. Such holistic inquiry must be carried out in a spirit free of both self-adulation and self-flagellation. What one has to log on to is the overriding fact that the Hindu society is not a static society, certainly not in the sphere of women, and that it is amenable to reform by law. It is a society that is visibly different today from what it was, say, even two decades ago. It is desirable, therefore, in the interest of total understanding, to put this dynamism in the centre in every debate about the woman's condition in India and, further to look for the roots of this change, and amenability, to change, not just in contemporary Western thoughts but also, and more adequately, in the attested, long tradition of reformative, highly differential, dynamic sociological thought of India.

8

Sciences in Ancient India

Pankaj S. Joshi

Introduction

A FEW years ago, when I was visiting South Africa, in the city of Durban I had a meeting with the iron lady of African freedom struggle, Fatima Meer, who was a close associate of Nelson Mandela. She asked me what I was doing, and I told her I study cosmology and astrophysics. She immediately asked me if I had studied Indian cosmology, as described so vividly in various Purāṇas, and other ancient Indian texts. She then went on to tell me how impressed she was with some of those ideas and descriptions and asked me if any of those concepts could be tested and described from a modern scientific perspective. While I had no immediate answer for her, she certainly had a point well made, and the question she raised still very much stays in my mind.

While it is exciting to think and believe that India had already, in her impressive past, discovered all the modern sciences available to us today, when you actually try to figure out *exactly* what all was discovered in India in terms of concrete scientific achievements, it is never an easy task. One is hampered by the lack of precise references, and only some general information becomes available.

Our Scientific Inventions

In fact, whenever some modern scientific invention is announced, whether it is space travel, or planets of the far away stars, or genetic engineering, some of our people have always a habit of saying. "Did not our *ṛṣi-muni*s already discover it?". But if you ask when and where, no body is ever able to give any specific answer. This reminds me of a very interesting conversation I have had with Dr Satyavrat Shastri, a renowned Indologist and Sanskrit scholar. He mentioned to me, "Whenever people talk to me as above, I always ask them that in that case, why are you telling this only now, after the discovery has been announced by other countries, and *never* before that?" Obviously, the point made is that, while we can be always proud of our rich heritage, there is no point in unnecessarily gloating at the cost of rational thinking, which only prevents our own progress in the correct directions.

When you try to figure out the exact scientific achievements of ancient India, that has never been an easy task. There are, however, several evidences available that India must have indeed made serious and remarkable achievements in various sciences in our long and hoary past which stretches to thousands of years at the very least. It is by all means an issue of serious research to which considerable attention needs to be paid, and much study and effort will be required which may possibly yield important results.

I shall try to raise here a few questions and hints, together with some comments, which I think are of basic importance. Hopefully, that may spur us to undertake and initiate serious researches into this topic from various dimensions, leading to further details and data. In fact, it is possible that modern scientific techniques can come to our aid here in this task, when we started thinking systematically in these directions.

Of course, the thoughts and comments given below express my thinking where there may not be a complete agreement. But it is possible that some of it may inspire us to undertake and initiate some intensive studies into these issues from different angles. Also, the subject is vast, hence by no means I claim to cover here all the interesting and important topics, and what is referred to below reflects my own personal choices.

So, let us consider a few important questions:

Q. *Is it true that great scientific discoveries were made in ancient India?*

From the information we have this looks possible, and I give some reasons for this below.

Science and Ancient Indian Literature

When we look at the ancient Indian literature, such as the Vedas, Upaniṣads and so on, we get impressed at the enormous intellectual heights which have been achieved and expressed in these creations. There can be no doubt that highest order of logic and finest reasoning existed with those who created these ideas and knowledge, independently of our agreement or otherwise with all the contents. What has survived now in ancient Indian literature, surely gives strong evidence of the great intuitive power and mental abilities of those who created it.

Q. *But then, we are asking about the scientific discoveries, and so let us first ask: What is science?*

We observe and experience, all the time, the *universe* or the *nature* around us. This is primarily through the agencies of our senses of vision, touch, hearing, taste and smell. Just as a stone thrown in a quiet pond causes waves in the water, these experiences and perceptions cause ripples in our mind, giving rise to different sensations and thoughts. These could be the feeling of joy and vastness (e.g. when we observe the night sky on a clear summer night), or surprise, or amazement, and so on. One of these most primary feelings is that of curiosity, when we try to understand and comprehend the nature of phenomena around us, and when we start asking questions such as how big the universe may be, how do seasons operate, why do eclipses take place, why the sky looks blue, and so on.

Thus, the observations of the universe around us lead us to the attempts to understand how things really work. In other words, we start trying to decipher the fundamentally basic laws governing the nature and structure of the universe. Our intuitive and logical thinking helps us to do that, and that is often supplemented by the mathematical ways of looking at things, when we look for and start recognizing definite shapes and patterns in the nature around us. The amazing thing is that the universe around us turns out not to be some kind of a haphazard and arbitrary entity, but frequently we find the phenomena to be systematic and organized, where certain basic laws appear to govern the happenings. The job of science is to recognize and formulate these laws.

In this broad sense, it may not be incorrect to say that any intelligent human being, who keeps on making keen observations on things and phenomena around us, and then tries to classify and understand these phenomena, trying to formulate basic laws and patterns governing these, is a *Scientist*. In fact, in the earlier days of modern science, the aim was to discover the *essential* and *real* constitution of things, which the ancient Greeks called *physis*. The term *Physics*, which represents today one of the most fundamental and basic modern sciences, at the foundation of much of our current scientific knowledge came from there, meaning originally the endeavour of seeing the essential nature of all things.

From such a perspective, I would like to suggest that it is unlikely that those who created the finest works such as above were totally unaware of the laws according to which the *Nature* around us operated. In other words, it is unlikely that they achieved all this, but have had no idea on different fundamental aspects of nature, including what we call *Scientific Laws* today. Some support for such a hypothesis comes from certain advances made in mathematics in ancient India, which are fortunately better documented, and have survived through history. Obviously, those who created such fine mathematics and counting system must have used these for various applications.

Intensive Research in Ancient Science

I am trying to make a case for undertaking intensive researches in *Ancient Indian Sciences.* This will be necessary in order to support and complement any of the conclusions such as above as to what we exacly achieved scientifically in ancient India.

Q. *Did ancient India make great progress in mathematics?*

Fortunately, this is one area where one can make some statements with definiteness. Research has been done on the development of mathematics in ancient Indian texts and it is found that books such as *Taittirīya Saṁhitā, Śatapatha Brāhmaṇa,* and *Yajurveda, Atharvaveda, Ṛgveda* besides additional Saṁhitās do contain many mathematical works and references.

There was a need to determine the correct times for Vedic ceremonies and an accurate construction of altars was required, which apparently led to the development of astronomy and geometry.

Several topics discussed here include use of geometric shapes, including triangles, rectangles, squares, trapezia and circles. There have been discussions on equivalence through numbers and area. Equivalence led to the problem of squaring the circle and vice versa, and early forms of Pythagoras Theorem were also discussed. Subsequently, the works of many mathematicians such as Āryabhaṭṭa, Brahmagupta, Bhāskarācārya, Varāhamihira, Śrīdhara, etc. have become known and studied. These researchers studied several different topics, mainly related to astronomy and geometry.

Indian Scholar's Contribution to Mathematics

The mathematical verses of the Āryabhaṭṭa cover some of the following topics in arithmetic, such as method of inversion, various arithmetical operators which include the cube and cube roots, which probably originated in Āryabhaṭṭa's works. The "new" operations of squaring and square root also originated with his work, it is believed. Again, in algebra, he discussed topics such as: Formulae for finding the sum of several types of series; Rule for finding the number of terms of an arithmetical progression; Rule of three — improvement on Bakshali Manuscript; Rule for solving examples on interest — which led to the quadratic equation. It also appears clear that Āryabhaṭṭa knew the solution of a quadratic equation. He appears to have used trigonometry in the modern sense for the first time.

In addition to important contributions to all the main areas of mathematics, Indian scholars were responsible for the creation, and refinement of the current decimal place value system of numeration, including the number zero, without which higher mathematics and modern science would not be possible.

Indian scholars made vast contributions to the field of mathematical astronomy and as a result contributed mightily to the development of arithmetic, algebra, trigonometry and secondarily geometry (although this topic was well developed by the Greeks) and combinatories. Perhaps most remarkable were developments in the fields of infinite series expansions of trigonometric expressions and differential calculus.

Surpassing all these achievements however was the development of decimal numeration and the place value system, which without doubt stand together as the most remarkable development in the history of mathematics, and possibly one of the foremost development in the history of humankind. The decimal place value system allowed the subject of mathematics to be developed in ways that simply would not have been possible otherwise. It also allowed numbers to be used more extensively and by many more people than ever before.

Again, very large numbers have been named and used in ancient Indian literature. For example, we have *prayutam* (a million, 10^6), *arbuda* (a billion, 10^9), and *śaṅku* (a trillion, 10^{13}). Likewise it goes on to *padma, mahāpadma, kharva, nikharva,* and *paradha* which is 100,00,00,00,00,00,00,000, i.e. seventeen zeros after 1.

This number system goes still much higher, and the point one wants to make is, only if they were using it somewhere, they would have created it all. It also goes on to show that they were fully aware, and used extensively the concept of powers of ten.

Contribution of Yoga

Q. Could one name some other areas where we can say with confidence that ancient India did make considerable progress, and which is also vindicated by modern scientific discoveries?

It appears to be the case that much progress was made in ancient India in the Science of Mind. The numerous Yoga traditions and related disciplines developed in ancient India are a clear evidence for that. After all, all our knowledge is generated, perceived and created through mind and the senses, as they perceive the nature around us.

The modern scientists are certainly aware of our limitations towards understanding the universe through the means of sense perception, and the finite process of intellectual thinking. The subject of cosmology that I study, and which deals with the origin and evolution of the universe, tells us vividly how small and insignificant we are when compared to the vastness of the cosmos. The story of the Blind Men and the Elephant, illustrates the fact that frequently people tend to understand only a tiny portion of reality and then they extrapolate various dogmas from that, while claiming only his is the correct version. In fact, well-known British astronomer Sir Arthur Eddington pointed out:

> Man in his search for knowledge of the universe is like a potato bug in the hold of a ship trying to fathom from the ship's motion the nature of the vast sea. . . .

Thus, there is apparently a limit of how far the logical thinking and intellect could go. The ancients must have realized, however, that unlike other instruments of knowledge, it is possible to extend the limits of mind enormously, and that in fact the mind could be the most powerful instrument of all.

The various yoga disciplines may be considered the means to develop and enhance the capacity of mind, and to take it to higher and higher stages and planes. And while in the process of strengthening the mind, the body is also healed, and is made disease-free.

The mind-body relationship, as espoused by the Yoga philosophy, appears to be increasingly being validated by the medical science today. Certainly, it is nobody's claim that ancient Indians knew everything, but all the same, it goes beyond doubt that much can be learned by the modern man by means of a study of ancient Indian sciences.

There are also examples such as Āyurveda, the ancient Indian science of medicine, astronomy, Jyotirvigyan — that is the science of celestial bodies, and such others. There are good evidences that the art of ship-building and navigation were well developed in ancient India. The magnificent temples that stand today in India tell us about the architecture and civil engineering of those times, and of course, about the fine arts of the day. It appears that the earliest recorded use of copper-ware in India has been around 3000 BCE. Apparently, the earliest documented observation of smelting of metals in India is by Greek historians in the fourth century BCE.

Q. *Why should one bother to study ancient Indian sciences in this modern age when science and technology are making amazing progress?*

The important point to bear in mind is, there is absolutely no reason to think that today mankind is at its highest and topmost peak of knowledge! It is totally plausible that there could have been higher advancements in the past, or future can again bring forth revolutionary changes in our ways of thinking and behaviour. Hence we must think with an open mind both of our past as well as of future. And as for the past, there could not be anything better than a careful study of ancient Indian traditions and sciences in its broader sense, because that can provide us with important and beneficial hints for a good future.

Q. *If we made great scientific discoveries in ancient India, then why so little is known on that? In other words, why we have been so bad at documenting and preserving?*

There is no doubt that we have done rather poorly in documenting any discoveries, that were made in ancient India. Hence, practically little evidence survives on what ancient Indian science we have had. It is also possible that much literature, evidence and knowledge was destroyed during the invasions India faced during the past several hundred years.

This has also to do with a certain attitude that we Indians have on life as a whole. For example, I was talking to an eminent Sanskrit scholar a few years back about the possibility of preserving great Indian scientific traditions. Of course, many such sciences have developed (and vanished) in ancient India. He said, this is an ongoing phenomena, and it is like the ash on fire. There are times when the fire is hidden under the ashes, but at times a breeze of air comes, just brushes away the ashes, and the fire again kindles and shines bright! Similarly, he pointed out, such sciences emerge and vanish in time. He then added, that the one which is eternal does not vanish and is never destroyed. So there is no need for me to worry so much and get disturbed that Indian sciences must be preserved.

With this kind of frame of mind, obviously there were no *Intellectual Copyrights,* and anybody was allowed to learn a given subject further to the necessary scrutiny to make sure he or she was found to be worthy of that knowledge.

Q. Do we have some specific examples of possible scientific advances in ancient India?

I mention below a few points without going into details, which may be considered to be some such examples. Such cases again require further investigation:

- The *lauh stambha,* which is made of a non-rusting alloy, at the Kutub Minār site in Delhi gives an idea of the well developed level of metallurgy of those earlier times.
- A well-developed architectural knowledge has been used in several very large temples.
- A knowledge of various acoustic effects is used in construction of some temple halls and forts (e.g. Golconda Fort near Hyderabad).
- There was apparently a well developed war-science existing in ancient India, as can be inferred from several different references.
- Recently I had been to a Fort close to Ramtek, at Nagpur, excavated in recent decades. While it was pretty hot outside, some of the interiors were so designed as to preserve a very pleasing cool atmosphere, even in the absence of trees at the moment.
- Some principles of optics are seen to be in operation at the Virūpākṣa temple.

Q. Is jyotiṣa (astrology) a science?

Earlier I used to avoid getting into this question, but I have realized that my surname being Joshi does not help and I am always asked a question on astrology, so let me include a brief comment here.

Based on my discussions with some eminent Sanskrit scholars, I understand *jyotiṣa* has two parts. One is the mathematical part, or *gaṇita,* which I think is fairly accurate. The other is *phalita,* or prediction part, and that depends very much on intuition and guesswork, and is generally not regarded as scientific.

Conclusion

Finally, I would like to end with a word of caution. Even if we did make a good scientific progress in the past, we must save ourselves from the danger of being complacent and from ending up in being merely self-congratulatory. Because, any such progress in the past does not mean anything if we cannot revive it today, and use it towards our present material and spiritual benefits.

While it may be good to be proud of our heritage, we should certainly not overdo it, at times bordering on egoistic patterns, that can only be harmful. Let me give you a recent example of such attitudes that I have come across. I was just looking sometime ago at the science text book of my daughter, and saw a picture of a brāhmaṇa with a shaved head, and with a *coṭī* at the back, and below the picture it was written, "Kaṇāda Ṛṣi," who discovered atoms. It may be alright to give pictures of a Newton or Raman, Rutherford or Einstein in a textbook, because we have definite information on these persons who have just lived in recent past. But to give a picture of Kaṇāda Ṛṣi, on whom we have no information as to how and when he actually lived, what he really looked like and so on, can clearly cause misconception. In my view, such attitudes do not produce any benefit to our cause, or enhance our glory in any manner.

In fact, it is quite possible, that it is these kinds of attitudes and self-satisfying ways of life, that lead us to be captured by foreigners, when we could not save from the scientifically advanced attacks from across the borders. While we were sleeping under the self-satisfaction of our past glories, without really understanding their content, outsiders made important scientific progress by understanding and applying useful laws of nature. These were then used to conquer and capture us, leading us to several hundred years of slavery in the recent past, causing abject poverty and ignorance throughout this nation. What is needed is a serious attention and research into these aspects of India, so that we could bring out some gems out of this vast ocean of ancient Indian wisdom, and use it towards the betterment of mankind.

9

Comparative Philosophy
Problems, Assumptions, and Possibilities

Bina Gupta

I

IT is not an exaggeration to say that comparative philosophy is gaining in prestige and yet there are many unexamined presuppositions that lie behind what is entailed in such an endeavour. First of all, what or with whom does one compare, and how does one compare those that are compared? Given that a lot of actual work in comparative philosophy is concerned with comparing the East and the West, are we to assume that comparative philosophy as a discipline requires that only the East and the West can, or need be compared? We all know that this is not necessarily the case. Within the East there are two large ancient traditions of thought, the Indian and the Chinese, which are often, although less often, compared. One could add to these two the Tibetan and the Japanese traditions; in that case, we would have more possibilities. If as a researcher in comparative philosophy one compares the major traditions within Asia, then the same could be done with regard to the major traditions in the West, for example, the Greek and the Roman, the Judaic and the Christian, the Anglo-Saxon and the Continental, the French and the German, and so on, leaving aside for the time being the American and the

African traditions. Thus to claim that comparative philosophy as a philosophical enterprise involves only comparing the East with the West is short-sighted; it cannot be accepted. However, for the present, I will not deal with this facet of comparative philosophy; I will restrict myself to another, perhaps more unsettling aspect, i.e. even after the researcher has chosen what to compare, she still has to decide *how* to compare?

This raises several skeptical questions; for example, is it possible to compare two *radically* different thought traditions? Where must the researcher take her stand, that is to say, from which position she should compare the two? Let us, for instance, consider the task of comparing the Chinese with the Western traditions, more specifically, Confucius with Aristotle. First of all, if one were not well versed in both the Chinese and the Greek languages, one must use English translations of the pertinent source materials. We very well know that the translations of the original source materials vary considerably; they generate controversies. For example, translations of Greek texts into any of the Western European languages are controversial enough, translations of the Chinese texts into any Western language are still more controversial, which the extant English translations of the *Analects* and the *Tao Te Ching* clearly demonstrate. We know that, despite the best intentions of the translators not to jeopardize the integrity of the original texts, all translations at one level unavoidably are interpretations in so far as they involve the translator's subjective frame of reference. when this is the case, then one is comparing interpretations and translations of those texts, and not the original texts themselves. Those of us who work with Sanskrit texts and compare their ideas to Western philosophical ideas know very well the risk of such comparisons. For instance, *Brahman* is often translated as "God" when the translator interprets it from a theological perspective, and more often, as "absolute" when tinged with a purely metaphysical sense. Either of these translations already predetermine whether the texts of the Upaniṣads lie closer to theology or to Hegelian metaphysics.

Still, the problem goes much deeper; it is not simply a problem of translating from one language to another. Comparing Confucius with Aristotle requires placing each one of the two in his original cultural and historical context; yet, a comparative philosopher cannot claim to be a cultural historian. One could argue that, although the thoughts of a thinker are embedded in her historical-cultural milieu, they are not inseparable from it, because it is possible to separate the content from the background irrespective of whether one is dealing with Confucius or with Aristotle. If this is possible, then a comparative philosopher need not worry any more about history, and should go directly to the contents of the systems to be compared. That this is possible, however remains to be shown.

Comparison proceeds smoothly as long as the compared systems exhibit obvious similarities. When this is the case, the comparative philosopher runs the risk of overlooking what are otherwise critical differences, because it is possible that the comparative philosopher has so interpreted her material that their radical differences have been subdued and eliminated in order to support her conclusion. This perhaps is the greatest danger in comparing two historically and culturally distinct traditions. The purpose of a comparison is not only to bring to light what is common between two systems, but also to show what are the differences between them. Such fruitful comparisons do not require that the two systems be radically different. In fact, when two systems are radically different, one does not take the trouble to identify what is common and what is different, something one can very well do within each tradition. One can, for example, state where Kant and Hegel agreed and where they differed; they belong to the same tradition. To treat Confucius and Aristotle, or Śaṅkara and Husserl, or Śaṅkara and Hegel, in the same way, would be the result of some hasty decisions on the part of the philosopher engaged in such comparisons; there is more to the story than what a hasty comparison reveals.

Let me elaborate a little more on this skeptical question. If T_1 and T_2 are two *radically* different theories, the real problem lies not in comparing them, but establishing the possibility of any mutual understanding between them at all. This is easily demonstrable in cases of formal theories with different axiomatic bases. Consider, for example, classical mathematics and the intuitionist mathematics. It is not enough to say that the former accepts the principle of excluded middle, and that the latter does not; it is important to keep in mind in this context that their fundamental concepts of existence, negation, and proof all differ. Thus, the issue becomes: How to make them engage in a meaningful dialogue whereby any fruitful comparison is even possible?

A comparative philosopher assumes that such seemingly different systems as Husserl's transcendental phenomenology and Śaṅkara's Advaita Vedānta, or Rāmānuja's qualified non-dualism and Hegel's absolute idealism are not like T_1 and T_2 in the above example. A philosopher might assume that she is doing comparative philosophy only if she speaks the same language as the philosopher she is comparing, irrespective of whether it is Sanskrit or German, so that she might talk to each thinker and settle their differences as well as discover commonalities. However, in reality a comparative philosopher is really trying to initiate a fruitful dialogue between, not two philosophers, but their texts. Still what justification is there for the assumption that such a dialogue is possible? Shared language, whether original or translated, cannot be justification enough. What justification could there be except for the belief that the human mind works in the same way irrespective of history and geography, culture and language? But to assume that, implies that half the work is already done.

The above objection to comparative philosophy really takes its stand on what is known as cultural relativism. Radical cultural relativism implies of course that though one may compare philosophies of different cultures; no judgement of one in terms of another is possible. When one considers the fact that one of the motives of comparative philosophy is to show that different philosophical traditions can engage in a meaningful conversation, thereby implying that a radical form of cultural relativism is mistaken, it is ironic that the very same cultural relativism is used as an objection to the very possibility of carrying out that project. I will not use this occasion to refute cultural relativism. However, I believe that cultural relativism cannot be used as an objection to the very project which is meant to undermine it. The real issue is: Can we understand a culture that is radically different from our own culture? If we fail to establish that we can even begin the project of comparing a philosophy belonging to any culture with a philosophy belonging to any other culture, then we can never begin to do a comparative study. Like any scientific research, the work of one generation in a field has to be improved upon by the scholars of the next generation. But, if one waits for a prior assurance that we understand the subjects of comparison faultlessly, an assurance that is never to be forthcoming, then the research will never begin. The point that I am trying to make is as follows: the project of comparative philosophy cannot be held hostage to the thesis of cultural relativism which itself cannot simply be taken to be true a priori. In fact, an evaluation of cultural relativism requires that comparative work be undertaken.

Once begun, comparative analysis presents the problem of perspective; the question arises: from which perspective should the comparison be done? The problem here is not simply one of the insider *vs.* the outsider. When a Chinese philosopher [a philosopher of Chinese ethnic origin] compares Confucius with Aristotle, in a certain sense it is true that he has an inside understanding of Confucius, while being an outsider in relation to the Greek philosopher. While that is true in a certain sense, it is not, however, entirely true. The point that I am trying to make is as follows: A Chinese philosopher does seem to share with Confucius a cultural background, so in that sense has an inside perspective when comparing Confucius and Aristotle. The modern Chinese scholar, however, in another sense, is removed from the Confucian tradition by 2000 years at least, and may have never gained the sense for the Chinese language of that time, and in this sense is also an outsider in relation to Confucius. Similarly, a modern Greek scholar may not be completely at home with the Classical Greek of the Periclean age. Does a modern Indian scholar have an inner understanding of the Vedic literature? She may think that she does, but she is also an outsider in many respects. So, with few exceptions perhaps, any comparativist on any topic is an outsider. Again, the scholar who embarks upon a comparison between Confucius and Aristotle may be an Indian, in which case she may not make any claim at all to being an insider with regard to either of the two philosophers being compared. The problem in comparative philosophy, then is not that there is an imbalance between the insider's special understanding and the outsider's lack of it; the problem is rather that which the relativist points out regarding the impossibility of comparing radically different systems. But as stated earlier, this is a spurious problem and begs the question. The relativist is like the one who is afraid of getting into the water, lest he may get drowned, and so never learns to swim. The comparativist takes risks, proposes results, which then can be checked by other scholars, whereas the relativist assumes that the project is hopeless, and so never enters into the field of comparison.

Accordingly, there are two fundamental and conflicting assumptions that a comparative scholar may choose from: one may either choose to accept that there are radically different conceptual frameworks among which there can be no meaningful dialogue, and hence no comparison; or, one may choose to assume that in spite of seeming differences no difference is so radical as to disallow any dialogue, and that with persistent pursuit of conversation one can discover more and more points in common. A comparativist has to proceed on the second assumption. Neither of the two assumptions can be proven or refuted a priori. Comparative philosophy provides empirical research; and as it progresses, it makes the second assumption more plausible.

Thus far I have only argued for the project of comparative philosophy. For those scholars who depend upon the translation of original materials, as well as for those who are the translators, some comparison is almost unavoidable. In translating a Sanskrit text from Vedānta or Buddhism, one almost unavoidably uses technical vocabulary of her contemporary philosophers' writings in the language into which she is translating. Thus, when Stcherbatsky translated *Dharmakīrti* into English, his translation was mediated by the philosophical vocabulary of the German Neo-Kantians. I think the same characterizes any translator. One may discard the antiquated language of the philosophers in the beginning of the twentieth century, but one would instead be using the language of more recent analytic philosophers. Any such translation then is covertly, and almost unavoidably, doing comparative philosophy.

Let us now consider a different question: What to compare? Shall we compare systems as a whole or shall we compare bits and pieces of those systems separately? For example, shall we compare Śaṅkara's Vedānta with Husserl's transcendental phenomenology both taken as total systems, or shall we begin with comparing more specific aspects of the systems, e.g. by asking whether the Husserlian concept of intentionality is found in the Advaita Vedānta school of Indian philosophy. In other words, there are two possibilities: either compare systems as wholes or compare the constituent concepts separately? If it were the case that the system is so tightly unified that no concept can be torn from the whole, then there is no alternative but to choose the first option. But most philosophical systems are not such closely-knit systems. In that case, it may be a more fruitful beginning to focus upon specific concepts, and not worry about the totality of a philosopher's thought. No a priori judgement on this issue is possible. If one compares modern Western logical atomism, for example, Bertrand Russell's with the Nyāya ontology, then one can do it in a piecemeal fashion. However, if one is comparing a philosopher X, say, with Hegel, then since in Hegel's system every concept internally implies other concepts, there would be no other option but to deal with the system as a whole.

It is at this point that some would object to comparing philosophical ideas piecemeal. They would warn that, although an idea in one tradition may look to be very similar to another idea in a quite different tradition, that similarity may only be deceptive. We have to take into account the total contexts in which the idea functions in the two traditions. Comparing the

East and the West, for example, one may focus on the role the idea of causality or the idea of truth plays in both traditions. One may loosen these ideas from their contexts and then proceed to compare them; however, such an exercise, we shall be told, runs the risk of oversimplification and decontextualization. I have no doubt that decontextualization does seriously transform a concept. Therefore, the comparativist should strive to identify the overall *context* and proceed on the basis of this overall context.

II

To explain how such a work would proceed, I will make use of E.A. Burtt's essay entitled "How can the Philosophies of the East and West Meet?"[1] By "context" Burtt means an "all inclusive orientation conceived to be required for the understanding of this or that philosophically relevant detail,"[2] which expresses, in his words "something of the genius of its point of view toward life and the world as a whole, and using that insight to throw light on the ideas which have perplexed him and their pattern of relationship with others."[3] Burtt argues that an appreciation of such an "all inclusive orientation" is essential to comprehend the philosophy embedded within it.

For Asian philosophy, at the risk of reiterating the obvious, Burtt notes how different is the cultural, historical, and metaphysical "context" of Asian thought from the West. The philosophies of South Asia, generally speaking, take as one of the central themes the quest of the each individual for self-realization. For Indian philosophy, this context is provided

1. E.A. Burtt, "How Can the Philosophies of the East and West Meet?," *The Philosophical Review*, vol. LVII, no. 6, 1948, pp. 599-604.
2. Ibid., p. 591.
3. Ibid.

by the idea of each individual's "quest for ultimate self-realization" as consisting in "the discovery of the oneness of his soul with the universal soul or the Absolute." It is only in light of such a context that the Indian idea of *karma*, otherwise so baffling for and so misappropriated by the West, begins to make sense. These characteristics reflect Indian tradition's antecedent context, a frame of reference more closely influenced by religion, for example, than is the case with Western philosophic thought.

Likewise, the "architecture of discourse" (if one may use such a phrase) typical of, say, Chinese thought similarly derives from a specific historical and cultural context. One might argue, for example, that the feudal anarchy of late Chou China, more than any other single set of factors, was the major determining influence upon the development of the entire Confucian tradition. Confucius and his disciples — not to mention his later followers — were obsessed with matters of practical ethics. Their concern was the relationship between the person and the state, between social harmony and personal responsibility. It is not altogether unreasonable to claim then that the exploration of this distinction was to prove absolutely critical to Chinese thought in general, and further, that in some sense at least the "flavour" or character of Chinese thought is owed more than anything else to that original preoccupation. Similarly, once we grasp the Chinese idea of human beings as social beings and yet inseparable from nature, the idea of the *Tao* as the ultimate order of regularity "in which all processes of the universe find their place" loses its metaphysical obscurity and takes on a fairly intelligible meaning. The key to the intelligibility lies in the knowledge of the relevant cultural contexts.

In any event, the point to be stressed here is that the context of Chinese philosophy, for instance, is negotiably different from that of either Western or Indian thought. Burtt (following Fung Yu-lan), comparing Chinese philosophy to its Indian counterpart, phrases the point thus:

> Its practical orientation toward the problem of harmonious adjustment to an inclusive whole is just as definite as is that of Indian philosophy . . . but on the one hand it tends to avoid claims of metaphysical insight into the nature of that inclusive totality, and on the other it emphasizes the fact that the individual who seeks such an adjustment is essentially a social being. He is what he is through his relations with his fellows in the here and now, especially his family relations, and whatever self-realization he attains involves a deepening of those relations and the responsibilities which they entail, even though it also transcends them.[4]

Is there a parallel context of Western thought? The presuppositions behind Western philosophy, which give it its unique character and flavour, are the product of a particular history and a set of discrete cultural traditions. In the West, philosophic thought has proceeded on the assumption of a universe of external objects, confronted by independent knowing minds, whose experiences and logical operations are capable of generating true knowledge of the external world, at least when guided by adequate theoretical safeguards. The Western stress has been upon objectivity, objective understanding, precision of meaning, and predication. Its philosophy has relied upon such familiar distinctions, such as subject-object, knower and the known, and the external world and internal or subjective consciousness. Both the content and forms of inquiry distinctive of Western philosophic inquiry have been shaped to some indeterminate extent by — for want of a better term — the "meta-philosophical" assumptions, presuppositions, and values

4. Ibid., p. 594.

which, historically have given Western philosophy its own unique and distinctive character.

Underlying the Western zest for analytic thinking, its separation of theory from practice, for the individualism and with an overwhelming interest in the external world, there is the idea of "experience" which determines the West's conception of fact and of the relation between mind and fact, for instance. The East does *not have this* concept of *experience.* The Indians have, according to Burtt, a concept of "experience" which for the West is irrelevant, a concept which is exemplified in their distinctions between waking, dreaming, and dreamless sleep and *turīya* (states leading to the realization of oneness with the absolute). In other words, "experience" plays a different role in the context of Indian though than it does in the Western context.

In another paper, instead of context, Burtt speaks of "presuppositions and framework of presuppositions."[5] In this paper, Burtt slightly changes his task: here the basic idea of the West is that of "rational understanding" embodied in logic and the empirical sciences, and the basic idea of India is *liberation,* necessitating transcending of reason (and ethics). The rest of the story is pretty conventional by now, but the issue at hand should be clear. Comparing concepts across different traditions requires that the comparativist be extremely sensitive to both her own presuppositions and those of the traditions that she works with.

To sum up, Burtt's point is as follows: the context of Asian philosophy is different from the context of Western

5. E.A. Burtt, "A Basic Problem in the Quest for Understanding between East and West," in *Philosophy and Culture: East and West,* ed. Charles A. Moore, Honolulu, Hawaii: University of Hawaii Press, 1962, pp. 673-91.

philosophies. The perspective of Chinese thought is particular to a given set of cultural conditions, so too is Indian philosophy, and its lineage is likewise different from the complex set of social, cultural, intellectual and socio-political forces that have formed Western philosophy. Burtt's detailed remarks on the apparent incommensurability of certain terms or concepts in Western and Eastern philosophies are designed to demonstrate that such notions as *karma* or *tao* cannot be easily rendered in terms of any familiar Western philosophic category. Some ideas, as he phrases it, force one to "confront something quite alien and opaque."[6] His settled conclusion is that one ought not try to force equivalences across philosophies drawn from disparate cultures; instead, in order to penetrate the philosophy of a different culture, one must attend to its "context," catching, as it were, "something of the genius of its point of view toward life and world as a whole."[7]

III

My reflections on Burtt's theses are also my comment on a very conventional way of juxtaposing the East and the West. We cannot assume that Burtt is unaware of the enormous complexities of the intellectual worlds of the East and the West. But he feels secure that, in spite of these complexities, the idea of liberation as oneness with the universal self stands out as the overall guiding context of Indian philosophies. Likewise, he was aware that the Indians developed logic, but argues that "any proposed pattern of inference was supposed to derive its validity from some ultimate purpose which, it was believed, thought ought to serve."[8] Likewise, as stated

6. "How Can the Philosophies of the East and West Meet?" p. 590.
7. Ibid., p. 591.
8. "A Basic Problem in the Quest for Understanding Between East and West," p. 680.

earlier, the only discussion of "experience" he ascribes to the Indian thinkers is the doctrine of the four states of the self. He did not say, though he could have said, that the Indians did not have a concept of truth as agreement with fact, but regard truth to lie only in the experience of the oneness of all beings with the *Brahman*.

All this is just mistaken, and the mistakes are due not to Burtt, but rather to the Indian philosophers to whose expositions in an East-West conference he was responding. Of the six *āstika* systems (itself an oversimplification) of Indian philosophy that one generally talks about, only Advaita Vedānta which alone takes liberation to be "oneness" with the *Brahman*. Neither Sāṁkhya-Yoga, nor Nyāya-Vaiśeṣika, none of the Mīmāṁsā schools, and none of the schools of Vedānta with the exception of Advaita, subscribe to this belief, and it is unfortunate that in an international East-West conference, only the Advaita Vedāntins represented the Indian side. Indian logic, that of the Nyāya and the Buddhists, and even of the Advaita, did not validate inference patterns by referring to some "ultimate purpose." Logical inference was tested in its own terms no less than the Aristotelian syllogism was. "Experience" translates into Sanskrit *anubhava*, which, in turn, translates into "perception," and the theory of perception (sensory perception, to be sure) was developed in all the schools including the Vedānta.[9] The Nyāya (and the Mīmāṁsā) defined truth of cognitions or *pramāṇya* as *tadvati tatprakārakatva* (knowing an X, which is F, as having F as its predicate).[10] These examples would show how treacherous it is *to look for* some ultimate presupposition or some global context for a

9. Bina Gupta, *Perceiving in Advaita Vedānta*, PA: Bucknell University Press, 1992.

10. J.N. Mohanty, *Gaṅgeśa Theory of Truth*, Delhi: Motilal Banarsidass, 1989.

rich, variegated intellectual tradition. One has to look hard, wide and deep. Similar remarks can be made about characterizing Western philosophy; in the context of Western tradition, one should not lose sight of the fact that Western philosophy encompasses within its fold Aristotle and Sartre, Carnap and Heidegger, Quine and Plato, Kant and Bergson, to name only a few.

That is why piecemeal work is still safer to begin with. Causality in Indian thought is not so unintelligible that we can only illuminate it by placing it in the context of soteriology. The cause, for most Indian thinkers, is that which immediately, unconditionally, and as a rule precedes the effect. Is that so different from the traditional Western conception? I must, however, add that one's optimism at this point may be offset by an unexpected turn or twist, a *mode of questioning* which is not available in the West, or by an answer to a familiar question that comes only in a rather unexpected manner. It is at this point that one has to look deeply for presuppositions, even when they appear obvious. But on this occasion I do not intend to do comparative philosophy; I am only talking about it. As a comparativist, I have experienced the pleasure of finding similarities, soon giving way to the discovery of unsuspected differences. Again, the discovery of deep differences may also be a source of satisfaction, but that satisfaction may level off when one also realizes that, despite differences, there are large similarities in context and structure. The details are what make the experience so lively, the broad sweeping generalizations by comparison feel stale and on weak grounds to be demolished by a single contrary instance.

It is enough for my present purpose to underscore my central contention: that any philosophy or array of philosophic systems does not exist in vacuum. A philosophy neither originates nor develops bereft of some undergirding context. As all human activity, philosophical takes its distinctive shape within a cultural setting, and it tends to bear the mark of that culture. Needless to add, one hopes, that no good purpose is served by denigrating one type of philosophy or attacking its very legitimacy solely upon the basis of its having been derived from one cultural context that differs from another. This is not to imply or to suggest that cross-cultural philosophical judgements are impossible. The foregoing need not be construed simplistically as an argument for philosophies as cultural artefacts whose validity or relevance extends no further than the cultural settings within which they evolved. To say that a philosophy is a product of a culture, and that it cannot be understood fully without reference to that culture does not entail the broader claim that any philosophy is entirely culture-bound. Although shaped by culture, it has meaning and relevance beyond the given culture. Moreover, proper appreciation for, insight into, or understanding of, the specific doctrines of any given system of philosophy requires that allowance be made for its contextual development.

Trans-cultural dialogue is both necessary and desirable — indeed, it is perhaps inevitable. When it is fruitful, it begins with sensitivity to both differences and commonalities, which neither attempts to reduce the former to the latter nor ignores either of them. Cross-cultural philosophic inquiry must be based upon a profound appreciation for diversity, and for uniqueness; when similarities are uncovered, so much the better. They are potentially revealing, as are differences. Whatever unique insights or perspectives are afforded within one philosophy can and should be grist for other philosophic mills; this is the promise of comparative philosophy.

10

Atomistic Formulations in Indian Thought

Victoria Lysenko

> *If, in some cataclysm, all of scientific knowledge were to be destroyed, and only one sentence passed on to the next generations of creatures, what statement would contain the most information in the fewest words? I believe it is the* ***atomic hypothesis*** *(or the atomic* ***fact****, or whatever you wish to call it) that* ***all things are made of atoms*** *— little particles that move around in perpetual motion, attracting each other when they are a little distance apart, but repelling upon being squeezed into one another. In that one sentence, you will see, there is an* ***enormous*** *amount of information about the world, if just a little imagination and thinking are applied.* — ***The Feynman Lectures on Physics****,* lecture 1, p. 2.

I HAVE chosen this well known statement of Richard Feynman, one of the greatest modern physicists, not because it may have some relation to certain aspects of ancient Indian atomism, but because I would like to underline, to make more evident the importance of the atomistic ideas for the development of theoretical thinking in general. How was it possible that long before the experimental discovery of atom and the appearance of the quantum physics with its theories and sophisticated equipment in two great civilizations of antiquity — Greek and Indian — there arose the idea of the ultimate constitutive part of things. If we suppose that it was a result of the observation of some general modes of human activity like constructing something from parts, for example a house or an altar from bricks, or of the destruction of things up to some further indivisible parts, then why this idea did not arise in other civilizations, like Egypt or Messopotamia or China with their highly sophisticated construction techniques? That makes us assume that the presuppositions of this idea may be more of a mental order than of a purely practical one.

Similarity Between Languages

What ancient India has in common with Ancient Greece concerning this kind of presuppositions? The first thing that comes to mind is their common Indo-European substrate, a rather similar principle of construction of their respective languages — the Sanskrit and the Greek. We know that Democritus directly referred to the letters as an image of atoms. In spite of the fact that Indian tradition was mainly an oral one, this common linguistic background may nevertheless be quite important. Besides the parallel between atoms and phonemes in the *Abhidharmakośa* of Vasubandhu (III.85), I can refer to a well-known fact — one of the text containing the idea of atom was translated into Chinese language as early as the fifth century CE, but it has not produced any impact on the Chinese thought. There was no place in it for this idea, because the Chinese language is not constructed, according to principles from letters to syllables, from syllables to parts of the word (prefixes, radicals, suffixes, endings), from words to phrases.

With this fact in mind we pass over to another important hypothesis relevant to the explication of the more or less parallel arising of atomism in Greece and in India — the possibility of a influence or of a borrowing. Till now we do not dispose of any facts proving that Indian thinkers have borrowed this idea from Democritus or vice versa. As far as I am concerned, this kind of borrowing is hardly probable not because there was no contact between the two civilizations, but for reason of a more cultural order. From the Indian side, it was a rather self-centric and close tradition which resisted any external influence. Thus, excluding the influence as an explanatory model, we are left with at least two series of facts. First, some common linguistic factors, morphology of words, and second syntactical structure of sentence — all these facts may serve as prototypes of the idea that one can compose an indefinite number of objects on the basis of some definite types of simple constitutive elements. This idea may serve as a necessary but not an indispensible condition. Otherwise, why could we not find any traces of atomism in Ancient Persia?

But what then constitutes a necessary and indispensable condition? In my opinion, it is a certain level of development of theoretical thinking, of abstract reasoning. It is absolutely inconceivable that mythological imagination or a simple common sense can produce anything like the atom. What does it mean to think theoretically? It means that we are trying to understand what things are by their internal, intrinsic nature, by their essence in spite of their appearance? The atoms are something that we could not see as we are seeing ordinary things, they are not simple observable facts but pure concepts, even if we believe in their reality we can prove it only indirectly, by analogy with observable facts, like Democritus with his example of letters. But we will be mistaken if we suppose that Democritus or his teacher Leucippius have just invented their theory of atoms. When I spoke about a certain level of theoretical thinking I had in mind that certain philosophical problems were already not only posed but received different interpretations and resolutions.

Democritus' Theory of Atoms

What are these problems? Whole and part, cause and effect, essence and appearance, one and many. It is often supposed that in Greek philosophy, Democritus' theory of atoms and void was a reaction against Parmenides' idea of one and singular immutable eternal being and his claim that the multiplicity of existing things, their changing forms and motions, are but an appearance. To account for the multiplicity and changing of physical phenomena, Democritus conceived of the void as an infinite space in which an infinite number of atoms was moving. These atoms are eternal and invisible; small, and their size cannot be diminished (hence the name atomon, or "indivisible"); they are without pores and differing only in shape, arrangement, position, and magnitude. As an ideal object, an atom is easy to manipulate, in that way it has become an important constitutive element in the mental pictures of the real processes. We may perhaps say that the idea of the atomic structure was one of the first theoretical explanatory models in the history of mankind having a universal expository power.

If we know for certain that Greek atomism arose around the sixth or fifth century BCE, turning to India we find ourselves in a total chronological uncertainty — we have nothing or almost nothing which permits us to date the beginnings of Indian atomism. The principal difficulty with dating in India is due to the fact that the body of knowledge in different areas was transmitted orally and the majority of texts that were preserved from these times were exclusively the oral texts. Even if we will establish that this or that mention of *paramāṇu* (in the sense of atom) in some text which reached us was the earliest one comparing with some other texts, we could not conclude from that that it was really earlier, because before their fixation in a written form all these texts were part of an oral tradition which could be in existence over a long period of time.

As compared with Greece, the atomistic ideas were much more widespread in India. At least three traditions of Indian thought have their own versions of the atomism: Jainism, Buddhism, and Vaiśeṣika. In a more late period it is due to Vaiśeṣika that some other orthodox schools, that is, schools which accepted the authority of the Vedas, have introduced the atomic conception in their world pictures (first of all Nyāya, then Mīmāṁsā, Sāṁkhya, Yoga and even Vedānta in its Madhva's dualistic version).

Comparison of Atomism Forms

If we compare the three forms of atomism developed in India with one another, the most ancient among them seems to be the Jaina one. The Jaina atoms have preserved an evidently archaic character. The Sanskrit word for atom is *parama+aṇu* — super fine, super thin, super minute. The Jaina *paramāṇu* are not devided in classes according to the classes of elements, like in other Indian schools. They contain all the properties of gross objects but in their unmanifested form. What is the most important about these atoms concerns not so much their indivisibility as in Greece, as their minuteness or subtleness (the adjective *aṇu* means thin, subtle, minute). Being the smallest unit of matter (*pudgala* — not sentient matter), the individual *paramāṇu* is nevertheless devoid of impenetrability. In the most important Jaina Sanskrit philosophical work, composed earlier in the Common Era, the *Tattva-Artha-Aghigama-Sūtra* by Umāsvāti, it is said that the infinite number of *paramāṇu* could be found at one and the same spot just as the infinite number of light beams could intersect at one and the same point of space. Two *paramāṇu* can form a combination which is held together by the force of cohesion due to the fact that one of them possesses viscosity and other dryness. These are the most important characteristics of the Jaina atomism.

Atomistic Doctrine of Buddhism

Quite probably around the same time (from third century BCE up to the first century CE) besides the Jaina atomism some Buddhist atomistic formulations were also developed along with the development of the Buddhist philosophy. We can find them in the famous *Abhidharmakośa* of Vasubandhu (a text of the fourth century of the Common Era), being itself a compendium of *Mahāvibhāsa*, a Buddhist text, composed around the first century BCE. The Buddhist atomism is even more vague that the Jaina one. The Buddhists stress above all the momentary and changeable character of their atoms. As they make no distinction between the substance and its qualities, their atoms are classified into as many as 14 classes or types, distributed among the three larger groups: the atoms of the great elements (*mahābhūta*): earth, water, fire, wind, the atoms of the qualities of these elements (atoms of smell, taste, colour, etc.) and even the atoms of organs of sense (smell, taste, vision, etc.). These heteroclitic atoms cannot form any regular stable "molecules," but only temporary aggregates (*skandha*), divisible by 7. In this way, the Buddhist thinkers explain the changeable and unstable nature of reality.

But the most elaborated and sophisticated atomistic doctrine belonged to Vaiśeṣika. The origins of these school were quite obscure. It is often supposed that in its earliest forms it was developed independently of the Vedas, but in the course of time its thinkers got into the sphere of the Brāhmanical influence. The *Vaiśeṣika-Sūtras*, the basic text of this tradition (codified around the first century CE) mentions the atoms quite incidentally as though they were dealing with something obvious and self-evident. One may have an impression that in Ancient India the atomistic ideas were so universally known that there was no need to prove or explain them. Only in the sixth century of our era the commentator of the VS Praśastapāda presented this doctrine in a clearer way, but still without any attempt to prove the existence of atoms. Nevertheless, these proofs existed and we learn about them from outside of the Vaiśeṣika tradition. The first of these proofs possess pure logical character. It consist in establishing the atom as a mean to stop short of the regressus to infinity in the process of division (I will return to it later on).

Presentation of Atomistic Doctrine in the Vedānta-Sūtra

Now, I would like to turn your attention to the second proof. Though we know about it from the Commentary of the great Indian philosopher Śaṅkara to the *Vedānta-Sūtra* — and that text was composed in the eighth century of our era, much later than the *Nyāya-Sūtras* where the first proof was announced — we have some rather substantial reasons to believe that Śaṅkara referred to some early Vaiśeṣika text that did not come to us.

Śaṅkara presents the arising of the Vaiśeṣika atomistic doctrine in the following way (I quote from *Brahma-Sūtra-Bhāṣya,* the second *adhyāya,* second *pada, sūtra* 12):

> We see that all ordinary substances which consist of parts as, for instance, pieces of cloth originate from the substances connected with them by the relation of inherence, as for instance, threads, conjunction co-operating (with the parts to form the whole). We thence draw the general conclusion that whatever consists of parts has originated from those substances with which it is connected by the relation of inherence, conjunction co-operating. That thing now at which the distinction of the whole and part stops and which marks the limit of division into minuter parts is the atom.

> This whole world, with its mountains, oceans, and so on, is composed of parts it has a beginning and an end; an effect could not be assumed without a cause; therefore the atoms are the cause of the world.

What can attract our attention here is exactly this very philosophical way to deduce the existence of atom from the generalized observations on objects arising from their parts. Thus the postulation of atom was closely connected with two main philosophical problems — of whole and in parts, on the one hand, and of effect and its causes, on the other. It were namely these two problems which, perhaps, gave birth to the Vaiśeṣika atomism and which at the same time put under doubt its coherence while discovering its weakest points.

Atomistic Doctrine of Nyāya-Sūtra

Let us now turn to the Nyāya proof of existence of atom. In the *Nyāya-Sūtra*, three possibilities of division of a whole into its parts are examined (*Nyāya-Sūtra*, 4.2.15-17): the first one is a division till the full destruction, or rather dissolution of the thing (*pralaya*). But that will mean that all things consist of *pralaya* (dissolution) and they simply do not exist (*Nyāya-Sūtra*, 4.2.15). The other possibility is an infinite division (*Nyāya-Sūtra*, 4.2.17) — in that case the very large object as well as the Dyad (molecule of two atoms) would both consist of an endless number of particles (the famous paradox of the Mount Meru and a grain which would consist of equally innumerable parts). The third possibility is the only valid one — neither destruction, nor regress in infinity are admissible, because there remains the Atom which is something (a physical object) that has no parts into which it may be divisible. As a commentator puts it, "When a cloud of earth comes to be divided into smaller and smaller pieces, that point at when the division ceases, and then when there is nothing smaller, is what we call *paramāṇu* (the atom) — (*Nyāya-Sutra* 4.2.16 — *Vārttika*). But the polemics which follows shows that the fact of being something material even if this atom is of the smallest dimension, is logically hardly compatible with being without constituting parts. In other words, the purely physical character of the atom threatens its status of a metaphysical entity — ultimate cause and origin of all composed things.

The first argument runs as follows: There can be no such thing as the indivisible eternal atom, because it is surely permeated by *ākāśa*, ether; both inside and outside the atom must be surrounded by *ākāśa* and permeated by it; and being so permeated, it must be made up of parts, and being made up of parts, it must be non-eternal (4.2.18). Otherwise, *ākāśa* would not be all-penetrating (4.2.19).

The other argument concerns the way the atoms are connected with one another. Because the atoms are capable of conjunction they must be made up of component parts (*Nyāya-Sūtra*, 4/2/24). That is, explains a commentator,

> When an atom comes between two other atoms and becomes conjoined to them, it brings about separation between them; and from this separation it is inferred that the intervening atom is conjoined, in its fore-part, with the atom lying behind it, and, in its after-part, with the atom appearing in front of it; and these fore and after parts are "the component parts" of the Atom. Similarly, when the atom becomes conjoined in all its parts, it must be regarded as having component parts all over.

In other words, if we assume that an atom may enter in conjunction with other atoms, we must agree that it has its own component parts, but if it has its component parts, it is no longer the atom, the smallest and further indivisible corpuscles. This is a kind of difficulty that arises in all the forms of the philosophical atomism as distinct from the scientific one. As a matter of fact, if we consider an atom to be a kind of a physical body, we may always put under question its indivisibility, but if we try to see in it a kind of non-spatial mathematical point, we could not explain in what way these points may form a physical body. We know very well that the addition of mathematical points is still a mathematical point and no increase of physical volume could be obtained in this way, because these points, unlike the atoms, are devoid of impenetrability. That means that two atoms cannot occupy one and the same place, but as regards the mathematical points even if they are innumerable, nothing prevents them from occupying one and the same point of space.

Facing this kind of difficulty, the Greek and later the Arab atomists, tried to distinguish between the real physical and the imaginable mental divisibility. According to some fragments, Democritus drew a distinction between atoms, on one side, and logically or mentally discernible parts of atoms — the ameros, on the other side. This division has become much more clear with Epicures. For Democritus, the indivisibility of the atoms does not entail the minimality of their size. As we know, the atoms of Democritus differ not only by their forms, but also by their size. On the contrary the atomism of the Vaiśeṣika and Nyāya traditions is based on the idea of the minimal size of the atom which is called *parimaṇḍala* (spherical). The *parimaṇḍala* is a kind of ideal form which is indivisible in logical, or in metaphysical sense. It neither generates the other forms, nor is generated by the other forms. It is a pure metaphysical cause.

But the Vaiśeṣika atom is nevertheless not a pure geometrical figure, it is the smallest physical body endowed with the properties or qualities of the element to which it belongs. Thus, the Vaiśeṣika classify the atoms into four main groups: the atoms of earth, the atoms of water, the atoms of fire and the atoms of wind. The European atomism in its strict sense, beginning from the Greeks is characterized not only by the indivisibility of atoms, but also by their qualitative identity (they are distinct only in shape, size, and motion). In India, on the contrary, the atoms were quantitatively the same (all of them were spherical), but qualitatively diverse. The atoms of earth possess smell, taste, colour and touch; the atoms of water — taste, colour and touch; the atoms of fire — colour and touch; and the atoms of wind — touch only.

But as to the individual, separate atom, the question arises whether it is endowed with qualities? Till now I could not find a direct answer to this question in any of the Vaiśeṣika text I examined, but learning on some indirect clues we may conclude that the physical qualities of the separate atoms were somehow present but non-manifested to the point that we may grasp them. What we perceive as smell, taste, etc. is well and truly the taste and the smell of atoms, but only when they are combined in "molecules." The Vaiśeṣikas talked most often about two kinds of combinations — diads (*dyānuka*) and triads (*tryānuka*), but in what way were they formed? That brings us to the one of the most complicated issues of the Vaiśeṣika atomism — the formation of perceptible objects from imperceptible atoms.

According to Praśastapāda, there are three ways in which ordinary objects are formed:

(1) summation of the component's magnitudes,

(2) loose combination (*pracaya*) of components,

(3) increasing the number of components.

For example, the cloth and threads.

But, concerning the beginning of the world cycle (*sṛṣṭi*) when all the atoms are in their non-combined state, the most sophisticated argumentation was elaborated by Praśastapāda's commentators Śridhara, Vyomaśiva and Udayana. As maintained by Śridhara, a single atom cannot be productive, because if it could, it would produce its effects eternally and these effects would be indestructible. Nor could the combination of three atoms be regarded as productive, because being a perceptible and thus made up of parts, a *tryāṇuka*, has to be equally made up of constitutive parts which would be in their turn effects. Therefore, its parts were *dvyāṇuka* (a substance-effect), but not three single atoms (substances causes). And finally, two dyads do not produce perceptible things because it is not the number "two," but the number "three" which is productive of large measure of things.

We can see here a general problem pertaining to metaphysics in general, regardless of its concrete forms, Western or Eastern. I am referring to the problem of the transition from Metaphysical to Physical, from One to Many, from Eternal to Transient, from Absolute to Phenomenal, etc. The metaphysical *prima causa* seems to be too pure and too perfect to initiate a production. Actually, the Absolute in metaphysics cannot be nothing else, than a sterile entity, incapable of production. To be productive, the One needs something which is more than One, the Pure needs something, say, not so pure, like for instance *māyā* (principle of illusion), or *prakṛti* (matter), or even *avidyā* (ignorance). Thus an implicit or explicit duality may suggest itself as the only way out from the blind alley of sterility. It is symptomatic that all metaphysical, as well as religious systems, as far as they have tried to explain the transition from any kind of Absolute to the phenomenal world, have *volens nolens* come to use dyads (like Self and non-Self in Fichte, matter and mind in dualist philosophical systems like that of Descartes and Sāṁkhya, etc.) and triads (Hegel's thesis, counter-thesis, synthesis, Hindu Trimūrti, Christian Trinity, etc.).

Though atomism is not a monistic system it is still a metaphysical system, that is why we find here the same problem. Any atomistic theory can be interpreted as an attempt to reconcile the thesis of the unity and immutability of being with the fact that the senses observe multiplicity and change. Democritus tried to reduce all the observable qualitative diversity of objects to quantitative differences between the atoms. In Vaiśeṣika, all kinds of properties of elements have their origin in the appropriate kinds of atoms. But that does not mean that a singular atom has some particular properties, say as if a single separate atom could possess the properties of sugar. Sugar becomes sugar only at the level of the *tryānuka*, the triad. Why the *tryānuka* and not the *dvyānuka*, the dyad?

As follows from the Vaiśeṣika viewpoint, the minute size of a single atom cannot bring into being the magnitude of gross things, because an addition of the ultimately small measures may produce an increase of only the same small measure. But as the *aṇu* is already the limit of the minuteness which could not be overpassed, the size of a diad continues to be as minute (*aṇu*) as the size of the single atom. As the Vaiśeṣikas did not see any quantitative difference between the size of one and of two atoms, they did not recognize different degrees of minuteness with regard to a single atom and a diad. The triad was held to be a combination not of three singular atoms, but of three dyads; and only this triad, neither dyads, nor single atoms, were endowed with a capacity to bring about the gross things. Are we dealing here with a kind of Pythagorean ontology of numbers, which endows them with the capacity to produce things? What can we say with a certain certitude is that the number three is associated in the Vaiśeṣika thought with the minimal plurality (*bahutva*) and what is even more important — with the possibility of perception. We begin to see things starting with the triads composing of six atoms. The favourite Vaiśeṣika natural example of triad is *tresāreṇu* — a speck of dust moving in a sun-beam.

Thus our sugar becomes sugar only at the level of triads. If we divide it into its component parts, the smallest possible particles will be the triads. But what about further parts, which are not perceptible (we can easily imagine that the division of the sugar material could be continued beyond the threshold of perceptibility). Do the atoms and the dyads of sugar possess the same sweetness and whiteness as our "gross piece" of sugar? I suppose that at this level, neither atoms, nor dyads have any particular properties. Our pre-sugar atoms and diads may have some general qualities/characteristic of this class of atoms — the earth atoms which have some indefinite smell, some taste, some touch, etc. In other words they may have some possibilities, potentials of smell, taste, colour or touch.

My supposition is indirectly confirmed by Praśastapāda's commentator, when he mentions that the atoms of earth haven't any species. That means that the atoms are not divided on the basis of their belonging to species corresponding to the earth substances like class of cows, or class of pots, etc. If they do, they will be something like the homeomeria of the Greek thinker Anaxagoras who believed that the smallest parts of some things are a kind of miniature copies of these things, he assumed as many qualitatively different "atoms" as there are different qualified substances in nature.

But if the Vaiśeṣika's atoms of one class are not responsible for the diversity within this very class, how could it be explained? In other words, what was the Vaiśeṣika explanation of the structural and material diversity of this universe? To understand this problem properly, we should address ourselves to another facet of the Vaiśeṣika system — its ethics and soteriology. According to Praśastapāda this universe undergoes periodical emissions and absorptions (*sṛṣṭi* and *pralaya*). During *pralaya* there are only atoms of great elements, and souls experiencing either pleasure or pain according to their previous deeds, the traces of which were preserved in *adṛṣṭas* — invisible forces of *karman*. It is due to these *adṛṣṭas* that our universe at the beginning of its emission takes the same form as it had had before the *pralaya*. Thus, there is a progressive formation of the great elements and then of the living beings. All this process proceeds through Īśvara, the Demiurge, and with the assistance of the *adṛṣṭas*.

According to Praśastapāda, "A multitude appears in the atoms and the dyads due to the *apekṣābuddhi* of Īśvara, and when these dyads produce effects in the form of the triads, etc. the multitude produces in them a colour along with a longness and a magnitude." Thus, along with the perceptible size, the multitude, in the form of the number "three," produces in effects (the gross things from *tresareṇu* onwards) the perceptible qualities like colour, taste, smell, etc. And this very multitude is introduced into atoms by the *apekṣābuddhi* of Īśvara. What is *apekṣābuddhi*? Literally it means "depending on *buddhi*," or depending on the cognitive act. Being fundamental, the single atoms, at the beginning of the new world cycle, are nevertheless non-productive and thus in need of the *apekṣābuddhi* for their effects to be produced. One is tempted to look at the *apekṣābuddhi* as quite similar to the Greek Nous, the Cartesian Mind or the Newtonian Reason. But in my opinion, the *apekṣābuddhi* is rather a cognitive act grasping several things at a time, and not a substantialized intellectual capacity. In the course of *sṛṣṭi*, or emission of the world, dyads are resulting out of Īśvara's simultaneous cognition of two atoms, triads — of three dyads. As for the role of the "first impulse" that compels the atoms to combine into these "molecules" it is being played by the above-said *adṛṣṭa*s. Thus, during the *sṛṣṭi,* the physical universe is created according to a certain moral and religious design kept and carried on by the *adṛṣṭa*s through the time of *pralaya* (a cosmic night). The role of Īśvara, in the final analysis, is like that of the Demiurges in Platon's *Timeus;* as for the *adṛṣṭa*s, they may be compared to the *eidoi,* the original paradigm that serves Demiurges as a model of creation, or in more modern terms to a kind of genetic programme for each living creature and for the whole universe.

In the normal state of universe, when its karmically determined structure is well established, Īśvara interferes not more in any process of production. It is *adṛṣṭa* or rather *adṛṣṭa*s (in plural) that play the role of the so-called teleological factor in the production of ordinary things. What makes such a thing as a pot is not only its material, but its form as well. The Vaiśeṣika authors are talking of *vyūha* — configuration of atoms — as such form-making factor. It is mainly this configuration due to which the combinations of atoms from triads onwards may be regarded as constitutive parts of sugar or of some other particular substance. But this *vyūha* is not something spontaneous or casual, being the result of a certain *adṛṣṭa*. The *adṛṣṭa* is a quality of the soul (*ātman*), a cosmo-ethical factor representing individual *karman*. How could *adṛṣṭa* as a quality of the soul have anything in common with the production of sugar or of pots, or of any other composed thing? According to the Vaiśeṣika, our souls are *vibhu,* that means, all-pervading, omnipresent. The whole universe is permeated by the infinite number of souls of all living creatures. But that does not mean that the entire universe is animated or intelligent, because the soul can serve as an animating or intelligent principle only when it is in contact with a *manas*, or internal organ, coordinator of the senses, which exists within the particular body. Outside the body our *ātman* is deprived of consciousness, but it still continues to be the support of *adṛṣṭa*s from our previous existences. Thus we can imagine that all the artefacts produced by men are determined not only by the professional capacities of their producers, but also by their *adṛṣṭa*s. As for the things produced in nature they are also influenced by the *adṛṣṭa*s. What kind of *adṛṣṭa*s? Our texts are silent on this subject, but we can suppose that these could be the *adṛṣṭa*s of men or animals which make a kind of summary formative karmic force taking part in all sorts of natural productions, like that of stones, salt, snow, etc. What we know for sure is the fact that in the Vaiśeṣika world-view, the material universe is inseparable from the moral order created and sustained by human beings; it is, so to say, programmed by the human, moral factor at the most deep level of reality — that of its atomic structure.

If you ask me what the most striking feature of Indian atomism is, I would first of all mention this, so to say, anthropic, or moral factor. If we compare *adṛṣṭa*s as final form-making factors with the *eidoi* (image-making) or forms of the Ancient Greece, we will see it even more clearly: for the Greek thinkers, the *eidoi* as well as *atomoi* are tightly connected with individuality, uniqueness, originality, and specificity. Being direct heirs of the Ancient Greek civilization, we, Westerners, consider ourselves as individuals (the words *in-dividus* is a Latin synonym of the Greek *a-tomos*). In its extreme forms the so-called social atomism appears in the tragic solitude of the Protestant self-made man or in the existential estrangement of the modern man. In India, the idea of the atom never became either a scientific theory, or a prototype of social individualism. Through the *adṛṣṭa* it was always connected with the specifically Indian view of the universe as a place where living beings are involved in the incessant trial of reincarnation (*saṁsāra*) and where their present individuality is far from being single and unique, as many other ones will follow in future existences. At the same time, due to the concept of *adṛṣṭas*, the Indian atomism in a much higher degree than the Greek one — may serve as an example of the real confluence of physical and ethical orders (the idea of *dharma*).

See my Other Contributions to the Same Topic:

"The Atomistic Theory of the Vaiśeṣika: Problems of Interpretation" in *History of Indian Philosophy: A Russian Viewpoint,* Indian Council of Philosophical Research, New Delhi, 1993, pp. 56-71.

"Atomistic Mode of Thinking as Exemplified by the Vaiśeṣika Philosophy of Number," in *Asiatische Studien/Etudes Asiatiques,* Bern, etc. 1994, vol. XLVIII, no. 2, pp. 781-806.

"La doctrine des atomes chez Kaṇāda et Praśastapāda," *Journal Asiatique,* Paris, 1996, vol. 248, no. 1, pp. 137-58.

"The Vaiśeṣika Notions of *ākāśa* and *dik* From the Perspective of Indian Ideas of Space" in *Beyond Orientalism,* "The Work of Wilhelm Halbfass and its Impact on Indian and Cross-cultural Studies," *Poznan Studies in the Philosophy of Science and Humanities,* vol. 47, Amsterdam, 1996, pp. 417-47.

"The Human Body Composition in Statics and Dynamics: Āyurveda and the Philosophical Schools of Vaiśeṣika and Sāṁkhya," *Journal of Indian Philosophy,* vol. 32, no. 1, 2004, pp. 31-56.

"Śaṁkara, critique du Vaiśeṣika. Une lecture de Brahmasūtrabhāṣya (II, 2, 11-17)," *Asiatische Studien/Etudes Asiatiques,* LIX 2, Lausanne 2005, pp. 533-80.

11

Mahendra, the Poetic Emperor

R. Nagaswamy

Introduction

THE Pallava Emperor, Mahendra-vikrama-varman, who ruled the northern part of Tamil Nadu from Kanchipuram to the banks of river Kāverī in Trichy, from *c.* CE 590 to 630 is a unique poet in the field of Sanskrit literature. He was a multi-faceted personality who needs to be appreciated. He was undoubtedly one of the greatest artist poet among Emperors of India. His love for art and poetry sprang from his innate poetic genius, that enabled him to see and visualize every aspect of life from poetic angle. Mahendra was a born *kavi*, a poet to whom everything appeared either as a *dṛśya kāvya* or as a *śravya kāvya* (visual poetry or literary poetry) which he reveals in his interesting title *Vicitra-Citta. Citta* refers to his mental approach while the word *vi-citra* points to varied arts. Some scholars render the title *Vicitra-Citta* as "Curious minded," but judging from his works it seems the most appropriate meaning would be "varied arts" as may be seen from his another title *Citra-kāra-puli*, i.e. Tiger among artists.

Mahendra has left several monuments which are *dṛśya kāvyas*, and many Sanskrit portic works which are *śravya kāvyas* like the *Matta-Vilāsa-Prahasana* and *Bhagavad-ajjuka*, both in Sanskrit. His love of monumental art is revealed by his titles like *Citrakāra-puli, Cettā-kāri* and *Mahā-cettā-kāri*. Mahendra also invented a new *rāga Saṅkīrṇa-jāti*, which he assumed as one of his titles.

Mahendra's titles

As Mahendra's titles found in his monuments engraved by himself are indicative of his personality, his significant titles are given below. He assumed several titles which are inscribed in alphabetic order in his monuments. They generally begin with his *Paṭṭābhiṣeka* name coronation title, the rest fall in alphabetical order as follows:

1. *Anumāna*
2. *Avani-bhājana*
3. *Bhrāntaḥ*
4. *Cettā-kāri*
5. *Citra-kāra-puli*
6. *Guṇa-bharaḥ*
7. *Kalahapriyaḥ*
8. *Kāmārṇava*
9. *Lakṣita*
10. *Lalitāṅkura*
11. *Mahā-cettā-kāri*
12. *Mahendra-vikrama*
13. *Matta-vilāsa*
14. *Sankīrṇa-jāti*
15. *Satya-sandhaḥ*
16. *Upamāna*
17. *Vicitra-citta*

His cave at Mandagappattu was named *Lakṣitāyatanam*; and the trichy cave as *Lalitāṅkura-pallaveśvara-gṛham*; He emphasizes his title *Avani-bhājana* in his *Matta-Vilāsa-Prahasana* which he used in the invocatory verse. In the Trichy cave inscription he has used different titles, one for each verse as *Guṇa-bhara, Satya-sandhaḥ*, etc. He named his Trichy cave as Lalitam, i.e. beautiful.

His attachment to sculpture and painting is revealed in his title *Citra-kāra-puli*. Interestingly his Gaṅgādhara sculpture at Trichy is the earliest monumental sculpture in Tamil Nadu.

Two Sanskrit Satires by Mahendra-
Matta-Vilāsa-Prahasana

It may be advantageous to reflect on his two Sanskrit works *Matta-Vilāsa-Prahasana* and *Bhagavad-ajjuka*, before Mahendra's inscriptions are taken. Both are farces in Sanskrit with profuse use of Prakrit, that show the stature of Prakrit around CE 600 in Tamil Nadu. This requires a separate study. *Matta-Vilāsa-Prahasana* — clearly after one of his titles, *Matta-vilāsa*, portrays a Kāpālika and his consort Kapālikā, another drunkard. As they move around the streets of Kāñcī fully drunk, prattling, the Kāpālika noticed that his drinking bowl was missing. He found a Bauddha *bhikṣu* at that time, coming with his begging bowel tucked under his long robe. The Kāpālika accuses the *bhikṣu* of stealing his bowl. There ensues a verbal quarrel between the Kāpālika and the Bauddha *bhikṣu*, each one accusing the other of their respective philosophy. The Kāpālika seeing the Bauddha *bhikṣu* casting his lustful eye on the lady Kapālikā, accuses the *bhikṣu* of stealing and states that stealing is inherent in his Buddha's teachings. He accuses Buddha as "the foremost thief" who has stolen the teachings of Upaniṣads, claiming them as his own. The *bhikṣu* found the lady unsteady due to excess of drinks and catches hold of her hand to prevent her from falling down. The Kāpālika accuses him of trying to snatch his wife. The *bhikṣu* challenges the Kāpālika drunkard to come to the city court for arbitration. The Kāpālika promptly dismisses it saying the judges are corrupt, accept bribes and deliver partisan judgments. A Māheśvara appears on the scene and as the dual continues a dog came running with the Kāpālika's bowl. The Kāpālika now turns his attention saying he knew that the roguish dog would steal. There ends the drama. This drama may be seen against one of his titles, *Kalahapriyaḥ*.

Mahendra's grasp of *śleṣa alaṁkāra*, the different philosophical systems, and ridiculing the Kāpālikas, Buddhists, the then existing judiciary, etc. are in a lighter vein. That too coming from the pen of an Emperor *Matta-Vilāsa-Prahasana* is a unique work in the field of Sanskrit dramas.

Bhagavad-Ajjuka

Similarly the *Bhagavad-ajjuka* is another farce where the Yama's messengers who come to take away the life of a courtesan take the life of another courtesan by mistake. When the associates of the courtesan lament a *sādhu* out of compassion enters the dead body of the courtesan by his *siddhi* of *para-kāyā-praveśa*. Now as a courtesan he starts speaking noble paths suddenly which puzzles the associates. The Yama *bhaṭas* realizing their mistake returned to find that the courtesan's body is now occupied by the *sādhu*, found his original body without life. So they left the courtesan's soul in the *sādhu*'s body. The courtesan in the *sādhu*'s body now started talking sex to the disciples of the *sādhu* who were puzzled. This comedy of the courtesan speaking virtuous life and *sādhu* speaking the language of the courtesan, continues. Finally the Yama *bhaṭas* arrive to set the matter right.

These two satires of Mahendravarman are unique with no parallels in the history of Sanskrit literature. Mahendra shows his mastery over the then existing philosophies like the Kāpālika, Māheśvara, Buddhist, and Arhantas (Jainas) and also the corrupt judiciary. Playing pun on their vocabulary, he ridicules them quite refreshingly. His command over the Tarka-Śāstra is revealed throughout the text and as mentioned earlier he assumed the title *Anumāna* and *Upamāna* which are significant that are fully reflected in the text. These two satires have been preserved in Kerala where the Cākkiyārs, the traditional dancers, have been enacting these two satires in temples as offerings for the past 1200 years which is an extraordinary survival in the field of world dramatic history.

Mahendra's Mastery of Dance Tradition

The invocatory verse of the drama *Matta-Vilāsa-Prahasana* is an example that illustrates his mastery of Bharata's *Nāṭya* tradition.

> *bhāṣā veṣa vapuḥ kriyā guṇa kṛtān āśritya bhetān gatam*
> *bhāvāveśa vaśāt aneka rasatām trailokya yātrā mayam nṛttam*
> *niṣ-pratibaddha-bodha mahimā yaḥ prekṣakaśca svayam sa*
> *vyāpta avani-bhājanam diśatu vo divya kapālī yaśaḥ*

The *Nāṭya-Śāstra* deals with four types of *abhinaya*s namely *āṅgika* (bodily *abhinaya*), *vācika* (verbal), *āhārya* (costumes), and *guṇa* (like *sāttvikam*). All these are the essential components of dance recitals. Mahendra mentions these four aspects of dance in the very beginning of his invocation as *bhāṣā* (*vācika*), *veṣa* (*āhārya*), *vapuḥ-kriyā* (*āṅgika*), and *guṇas*. *Bhedān gatam* — assuming all variations. He uses these terms in connection with *Nṛttam* dance in which the four *abhinaya*s are used. *Bhāva-āveśa-vaśāt* refers to the Kāpālika *siddhānta* in which the Kāpālikas enter into *āveśa* by dancing to the violent rhythms of instrumental music. They believe that they reach the presence of dancing Śiva. Śiva's dance is considered *Trailokya-yātrā-maya* journey in the three worlds. The third phrase *niṣ-pratibaddha bodha mahimā* refers to faultless cognition through inference. The next phrase reminds us of the Śaiva Siddhānta system in which Siva's consort Pārvatī the personification of his own power, witnesses his dance. Pārvatī is described as the primordial spectator. By this process of dance Śiva becomes the abode of the entire universe which is mentioned in the last line *sa vyāpta avani-bhājanam.* The Kāpālika Siddhānta holds that Śiva as Dancing Bhairava is the ultimate reality which is revealed in the end of this verse which ends as *divyaḥ kapālī*, i.e. let the divine Kapāli; *yaśaḥ diśatu vaḥ* give us fame and prosperity.

Mahendra also plays pun on the word *Avani-bhājana* which was one of his titles. It invokes the blessing of Śiva as Kapālin on *Avani-bhājana*, that is Mahendra. It also seems to suggest that Mahendra himself played a lead role as an actor in the drama. According to tradition this verse alone used to be interpreted by the Cākkiyār actors of Kerala for seven nights, that indicates the depth of meaning contained in the very first composition of this Great Emperor.

Mahendra's Personality in his own Words

Mahendra also gives his own personality in the mouth of the *Sūtradhāra* as follows:

> *pallava-kula-dharaṇī-maṇḍala-kula-parvatasya,sarva-naya-vijita-samasta-sāmanta-maṇḍalasya, ākhaṇḍala-sama-parākrama-śriyaḥ, śrī-mahimānurūpa-dāna-vibhūti-paribhūta-rājarājasya, śrī-siṁhaviṣṇu-varmaṇaḥ-putraḥ, śatṛ-ṣaḍvarga-nigraha-paraḥ, parahita-paratantratayā mahābhūta-dharma-mahārājaḥ, śrī mahendra-vikramavarmā nāma.*
>
> The Pallava *kula* resembled a great mountain of which Mahendra shone as the lofty peak. He won over a large circle of commanders by all the skills and made them remain enclosing this peak; who possess all the valour and prosperity equal to Indra; who befitting his greatness surpassed Kubera the lord of wealth by his generous gifts; the son of Siṁhaviṣṇu Varma, who remains suppressing the sixfold enemies, is the emperor of virtues — *dharma-mahārāja* named Śrī Mahendra Vikrama. This is virtually the pedigree Mahendra has left of himself.

There is also a verse in continuation of this recited by the *Sūtradhāra*:

prajñā dāna dayānubhāva dhṛtayaḥ kāntiḥ kalā kauśalam
satyam śauryam amāyatā vinaya iti evam prakārā guṇāḥ ।
aprāpta sthitayaḥ sametya śaraṇam yātāyamekam kalau
kalpānte jagadādim ādi puruṣam sarga prabhedā iva ॥

Wisdom, bounty, mercy, splendours
Courage, beauty, and skill in arts,
Truth, prowess, honesty, modesty,
And all such qualities together,
Finding themselves without single abode
Tend on him the only one
To protect them in the *kali* age
As creatures reach the Primeval being at the end of Aeons.
— Tr. N.P. Unni, *Mattavilāsa-prahasanam,* Nag Publishers, Delhi, 1998, p. 65

Mahendra's Cave Temples

We have noted that Mahendra excavated the Trichy rock cut cave. There are two rock cut caves at Trichy one on top of the hill called upper rock cut cave and the other at a lower level called lower rock cut cave. According to the present writer both of them are the creations of Mahendra though some hold it might be somewhat later. The upper rock cut cave has Mahendra's inscriptions in Sanskrit consisting of verses and his titles. The inscription calls the temple as Lalitāṅkura Pallaveśvaragṛham. The Trichy inscription is undoubtedly a composition of the Emperor himself as he has shown in his other works.

The Trichy Cave Temple of Beauty

The inscription and sculpture are found in the upper rock cut cave which is near the summit of the hill. When one reaches the summit he will be attracted by the nature's beauty, particularly the great river Kāverī coming from a long distance and taking a delightful course with its crystal like water, visible from over fifteen miles on either side. The cave temple is a rectangular *maṇḍapa* type of temple, with a sanctum (*garbha-gṛham*) on one side and the image of Gaṅgādhara facing it on the other side. Mahendra's inscriptions are found (a) on both sides of Gaṅgādhara sculpture, (b) on the lintel, (c) on the base of the sanctum, and (d) on the pillars. They are both in verse form and just titles, arranged alphabetically. Mahendra's titles *Lakṣita, Lalitāṅkura, Anumāna, Upamāna, Avani-bhājana, Satya-sandha,* etc. are important. According to one verse the cave is called *Lalitāṅkura-Pallaveśvara-Gṛham* as mentioned earlier. Mahendra has certainly considered this as one of his best creations and names it as *Lalitam* among many other titles.

The Poetic Inscription

The inscription on either side of Gaṅgādhara is an excellent example of poetry. The first verse is a *utprekṣā-alaṁkāra,* in which Mahendra as a poet, describes in his own words *manye* what he thought of his creation.

> *kāverīm nayanābhirāma salilām ārāma mālādharām* ।
> *devō vīkṣya nadīpriyaḥ priyatamām apyeṣ rajyet iti* ।
>
> *saśaṅkhā girikanyakā pitṛ kulam hitvaiva manye girau*
> *nityam tiṣṭati pallavasya dayitām etām bhruvānā nadīm* ॥

Mahendra extols the river Kāverī as an attractive girl. She is delightful to look at by her crystal like waters. She is *nayanābhirāma* and also *abhirāma salilā.* By herself she is thus a charming attractive girl. In addition she wears lovely garland *ārāma-mālā-dharā,* i.e. wearing a garland of *ārāma*s. *Ārāma*s are sacred places — temples in the midst of beautiful groves and gardens. As Kāverī came from a distance, beautiful green gardens of flowers, coconut and plantain groves may be seen on both its banks for miles and miles together. Like velvet green spreads, paddy fields are seen on either sides.

There is no doubt it would be an attraction to onlookers. Mahendra being a great poet goes into poetic ecstasy and calls it a lovely garland studded with gems of temples on either sides, glittering in the midst of green fields, shining like emeralds. Kāverī, who is herself a perfect beauty, wears this garland of *ārāmas* as added beauty and looks pretty as a beautiful girl bedecked with beautiful garland. She is naturally the most lovable girl. So Mahendra calls her *Priyatamā*. When a girl has voluptuous beauty she would become a centre of attraction and any lover of beauty would fall in love with her immediately. Playing pun on the Gaṅgādhara figure by the side Mahendra calls him *Nadīpriyaḥ* lover of rivers. Śiva's attraction towards the river Gaṅgā is known. Not only he loves Gaṅgā but also he has given her a place on his head. This *Nadīpriyaḥ*, would fall in love with this beautiful Kāverī is but natural.

Pārvatī, as a daughter of Himavān (*giri kanyakā*) was fond of her father's abode (*pitṛ-kula*) as girls are greatly attached to their parents. This girl of the mountain, grew suspicious that her husband, a *Nadīpriyaḥ*, would fall in love with this beautiful river Kāverī. So she abandoned her parent's abode, hurriedly rushed to this mountain at Thiruchirapalli, and stays permanently with her husband, reminding him constantly that Kāverī is the consort of the Pallava (*pallavasya dayitā*) indicating that she is another man's wife.

There are many suggestions arising out of this poem. Mahendra is proud that the river Kāverī belongs to him and that it is more beautiful than Gaṅgā and that Śiva and Pārvatī are residing permanently in the mountain abode created by him rather than in the Himalayas. It is a novel way of suggesting the greatness of his creation. Also kindly note the soft, tender and highly sensitive title *Lalitāṅkura*, amongst his various titles, that he has chosen to name this temple as

Lalitāṅkura-Pallaveśvara-Gṛham. The term *Pallaveśvara gṛham* could be interpreted in two ways: (1) The temple of Īśvara of the Pallavas, and (2) *Pallaveśvarasya gṛham*, the temple of the Pallava king (i.e., the Pallava Royal temple). Mention has been made earlier that Mahendra chose his title *Lalitāṅkura* to name this temple as the most beautiful of his creations. Mahendra's love of environment is also suggested by this poem. It is also his deep interest in Sanskrit *Kāvyālaṁkāras* as seen from the use of the *utprekṣā alaṁkāra* in this verse. It is an excellent *dhvani kāvya*.

Mahendra's Love for Logic

Another verse in this inscription is also of historic interest for more than one reason. Before we study this verse it is necessary to keep in mind the following titles of Mahendra — *Anumānaḥ, Upamānaḥ, Guṇabharaḥ*, and so on — appearing in the same cave temple. The titles *Anumānaḥ* and *Upamānaḥ* clearly suggest his love for logic — Nyāya system. The relevant verse reads:

guṇabhara nāmāni rājāni anena liṅgena liṅginī jñānam ।
prathatām cirāya loke vipakṣa vṛtteḥ parāvṛttam ॥

Please note the Nyāya terminology used throughout the verse.

Liṅgena (hetunā), rājāni (sādhya viṣayaka pakṣe) vipakṣa vṛtteḥ parāvṛttam (vipakṣāt vyāvṛttam) liṅginī jñānam (anumiti jñānam) cirāya prathatām. The terms *hetu, pakṣa, vipakṣa vyāvṛttam, jñānam*, etc. are all Nyāya terminology. In Ancient Nyāya system the term *liṅga* is used for *hetu*, *liṅgin* is used for *pakṣa*, *jñānam* for *anumiti*, *vipakṣa vyāvṛttam* used as *vipakṣā vṛtteḥ parāvṛttam*.

Also in Śaiva Āgamas the term *liṅga* is used for *hetu* which has a special significance. It is through *Śivaliṅga* the Śaiva knowledge dawns. *Liṅga viṣayaka śaiva mārgī iti jñānam*.

This verse has two meanings. According to medieval literature like *Periya-Purāṇam*, the Pallava king was a follower of Jainism earlier, ill-treated the Śaiva saint Appar and later on turned a Śaiva when he saw the greatness of Appar. This verse seems to confirm by the term *vipakṣavṛtteḥ parāvṛttam* that Mahendra turned away from another faith, which he saught to prove by the *liṅga* he established here (*anena liṅgena*), That he, *Guṇabhara,* was now a Śaivite worshipping *liṅga* may spread throughout the world for ever (*loke cirāya pratathām*) is what is sought to be proved and established. That seems to be the meaning of this verse. It is well known a Śaivite is a worshipper of *liṅga* which is mentioned in the verse. Obviously the sanctum found on one side of this cave, opposite to the Gaṅgādhara panel, contained the *liṅga.*

The second point alluded to in this verse is that Mahendra is *Anumāna* and *Upamāna* (titles) proved by this verse *anena,* i.e. this verse itself. The term *māna* refers to greatness. The expressed meaning is in terms of his greatness but the suggested meaning is that he himself is *Anumāna* and *Upamāna.*

Mahendra's family was greatly devoted to Jainism is proved historically by two copper-plate inscriptions. In the royal charter extolling Mahendra's father Siṁha-Viṣṇu, a village grant is made to a Jaina Saṅgha at Thirupparuttikkunru. The copper-plate is known to historians as Pallankoyil inscription of Pallava Siṁhavarman, grandfather of Mahendra. There is another copper-plate charter known as Hoskote plates of Gaṅga king. It refers to the mother of Siṁha-Viṣṇu making a gift to an *Arhatāyatana* that is a Jaina temple. Mahendra's leniency towards Jainas is thus well attested. It seems this verse of Mahendra at Trichy seems to point to those historic events in the life of Mahendra.

Mahendra's Portrait

There is another verse in the same place in continuation of the above in which Mahendra mentions that he made a portrait of himself in the cave temple. He makes an interesting mention that what he made was a permanent stone image:

śilākṣarena janitā satya-sandhasya bhautikī ।
mīrtiḥ kīrtimayī cāsya kṛtā tenaiva śāsvatī ॥

The verse states that his physical body is made permanent along with his fame by this stone form. Also it may be seen his title *Satyasandha* is mentioned in this verse. Continuing this information the next verse says that Mahendra having made the image of Śiva bears him the one who was in his heart now on his head. By this he made Sthānu (Śiva) the immovable quite appropriate meaning and also made himself permanent. By this Mahendra suggests the term *Sthānu* (*Acala*) for Śiva is made appropriate as his image is made of stone that would remain permanent here. The king also says he also became *Acala* (immovable or permanent) by this sculpture. By this it is meant Mahendra made along with Śiva a portrait of himself on stone which becomes *acala* immovable.

sthānum vyadhatta vidhireṣa yathārtha samstham ।
sthānuḥ svayam ca saha tene jagatsu jātaḥ ॥

The meaning of the verse will become more clear when looked at the Gaṅgādhara panel carved nearby. In the centre stands Śiva as Gaṅgādhara receiving river Gaṅgā in his *jaṭā*. By the side of his leg is portrayed a royal figure bowing down to Śiva raising his hand suggesting that he is adoring the Lord by his head. This is the suggested meaning of the verse when it says he bears Śiva on his head.

There are a large number of inscriptions of Mahendra. A detailed study of them is a desideratum. But from what has been said above it would be clear Mahendra was an extraordinary ruler of great love for Sanskrit, poetry, art, religion and the like. Mahendra is indeed a great poetic emperor India has known.

References

Bhagavadajjugam, tr. by C. Minakshi, published in South Indian Studies, vol. 1, SHAER, Madras, 1978.

Cave Temples of the Pallavas, by K.R. Srinivasan, Archaeological Survey of India, New Delhi, 1961.

Kiratarjuniyam or Arjuna's penance, by T.N. Ramachandran, India Art, Calcutta, 1950-51.

Mahendra's Inscription at Tiruchirappalli, Studies in Ancient Tamil Law and Society, R. Nagaswamy, Tamilnadu State Department of Archaeological Department, Madras, 1978.

Mattavilasa prahasana of Mahendravarman, ed. and tr. by N.P. Unni, Nag publishers, Delhi, 1998.

South Indian Inscriptions, vol. 1, ed. E. Hultzch, Archaeological Survey of India, Madras, 1892.

South Indian Inscriptions, vol. XII, V.Venkatasubbha Aiyar, Archaeological Survey of India, Madras, 1943.

12

The Last Buddhist of Kashmir as Recorded by Jonarāja

Walter Slaje

KASHMIR and the north-western areas of peninsular India[1] have played an extraordinarily important role in the history of South and Central Asian Buddhism. This is a fact that needs no proof. Recent discoveries such as the Buddhist scrolls from Gandhāra,[2] now in the British Library, and a considerable number of Buddhist manuscripts from Bāmiyān,[3] now in the (Norwegian) Schøyen collection, to mention only the most sensational finds, fully tally with known facts. Influential scholastic traditions such as the (Mūla) Sarvāstivāda, an enormous number of great scholars and a high standard of learning have always been considered sort of a "trademark" of Kashmir Buddhism right until the beginning of the second millennium CE. So much so that J. Naudou's (1980)[4] historical outline of Kashmir Buddhism and the principal exponents thereof occupies some 300 printed

1. "India" as used here does not strictly refer to modern India in terms of its present political borders. What I have in mind is the cultural area as dominated by Indian thought in history.

2. *c.* first century CE, North-western [Gāndhārī] Prakrit written in Kharoṣṭhī script, Salomon, 1999.

3. *c.* second to eighth centuries Buddhist Manuscripts.

4. Originally published in French in 1968.

pages.[5] An agreement prevailed among different Buddhist traditions (Pāli, Tibetan, Chinese) as to Kashmir having been a sacred place for Buddhists.

Spread of Buddhism in Kashmir

The spreading of the Buddhist Dharma to Kashmir is attributed to a direct disciple of Ānanda, the Arhat Madhyāntika.[6] Under Kuṣāṇa rule[7] in particular, Kashmir was considered "a stronghold of Buddhism, in the possession of the Bauddhas."[8] It would also appear that from the seventh to the tenth centuries, Kashmir exercised a strong attraction for pilgrims from Central Asia and from East Asia,[9] when also the production of logico-epistemological works and commentaries reached its peak in this country.[10] A Central Asian itinerary,[11] drawn up in the tenth century during the reign of king Abhimanyu of Kashmir,[12] also confirms, by way of an interesting description of the route from the Tarim Basin to

---

5. Cp., also Kaul, 2003, and Funayama, 1994, who has analysed and evaluated additional sources, such as the *Nīlamatapurāṇa, Kalhaṇa's Rājataraṅgiṇī* and the accounts of Chinese visitors to the region in the seventh and eighth centuries.

6. On his name-form and on the whole subject see Funayama, 1994, pp. 367-73, n.1.

7. Year 1 of Kaniṣka has recently been determined by Harry Falk as corresponding with CE 127. From this calculation it follows that Huviṣka reigned from CE 153-91, Falk, 2001, Errington, 2002, p. 106.

8. *RT*, 1, pp. 171-77, Quoted from Witzel, 1994, p. 247.

9. For example, Xuanzang, Huichao, Wukong.

10. For example, Arcaṭa, Dharmottara, Prajñākaragupta, Jñānaśrī, Śaṅkaranandana, etc. See Funayama, 1994, p. 370 ff.

11. See Skjærvø 2002, pp. 524-26 (for text and translation). Cp. also von Hinüber, 2004: pp. 74 ff.

12. Ruled 22nd December, 958 until 13th October, CE 972. Calculated by Dr K.H. Golzio (Bonn).

Śrīnagar (Adhiṣṭhāna), an overwhelming presence of Buddhist sites. The anonymous contemporary, who authored this Khotanese itinerary, made the following reference to Buddhist monasteries in Śrīnagar at the time: "[. . .] there is a large monastery with a *dharmarāja* (*stūpa*) and 500 rock cells. Smaller monasteries are countless."[13] Kalhaṇa, too, informs us about big monasteries there, among them the one called after its founder Jayendra, the "Jayendra-Vihāra." Xuanzang had stayed in Śrīnagar for two years (CE 631-33), living and studying in this very monastery. He has left us a travel report (Xiyuji), which corroborates its existence at that time.[14] Another important monastery of Śrīnagar was the Ratnāvalī-Vihāra.[15] Galūna, who had named it after his wife, constructed that one. Galūna had been a minister of king Vikramāditya, the great-grandson of Pravarasena II (*c.* CE 580),[16] founder of Śrīnagar, and son of Raṇāditya,[17] who had built a Pāśupata-maṭha there on the Pradyumnaśikhara.[18]

---

13. Skjærvø 2002: p. 526, II. pp. 33-34.

14. Cp. Stein, 1900, 1, p. 103, note on *RT* III, 355; 1900, 2, p. 439; cp. also *RT* V 428.

15. *RT* III 476. Cp. also the *Mokṣopāya*: *Adhiṣṭhānābhidhe tasminn evogranagare tadā ratnāvalīvihārākhyo vihāro 'pi bhaviṣyati* (MṬ IV, 32, 18) "Then, in the same mighty town called Adhiṣṭhāna, there will be a monastery also, going by the name of Ratnāvalīvihāra."

16. Cp. Witzel, 1994, p. 253.

17. Cp. Witzel, 1990, p. 35, according to whom Raṇāditya would have died *c.* CE 523. This, however, would come into conflict with the date of Raṇāditya's grandfather Pravarasena II, which was given by Witzel as *c.* CE 580 (see footnote 16, above). Thus, Raṇāditya, whose reign of three hundred years — according to Kalhaṇa — poses anyhow many problems, should, if at all, be assumed as shortly before or around CE 600, see Witzel, 1990: p. 32.

18. *RT* III, 460. The big number of Pāśupata ascetics present in north-western India at the time can also be gleaned from the numerous references made to them by Xuanzang, see Hara, 2003: p. 251 f.

Buddhism on Decline in Kashmir

Signs for a "decline of Buddhism in Kashmir," to use Naudou's expression, were — according to him — however emerging already at the time of Kṣemendra (*c.* 980-1060), and the "approximate time when the career of Kaśmīri Buddhism finishes" would have come by the end of the thirteenth century, when Marco Polo travelled through Kashmir (Chesimur).[19] Yet, as Witzel has pointed out, Buddhism was still flourishing during Kalhaṇa's lifetime,[20] and seems to have feebly survived the period of the early Islamization of the valley, when Hindu *maṭhas*, Buddhist *vihāras*, and Muslim mosques still existed side by side in Śrīnagar.[21] Witzel also emphasized that under Sultān Zayn al-'Ābidīn[22] "a Buddhist minister, Tilakācārya, [. . .] probably is the last Buddhist attested by name in Kashmiri history," and adds that the "disappearance of the religion was so complete that no Buddhist manuscript has been found in the Valley so far."[23]

Jonarāja, it is true, mentions to the end of his own *Rājataraṅgiṇī* a Buddhist called Tilakācārya (*JRT*, 823). He does so in connection with Śiryabhaṭṭa, who, after Sūhabhaṭṭa's death (CE 1417) successfully restored Hindu culture with the approval and by the orders of Zayn. Śiryabhaṭṭa had become very influential at Zayn's court in many respects. Together with him, Tilakācārya, too, had been holding a high executive post at the court, as it was also the case with Siṁha, the Sultān's

19. Naudou, 1980, p. 260 ff.

20. Kalhaṇa finished his *Rājataraṅgiṇī* in CE 1149-50.

21. Witzel, 1994, p. 255; 287, n. 135-38.

22. Zayn ruled from CE 1418 (spring) until 2 May 1470, interrupted by an interregnum of his elder brother Alī Śāh from autumn 1419 to spring 1420 (Slaje 2007, 343f.).

23. Witzel, 1994, p. 255.

chief auditor. Together, all the three were supporting the Brāhmaṇas' promotion to highest positions.[24] It is remarkable that at Zayn's (Muslim) court even Buddhists were accepted as officials.

Now, and this is the modest contribution I should like to make by the present paper, Jonarāja was referring to Zayn and Tilakācārya punningly, which has escaped the notice of scholars so far.[25]

Jonarāja's text runs as follows:

> *samyagdaśabalenātha sarvajñena mahībhujā* ।
> *saugatas tilakācāryo mahattamapade kṛtaḥ* ॥
> — JRT 823 (ed. Kaul)

The passage was not correctly understood by Dutt (1898, loc. cit.), who "translated" it as:

> Then the king, who had gone through all the circumstances of life, and who knew all things, placed Tilakācāryya, the Buddhist, in the highest position.

Kaul (1967, loc. cit.) explained the *śloka* by saying that the

> appointment of Tilakācārya, the Buddhist, as *mahattama* gives a clear proof of the Sultan's interest in the welfare of religious groups.

In making a statement on the term *mahattama*, Kaul noted down that it "designated an office whose exact position in the government is not clear" and rightly refers in this connection to Kalhaṇa's *Rājataraṅgiṇī* (*RT* VII 438), where the same term

24. *sa śiryabhaṭṭas tilakaḥ sa siṁhagaṇanāpatiḥ* । *sopanāny abhavann uccapadārohe dvijanmanām* ॥ 824 ॥ "*Śiryabhaṭṭa, Tilaka,* and the [Sulṭān's] chief auditor Siṁha became the Brahmins' ladders [to success, Promoting them] to highest positions." *JRT 824,* (ed. Kaul).

25. See Dutt, 1898: p. 68; Kaul, 1967: p. 106.

was used, the exact meaning of which still remains opaque to us. From Stein's commentary on the *Rājataraṅgiṇī* passage under consideration, it becomes at least clear that "there could be more than one *mahattama* at the same time" at the court, and that Kalhaṇa used the term rather frequently in books VII and VIII.[26]

Despite this unquestionable obscurity as to just what exactly the function of a *mahattama* might actually have been, Jonarāja composed his verse with the intention of a double entendre (*śleṣa*). On closer inspection, it becomes immediately clear that he throughout deliberately alluded to Buddhist semantics by using words of specifically Buddhist connotations. If we focus our attention once again on Jonarāja's *śloka*, this time considering Buddhist connoted notions, as emphasized by bold letters in the following quote, the result would come like this:

> ***samyagdaśabalenā****tha* ***sarvajñena*** *mahībhujā* ।
> ***saugatas*** *tilakācāryo* ***mahattamapade*** *kṛtaḥ* ॥
> — *JRT* 823 (ed. Kaul)

Translation:

> Then the *omniscient* king, a *perfect Buddha*, elevated the *Buddhist* Tilakācārya to the *highest status*.

The terminology used by Jonarāja is unambiguously Buddhist. Even a merely superficial consultation of Franklin Edgerton's *Buddhist Hybrid Sanskrit Dictionary* (*BHSD*) would suffice to prove this point beyond doubt. Thus, we find *sub voce*.

1. *daśabala*: "Synonym of (any) Buddha."

   Jonarāja's "*samyagdaśabala*" therefore clearly equals a "*Samyak-Sambuddha*."

26. Stein, 1900: p. 303, note *ad RT* VII, 438.

2. *sarvajña*: "Omniscient, as esp. of a Buddha."
3. *saugata*: "Buddhist."
4. *mahattamapada*: "Holding a great or high position."[27]

Most interestingly, Jonarāja, who died in CE 1459, not only went so far as even to identify Sultān Zayn with a Samyak-Sambuddha by way of a pun, but also displays his perfect acquaintance with typically Buddhist terminology. This shows that, although Buddhism might already have declined largely, the Paṇḍits of Kashmir were still astoundingly familiar with Buddhist lore in the middle of the fifteenth century.

Bibliography

BHSD, Franklin Edgerton, *Buddhist Hybrid Sanskrit Grammar and Dictionary*, vol. II: Dictionary, New Haven, 1953.

Buddhist Manuscripts, vol. 1.2. General Editor Jens Braarvig. [Manuscripts in the Schøyen Collection. 1.3.] Oslo, 2000-02.

Dutt, J.C., 1898, Medieval Kashmir. Being a reprint of the *Rājataraṅgiṇīs* of Jonarāja, Shrivara and Shuka, as transl. into Engl. by J.C. Dutt and publ. in 1898 AD under the title *Kings of Kashmira*, vol.III., ed. with notes, etc. by S.L. Sadhu, New Delhi, 1993.

Errington, Elizabeth, 2002, "Numismatic Evidence for Dating the "Kaniṣka" Reliquary," *Silk Road Art and Archaeology*, 8, 2002, pp. 101-20.

Falk, Harry, 2001, "The Yuga of Sphujiddhvaja and the Era of the Kuṣāṇas." *Silk Road Art and Archaeology*, 7, 2001, pp. 121-36.

---

27. Monier-Williams *Sanskrit Dictionary* (also Schmidt, 1924, s.v. *mahattamapada*), evidence recorded from the *Divyāvadāna* (247, 4) only, a Hīnayānistic work in its essence. Let it be noted that some consider the *Divyāvadāna* a work of the Mūlasarvāstivādins [Nakamura, 1980: p. 138], by which we come full circle (see page 1 of the present paper). Dr Klaus Wille (Göttingen) was kind enough to examine the entries of *mahattamapada* in his SWTF-files (letter dt. 14 Sept. 2006). Although he could not discern anything specifically 'Buddhist' in terms of usage, the occurrence of the word is undeniably linked to Buddhist literature.

Funayama, Toru, 1994, "Remarks on Religious Predominance in Kashmir: Hindu or Buddhist," in: *A Study of the Nīlamata, Aspects of Hinduism in Ancient Kashmir*, ed. by Yasuke Ikari, Kyoto, 1994, pp. 367-75.

Hara, Minoru, 2003, "Ashes," *Cracow Indological Studies*, IV-V, (2002/2003): pp. 251-67.

JRT (*Jonarāja Rājataraṅgiṇī*). *The Rājataraṅgiṇī of Kalhaṇa*, ed. by Durgāprasāda, son of Vrajalāla, vol. III containing the supplements to the work of Jonarāja, Śrīvara and Prājyabhaṭṭa, ed. by P. Peterson [Bombay Sanskrit Ser. 54.], Bombay, 1896.

———, *Rājataraṅgiṇī of Jonarāja*, ed. with text comparative and critical annotations and an elaborate introduction by Srikanth Kaul. [Vishveshvaranand, Inst. Publ. 432 = Woolner Indological Ser. 7]. Hoshiarpur, 1967.

———, *Rājataraṅgiṇī of Jonarāja*, transl. with critical notes in Hindi by Raghunath Singh. [The Jaikrishnadas-Krishnadas Prācyavidyā Granthamālā, 4.], Varanasi, 1972.

Kaul, Srikanth, 1967, *Rājataraṅgiṇī of Jonarāja*, ed. with text comparative and critical annotations and an elaborate introduction by Srikanth Kaul. [Vishveshvaranand Inst. Publ. 432 = Woolner Indological Ser. 7], Hoshiarpur, 1967.

Kaul, Advaitavādinī, 2003, "Bearing of Kashmir in the Development of Buddhist Thought," *Kalākalpa*,1, 1, 2003, pp. 179-91.

MṬ, (IV), Bhāskarakaṇṭhas Mokṣopāyaṭīkā. Ein Kommentar in der Tradition der kaschmirischen *Yogavāsiṣṭha*-Überlieferung. 4. (*Sthiti*)-*Prakaraṇa.* Hrsg. von Walter Slaje. [Materialien für eine kritische Ausgabe des *Mokṣopāya*. 4. = Geisteskultur Indiens. Texte und Studien. 2. (Indologica Halensis)], Aachen, 2002, 302 S.

Nakamura, Hajime, 1980, *Indian Buddhism. A Survey with Bibliographical Notes.* [Buddhist Traditions.1.] Reprint, Delhi, 1989.

Naudou, Jean, 1980, *Buddhists of Kaśmīr*, New Delhi.

RT — *Kalhaṇa's Rājataraṅgiṇī*, Chronicle of the kings of Kaśmīr, Sanskrit text with crit. notes ed. by M. A. Stein, Bombay, 1892.

Salomon, Richard, 1994, *Ancient Buddhist Scrolls from Gandhāra*, The British Library Kharoṣṭhī Fragments, Seattle.

Schmidt, Richard, 1924, *Nachträge zum Sanskrit – Wörterbuch in kürzerer Fassung von Otto Böhtlingk*. Reprint, Delhi, 1991.

Skjærvø, P.O., 2002, Khotanese Manuscripts from Chinese Turkestan in the British Library. A complete catalogue with Texts and Translations. [*Corpus Inscriptionum Iranicarum*, Part II: Inscriptions of the Seleucid and the Parthian Periods and of Eastern Iran and Central Asia, vol. V: Saka, Texts VI], London.

Slaje, Walter, 2007, "Three Bhaṭṭas, Two Sulṭāns, and the Kashmirian Atharvaveda," In: *The Atharvaveda and its Paippalādaśākhā. Historical and Philological Papers on a Vedic Tradition*, ed. by Arlo Griffiths and Annette Schmiedchen. [Geisteskultur Indiens 11, Indologica Halensis], Aachen, 2007, pp. 329-353.

Stein, Marcus Aurel, 1900, *Kalhaṇa's Rājataraṅgiṇī, A Chronicle of the Kings of Kaśmīr*, Transl., with an introd., comm. and app., vol. 1.2, Westminster, 1900.

Von Hinüber, Oskar, 2004, Die Palola Ṣāhis, ihre Steininschriften, Inschriften auf Bronzen, Handschriftenkolophone und Schutzzauber. [Antiquities of Northern Pakistan. 5] Mainz.

Witzel, Michael, 1990, "On Indian Historical Writing: The Role of Vaṁśāvalīs," *Journal of the Japanese Association of South Asian Studies*, 2 (1990), pp. 1-57.

———, 1994, "The Brahmins of Kashmir," in: *A Study of the Nīlamata. Aspects of Hinduism in Ancient Kashmir*, ed. by Yasuke Ikari, Kyoto, 1994: pp. 237-94.

13

Looking for Bricks as a Writing Material Through Epigraphic By-lanes

An Enchanting Evidence

Panchanan Bhoi

Introduction

IT has been argued that the tradition of writing in India has a history of its own despite some scholars of modern Indological and popular writing contend that India has no sense of history. And this view has frequently been justified by their observation that indigenous historical writing has been almost completely absent until fairly recent times. Despite several studies there still remain questions to be addressed on the issue of tradition of writing — historical writing and use of various writing materials. Thus, the evolution and growth of inscriptions could be ascertained only through specific studies on writing materials and writing instruments. The finds of tools and artefacts at various sites in India support the utility and necessity of investing on these issues. There is no denying the fact that few of the materials with inscriptions such as earthenware, potsherds and bricks are still surviving despite the rigours of the Indian climate and these were definitely used by the people for lettering purposes. Therefore, discovery of various inscriptions of these materials speak the antiquity of writing. We have scant specimens of these inscribed materials belonging to early period. So, it is difficult to get early and much information on writing from these materials. But according to this observation, one need not be surprised to see inadequate specimens of writing on these materials and their absence does not establish that they never existed or were never in use by the people.

Writing Systems in India

Due to lack of proper evidence there is a lacuna of dexterity between the development of different writing systems and the material used in it. For one, we have largely focused on the tradition of writing and ignored the various writing materials involved in it, i.e. bricks. The sources existing from literary, archaeological and other data nevertheless scantily refer to inscriptions on brick and only from these scant data we can examine the use of it. Therefore, the first question that confronts us whether the presence of inscriptions that exists on bricks could bear any testimony to their social and religious affiliation? Further to analyse the theme comprehensively we have to look into a wide range of information available from the epigraphical sources.

Although in Mesopotamia and other countries of Western Asia, the ancient people used bricks very commonly for writing purposes, but in India the use of bricks for lettering was somewhat sporadic.[1] Large specimens of inscribed bricks showing letters have been discovered in different temples of India and these are now preserved in various archaeological museums.[2] These are religious in nature. Some bricks relate to

1. R.B. Pandey, *Indian Palaeography*, Varanasi: Motilal Banarsidass, 2nd edn., 1957, p. 77.
2. G. Bühler, *Indian Palaeography*, New Delhi: Today and Tomorrow's Publishers, 2nd edn., 1973, p. 116.

royal epigraphs recording achievements of the *Aśvamedha* sacrifices performed by various kings and these can be referred to the horse-sacrifice performed by the kings Devīmitra, Dāmamitra and Śīlavarman. Brāhmanical inscriptions recording Vedic sacrifices are sometimes found on bricks, which were presumed to have been part of the sacrificial complex.[3] Bricks bearing inscriptions of such class were apparently fixed into structures like the platform constructed for the performance of the horse-sacrifice.[4] Inscribed bricks were also sometimes fixed into brick-made pillars. Generally the letters or characters were either embossed or scratched on moist clay of the bricks before they were dried and baked or burnt.

Excavations Reveal Script Mystery

The preliminary exploration of the *Aśvamedha* sites at Jagatgrām near Dehra Dun, Uttaranchal, where a king called Śīlavarman, of the third century CE performed *Aśvamedha* sacrifice four times. Subsequent excavations here noticed the other three sites. Bricks from the first site bore Sanskrit inscriptions in the Brāhmī script of the third century CE. The second site brought out a number of inscribed bricks containing verses in *anuṣṭubh* metre in the same language and script. The verses reveal the personality of the king as *varṣāgaṇya, yogeśvara* or *yugeśa,* and the lord of *yugaśaila.* The third site, which remains to be opened, shows the relics of another horse-sacrifice,

3. Richard Salomon, *Indian Epigraphy*, 1st published in New York: Oxford University Press, Indian edition published in New Delhi: Munshiram Manoharlal, 1998, p. 131, For the brick inscriptions referring to the horse-sacrifice performed by kings Devīmitra, Dāmamitra and Śīlavarman, see *EI*, vol. XXX, pp. 118 ff; *EI*, vol. XXXIII, pp. 99 ff.

4. D.C. Sircar, *Indian Epigraphy*, 1st edn., New Delhi: Motilal Banarsidass, 1965, p. 73.

performed by the same king, in the shape of bricks, one of which was again inscribed and bore his name. The inscriptions on the bricks read as follows:

(1) *siddham ou yugeśvarasyāśvamedhe yugaśailamahīpate,*

(2) *iṣtakā bārṣagaṇyasya nṛpateśśīlabarmaṇ*: meaning "this brick is from (or belongs to) the *Aśvamedha* of (or performed by) Śīlavarman, king of Yugaśaila and a Yugeśvara or the lord of the lustrum."

(i) *nṛpatebārṣagaṇasya poṇaṣaṣṭhasya ghimata,*

(ii) *caturthāsyāśvameghasya cityoyāṁ śīlavarmana*: meaning "this is the altar of the fourth horse sacrifice performed by king Śīlavarman, who was of *vṛṣagaṇa-gotra* and was sixth in descent from/of Pona(*vaṁśa*)."[5]

Bricks of Various Scripts

Most of the early inscribed bricks carry Buddhist *dhāraṇī*s and *sūtras*; the letters having been scratched on moist clay, before it was baked. Bricks with passages from canonical texts or *dhāraṇī*s have been found at several Buddhist sites like Nālandā. Bricks are round on square tablets of clay or mud dried and baked sometimes. Cunningham, Fuhrer and other archaeologists discovered specimens of inscribed bricks in different parts of India, containing a single or a few letters and originally set-up in the walls or the niches of temples or on the pedestals of images.[6] The remains at Bhītarī[7] consist of

5. *IAR*, 1953-54, pl. XV, *IAR*, 1953-54, pp. 10-11, pl. XV.

6. Pandey, p. 77, op. cit.

7. Bhītarī is situated on the left bank of the Gārgī river nearly midway between Banāras and Ghazipur; and five miles to the north-east of Saidpur in Uttar Pradesh.

several ruined brick mounds, an inscribed stone pillar, and a few pieces of sculpture. In the discovery at the foot of the pillar was an old brick inscribed with the name of Śrī Kumāragupta. From the mounds also recovered numerous other bricks inscribed with Kumāragupta.[8]

Some of the moulded bricks of Śorkoṭa[9] have been found bearing short inscriptions, which although they are simple mason's marks, are valuable on account of their antiquity, as their characters belong to the age of the Guptas, or from CE 79 to 319. As the forms of both letters and numbers in these inscriptions agree exactly with those of the later Indo-Scythian and early Gupta inscriptions, which belong to first and second century CE.[10] These inscribed bricks were obtained by General Van Cortlandt and are now in the Lahore Museum.

Sometimes religious texts were also inscribed on bricks. Some brick tablets recovered from Gopālapura village, in Gorakhpur district of Uttar Pradesh have Buddhist *sūtras* on both sides. These bricks are 11.5 to 9 inches in length and 4¾ to 4.5 inches in breadth containing 12 to 10 verses on one side and 12 to 9 verses on the other. The inscriptions on these bricks belong to third or fourth century CE.[11] Two inscribed bricks of third century CE were recovered from a fort named

---

8. A. Cunningham, *Reports*: *Archaeological Survey of India* (*ASIR*), vol. I, New Delhi, 1861-62, p. 97, pl. XXX.
9. The old fort of Śorkoṭa is the loftiest of all the mounds in Punjab, being just 100 ft. in height above the surrounding fields, is situated on the bank of the Cenāb river.
10. Cunningham, *ASIR*, vol. V, 1872-73, pp. 102-03, pl. XXX, Figs. A, B, C, D, E. Also see *CII*, vol. II, part-I, p.137 for Shāh jī-kī Ḍherī inscribed bricks.
11. *Proceedings of the Asiatic Society of Bengal* (*PASB*), 1896, pp. 100-03.

Ujjain located near Kāśīpur village in the Tarāī *parganā* of Nainital district. One of the bricks has an inscription, which reads on one side: *tasya rājñyoḥ śrīputhivimitasa*, and on other side: *rājñyo mātumitāpūta*.[12] A specimen of such an inscription was discovered by Hoey in the Uttar Pradesh where Buddhist *sūtra*s were engraved.[13] A number of inscriptions on bricks are preserved in the archaeological museum at Mathurā, which can be assigned to the first century BC on palaeographical grounds.[14] Further, an inscription (No. 477) engraved on a brick deposited in a wooden box in the Sarnath Museum reads *prābhṛtaka-dhānya* meaning "grain which is an offering." The brick appears to have been used as a label to mark the spot where the grain was stocked for religious offering in a temple or monastery.[15] On palaeographical grounds the epigraph may be assigned to the sixth century CE.

Earthenwares Used for Writing

Besides bricks, earthenwares were also used as writing material. An earthenware fragment of Guhasena of Valabhi inscription is on Valabhi characters and the inscription reads

---

12. The facsimiles of these inscriptions were first published in an English daily newspaper *Pioneer* (Allahabad) on 6th December, 1901. G.H. Ojha, *The Palaeography of India* (in Hindi), (1st edn.: 1918) Revised edition, New Delhi: Munshiram Manoharlal, 1993, p. 151.
13. *PASB*, 1896, pp. 99 ff.; for other interesting brick inscriptions, see N.P. Chakravarti, "Two Brick Inscriptions from Nālandā," in *EI*, vol. XXI, no. 32, pp. 193-99; A. Ghosh, "An Inscribed Brick from Nālandā of the Year 1997," in *EI*, vol. XXIV, no. 5, pp. 20-22.
14. Pandey, p. 77, op. cit.
15. D.C. Sircar (ed.), *ARIE*, Delhi: Dept. of Archaeology, Govt. of India, 1952-53, 1958, p. 17.

as: *200 40 7 śrīguhasenaḥ ghaṭā.*[16] Further, earthen seals[17] were also used as medium for writing, e.g. clay seals of Nālandā and inscribed clay seals recovered from the excavations at Basārh.

The most common inscribed earthen objects are seals and sealings of terracotta or unbaked clay. These are found in large numbers, especially in north India, from virtually all periods.[18] Buddhist votive inscriptions on clay bearing the Buddhist creed *ye dharmā hetuprabhavā*[19] and other formulae are common from many sites in India and elsewhere. Other less common types of inscribed terracotta include donative records. An earthen lid discovered in Sāñcī *stūpa* and the pottery belonging to the period of Grahavarman of Valabhi are instances where letters are written with ink.

For clay seals with inscriptions, we find Basarh Clay Seal Inscription of Dhruvasvāminī where it reads as *mahārājādhirāja śrī candragupta patnī mahārāja śrī govindagupta mātā mahādevī śrī dhruvasvāminī,*[20] Basārh Clay Seal Inscription of Ghaṭotkacagupta

---

16. Incription of Valabhi characters. E. Hultzsch, "An Earthenware Fragment of Guhasena of Valabhi," in *IA*, vol. *XIV*, p. 75.

17. T. Bloch, "Excavations at Basārh: Inscribed Clay Seals," in *ASIAR* 1903-04, pp. 107 ff., pls. 60-62; Hirananda Sastri, "The Clay Seals of Nālandā," *EI*, vol. XXI, no. 5, pp. 72-77.

18. For terracotta plaques and tablets, see *CII*, vol. II, part I, p. 177, for Kumrāhār terracotta plaque inscription; *Indian Archaeology*, 1955-56, pl. XLIII; *Indian Archaeology*, 1952-53, no. B 489.

19. T. Bloch, *ASIAR*, 1903-04, pls. 60-62, G.H. Ojha, *Bhāratīya Prācīna Lipimālā*, 3rd edn., Delhi: Munshiram Manoharlal, 1959, p. 151, fn.5.

20. D.R. Bhandarkar, B.C. Chhabra and G.S. Ghai, "Basārh Clay Seal Inscription of Dhruvasvāminī," in *CII*, vol. III, no. 13, pp. 260-61, pl. XIII.

reads as *śrī ghaṭotkacaguptasya*[21] and Nālandā Clay Seal of Vainyagupta reads as *sya candraguptas tasya putrastas tasya putras-tat pādānudhyātaḥ śrī-ma puruguptas tasya putras tat-pādānuddhyāto mahādevyaṁ śrī candra parama bhāgavato mahārājādhirāja śrī vainyaguptaḥ.*[22] Further in the *stūpa* mound in Nālandā site, Biharsheriff *tāluka* cf Patna district, broken pieces of terracotta are found, these frequently contain part of *Nidāna-Sūtra* or *Pratītyasamutpāda-Sūtra*. Again clay seals, votive tablets (with *ye dhamma*, etc.) in early Cāḷukyan script are recovered from Śaṅkaram in Visakhapatnam district.[23]

Conclusion

There are extant today more actual exemplars of inscriptions on bricks than what we realize, and many of them go back to the very places, times and events which they describe. Among the contents covered in this limited study comprise the association of bricks in social and religious affairs, which further needs to be studied. Therefore, scholars hope to edit

21. D.R. Bhandarkar, B.C. Chhabra and G.S. Ghai, "Basārh Clay Seal Inscription of Ghaṭotkachagupta," *CII*, vol. III, no. 27, pp. 294-96, pl. XXVII.

22. D.R. Bhandarkar, B.C. Chhabra and G.S. Ghai, "Nalanda Clay Seal of Vainyagupta," *CII*, vol. III, no. 33, pp. 319-21, pl. XXXIII. For other clay inscriptions see D.R. Bhandarkar, B.C. Chhabra and G.S. Ghai, "Nalanda Clay Seal of Budhagupta," *CII*, vol. III, no. 42, pp. 350 ff. pl. XLII; D.R. Bhandarkar, B.C. Chhabra, and G.S. Ghai, "Nalanda Clay Seals of Narasiṁhagupta," *CII*, vol. III, no. 44, pp. 354 ff. pl. XLIV, D.R. Bhandarkar, B.C. Chhabra, and G.S. Ghai, "Nalanda Clay Seals of Kumāragupta III," *CII*, vol. III, no. 45, pp. 355 ff. pl. XLV; D.R. Bhandarkar, B.C. Chhabra and G.S. Ghai, "Nalanda Clay Seal of Vishnugupta," *CII*, vol. III, no. 48, p. 364, pl. XLVIII.

23. Also see T.N. Ramachandran, *EI*, vol. 28, no. 25, pp. 133 ff., for an inscribed pot recovered from Sālihuṇḍām, Andhra Pradesh.

a substantial collection of writings on earthen epigraphy in the future. The subject is a fascinating one, and the brick documents of antiquity may yet turn out to deserve more than a casual footnote in the history of written materials. This stress on writing on bricks and the size of the area involved have prevented the composition of a universal approach of its use in India. However, even this is not altogether absent. It has been attempted in the Purāṇas, interestingly again in the Brāhmanical guise of Vedic sacrifices performed by different persons through the linking of certain royal families of the subcontinent. In short, the lack of enough availability of inscriptions on bricks and the alleged lack of proper finding is due. So, in the large measure, more findings of such bricks will enhance the efficacy and utility of investing this writing material in the sources of history, which will in turn provide an impetus to the religious and philosophical tenets of Indian history.

14

The Philosophy and Aesthetics of Rasa
A Note

Makarand Paranjape

Introduction

THIS chapter gives a brief discussion of *rasa*, one of the key concepts of the indigenous aesthetic system of our country. Along with other concepts such as *dhvani*, *alaṁkāra*, *vakrokti*, and *aucitya*, it helps to constitute a comprehensive aesthetic philosophy, which has affected our civilization from the earliest times to the present. Despite the impact of Western ideas on the Indian psyche, *rasa* aesthetics continues to underlie our sensibilities. One proof of this is its prevalence in the most popular and powerful of our artistic media, Bollywood cinema. I would argue that 90 per cent of all Bombay films are dominated either by *śṛṅgāra* (romantic) or *vīra* (heroic) *rasa*s. Also, that primarily ours is a cinema of emotion rather than action or intellect. We go to Bollywood movies to laugh and cry, to feel pain and pleasure, to escape from our daily routine, besides also to engage with our realities through exaggeration, fantasy, and romance. In our films, like in the older folk forms of performance, dance, song, and music are an integral part of the viewing experience. This distinct mode of performance, thus, harks back to Bharata's *Nāṭyaśāstra* (*c.* second century BCE to fourth century CE). Unfortunately, most of us are totally ignorant of our rich aesthetic tradition. This essay on *rasa* is thus an attempt to glimpse the deeper structures and values that underlie Indian aesthetic thinking.

Importance of Rasa in Our Daily Life

I have already tried to show how relevant *rasa* continues to be by citing the example of Bombay cinema. While I was writing this essay, I found another startling reminder of how *rasa* plays such an important role in our day-to-day life. No, I am not referring to the popular derivatives of the word such as *rasam,* the spicy soup so common in south Indian meals, or *Rasanā,* the flavoured cold drink mix, so frequently used in middle-class homes in summers. Nor am I referring to Indian cuisine, in which *rasa* is so important. All these examples no doubt link food and aesthetic sensibility, showing how some of the defining features of our way or life endure despite rapid changes and modernization. My reference was actually to the important role that *rasa* plays in celebration of all our festivals. I will consider the example of Holi, the festival of colours; *Holī,* because my paper was written during that period.

One can hardly chose a better occasion to discuss *rasa* than *Holī,* which is observed each year on Phālguna Pūrṇimā, the full moon night of the lunar month Phālguna roughly corresponding with March. Throughly corresponding with March. This ancient spring festival celebrated all over India is marked by the burning of the effigy of all impurities, symbolized in the story of Prahlāda and Holikā, before one welcomes one's own and others' renewal with a frenzy of colour, song, dance, and, at oftentimes, intoxication. *Holī* is the rite of the victory of spring over winter, or Eros over Thanatos, depicted in the frolic of Kṛṣṇa with his playmates, the *gopī*s of Vṛndāvana. Interestingly, the Śaivite legend associated with *Holī* has to do with the burning of Kāmadeva who tried to disturb the *tapas* or austerities of Śiva. After Rati, his wife, pleads for her husband's life, he is restored, but only in a mental form, hence his other name is Anaṅga or the bodiless one. *Kāma*, or desire, now becomes an abstraction, something that resides in the minds of all of us. *Holī* is also a carnival of transgression and subversion, erasing class and gender differences, upturning hierarchies, creating playful disorder, and above all, lots of fun and mischief. In such a celebration what is of paramount importance is the *rasa* of *Holī*, that is the relish of the festival. All the colours, fun, frolic, eating and drinking, lead to the tasting or the *rasa* of *Holī*. Similarly every festival in India — whether it is *Durgā Pūjā* or *Gaṇeśa Caturthī* or *Poṅgal* or *Diwālī* — must be enjoyed. Without this sense of participatory delight or *rasa*, the festival is drab or uninteresting.

Definition of Rasa

Rasa, therefore affects our daily life as it does to our aesthetic pursuits. But what is *rasa?* An obvious definition would simply be "juice." *Rasa* is actually juice, the sap, and the lusty-tasty meaning of life that we are craving to enjoy. *Rasa*, in all its various meanings, is thus akin to juice, which too is so rich in connotation and denotation. We all want to extract, as it were, the juice of life, or to use the word as a verb, to juice every experience, including the reading of this very essay. From this perspective, *rasa* has much to communicate to us.

Rasa is not only central to an understanding of the entire spectrum of the arts and crafts of India, but also to any understanding of India, especially of the lived reality of this complex and fascinating country. The first occurrence of the word goes back to the *Ṛgveda* (*c*. 1700 BCE), one of the oldest known texts of the human species. Here it simply means juice, particularly of the magical-medicinal plant, *soma* — the highly inspiring, symbolically charged elixir of the legendary plant. Agni and Soma of course like *yin* and *yang*, the male and female principles, must be in balance. *Agni* heats while *soma* cools; the sun is *agni* while the moon is *soma*. One flares up, the other calms down. These are not just metaphors, but spiritual principles.

Some have considered *somarasa* to be a hallucinogenic drug, a narcotic, an extract of a plant that could intoxicate those who consumed it. From that point of view, our progenitors, the great *ṛṣi*s, were often "intoxicated." But was this "high" they spoke of only a derivate of some material, mind-altering substance? Or did it refer to spiritual power, afflatus, the ecstasies of higher consciousness? The chanting of the Vedas in the proper manner was supposed to induce this heightened state, for instance. That is why the Vedas were performative, not scriptural. They were not literature or simply texts, but chants, *mantra*s, songs. By singing them properly one could subdue the elements, overcome one's enemies, fulfil one's desires, cure illnesses, and so on. The world, in other words, was linked to the word. The latter produced the former. Or to put it differently, the word was the juice of the world. The material, spiritual and the aesthetic were thus fused into a synergy right then. To cognize the world, to act on it, to alter it — all these were actually ways of enjoying the world. The object of knowledge was also the object of delight. The kinaesthetic and the aesthetic went hand in hand.

Rasa as Mentioned in Upaniṣads

In the Upaniṣads, especially in the *Taittirīya*, *Kauṣītakī*, and *Īśa*, *rasa* begins to acquire a more complex character. Here it means not only juice, but spiritual essence and flavour; furthermore, as something that moves or transforms the mind (*Īśa Upaniṣad*). In the *Taittirīya Upaniṣad* is the famous declaration *raso vai saha*

(14) — He (or That) is the flavour of all existence, by tasting or grasping which, our lives can become blessed. These examples from the Vedas show that the idea of *rasa* is as old as systematic Indian thinking.

As most of the major ideas migrated from the Vedic core to the other domains, so did *rasa*. In fact, Bharata made it central to his treatise on the arts, the *Nāṭyaśāstra*. *Nāṭya*, more specifically, the art and science of drama and performance, more generally, was itself the fifth Veda because like the Vedas, it was conducive to the *puruṣārthas*, or the cardinal aims of life, namely *dharma*, righteousness; *artha*, wealth and power; *kāma*, desire and sex; and *mokṣa* emancipation or liberation. Because the Vedas were not available to all, a new form of instruction that would appeal to all was required.

Central to this new art form was *rasa*. As Bharata says, there is no *nāṭya* or performance, without *rasa*:

> There is no *nāṭya* without *rasa*. *Rasa* is the cumulative result of *vibhāva* [stimulus], *anubhāva* [involuntary reaction], and *vyabhicārī bhāva* [voluntary reaction]. For example, just as when various condiments and sauces and herbs and other materials are mixed, a taste is experienced, or when the mixing of materials like molasses with other materials produces six kinds of taste, so also with the different *bhāvas* [emotions] the *sthāyī bhāva* [permanent emotions experienced "inside"] becomes a *rasa*.
>
> But what is this thing called *rasa*? Here is the reply. Because it is enjoyably tasted, it is called *rasa*. How does the enjoyment come? Persons who eat prepared food mixed with different condiments and sauces, if they are sensitive, enjoy the different tastes and then feel pleasure. Similarly sensitive spectators, after enjoying the various emotions expressed by the actors through words, gestures, and

> feelings, feel pleasure. This feeling by the spectators is here explained as the *rasa* of *nāṭya*. (Rangacharya, 54-55)

What is interesting is that nowhere does Bharata define *rasa*; he simply says that it is something to be experienced, savoured.

Rasa as Base for Aesthetics

After Bharata, *rasa* became the basis of a whole aesthetics, as Richard Schechner explains in his brilliant essay "Rasaesthetics":

> *Rasa* is flavour, taste, the sensation one gets when food is perceived, brought within reach, touched, taken into the mouth, chewed, mixed, savoured, and swallowed. The eyes and ears perceive the food on its way — the presentation of the dishes is sizzling. At the same time, or very shortly thereafter, the nose gets involved. The mouth waters in anticipation. Smell and taste dissolve into each other. The hands convey the food to the mouth. . . .
>
> *Rasa* also means "juice," the stuff that conveys the flavour, the medium of tasting. The juices of eating originate both in the food and from the body. Saliva not only moistens food, it distributes flavours. *Rasa* is sensuous, proximate, experiential. *Rasa* is aromatic. *Rasa* fills space, joining the outside to the inside. Food is actively taken into the body, becomes part of the body, works from the inside. What was outside is transformed into what was inside. (29)

One way to understand the salient features of *rasa* is to contrast it with the Greek idea of theatre. As Schechner argues, "An aesthetic founded on *rasa* is fundamentally different than one founded on the 'theatron,' the rationally ordered, analytically distanced panoptic" (29). In other words, in the European tradition, knowing is through seeing — theorem, theory, theorema, theatre, all linked to seeing, looking, gaze, all of which require distance and separation, while *rasa* is more immediate and experiential. As one of the foremost commentators on the *Nāṭyaśāstra*, the great Tāntric philosopher and mystic of the eleventh century, Abhinavagupta, put it, "Rather than being objectively known, it is to be understood though savouring" (Gopalakrishnan 143). If we apply such a definition, somewhat self-reflexively, to this very discussion of *rasa*, you will understand the concept of *rasa* only by knowing and enjoying how it is being presented to you *right now*. In other words, what the concept of *rasa* challenges us to do at the outset is to forge a causal and necessary connection between knowing and enjoying.

Bharata states this categorically when he declares: "Without *rasa*, there is no cognition" (*Nāṭyaśāstra*, Chapter VI). When I first came across this line, it certainly opened a door of perception. I never tire of repeating it to my students almost as a pedagogical imperative. If you're not having fun, you are not learning. That's the test. How can we be sure? That's because to learn is a basic human drive, as basic as ingestion, locomotion, or reproduction. Cognition or the constitution of meaning has to be accompanied by a certain enjoyment. Conversely, we cannot learn what we dislike or find unengaging, uninteresting, or tedious. *Rasa*, then, even if it suggests taste and savour, is actually a cognitive category.

Rasas as Identified by Bharata

Bharata identifies eight *rasa*s in the famous sixth chapter of the *Nāṭyaśāstra*: *śṛṅgāra* (erotic, effulgent), *hāsya* (humorous, happy), *karuṇa* (compassionate, full of pity), *raudra* (angry or inflamed), *vīra* (heroic, energetic), *bhayānaka* (terrifying, fearful), *bībhatsa* (disgusting, odious), and *adbhuta* (wondrous, enchanting). Each *rasa* has a corresponding dominant or stable mental state, or *bhāva*, which helps to produce it: *rati* (love), *hāsya* (mirth), *śoka* (sorrow), *krodha* (anger), *utsāha* (enthusiasm), *bhaya* (fear), *jugupsā* (disgust), and *vismaya* (wonder), respectively. *Bhāvas*, of course, are not just stable emotional states, but states of being. *Rasa* aesthetics is thus based on an understanding and conceptualization of the structure of human experience. It is more fruitful to consider it descriptive rather than prescriptive. Bharata also defines how *rasa*s are generated or produced in his famous *Rasa-Sūtra*: *vibhāvānubhāva-vybhicārī-saṁyogāt rasa niṣpattiḥ* — the combination of *vibhāva*s (determinants), *anubhāva*s (consequents) together with *vyabhicārī bhāva*s (contributory or transitory states) produces *rasa*.

These eight *rasa*s according to Bharata actually fall into two groups of four each: *śṛṅgāra, hāsya, vīra,* and *adbhuta* on the one hand, and *karuṇa, raudra, bhayānaka,* and *bībhatsa* on the other. If we examine their *sthāyī bhāva*s, we will see that the first group is pleasant, while the second is unpleasant. While we all like to experience *rati, hāsya, utsāha,* and *vismaya,* we try to avoid *śoka, krodha, bhaya,* and *jugupsā*. The *rasa*s promotes the *puruṣārathas* by pointing out the consequences of our actions; some actions will have pleasant results, while others will have deeply disturbing ones. The plot of a play will show which actions are conducive to a good, that is, virtuous life and which are not. The abduction of Sītā, for instance, will induce *bhaya, śoka, jugupsā* or even *krodha* — all these emotions suggest how immoral or terrible an act it is — and the corresponding *rasa*s, *bhayānaka, karuṇa, bībhatsa* or *raudra* will be experienced by the spectators of the performance. The consequences of Rāvaṇa's act, eventually, include not just the death of Rāvaṇa, the perpetrator of the deed, but the destruction of his whole city, along with many of its inhabitants. There is thus an intrinsic relationship between the *rasa*s and the *puruṣārtha*s.

Rasas as Debated in Later Years

In the subsequent literature, there has been much debate on the number of *rasas*, their relationship to the *bhāvas*, and on how they are produced in a work of art and perceived by the audience. In tracing the development of the concept of *rasa* from Bharata to present times, we come across the names of several commentators, notably Bhaṭṭa Lollaṭa and Śrī Śaṅkuka (eighth century), Bhaṭṭa Nāyaka (tenth century), and most importantly, Abhinavagupta (eleventh century). The latter added a ninth *rasa*, the *śānta*, or tranquil, which he considered to be the substratum of all the other *rasas*. According to Abhinavagupta, the appreciation of a work of art leads us to a state of joyous satisfaction that comes from the full savour of the performance. Just as a *yogī* reaches such a state of detached enjoyment of the world through a proper understanding of it, an auditor arrives at a similar state of blissful repose after fully juicing an aesthetically superior performance. Regarding the *sthāyībhāva* of the *śānta rasa,* Abhinavagupta considers it to be *tattvajñāna*, categorical knowledge or knowledge of the absolute reality. Because *tattvajñāna* leads to *mokṣa* it is the appropriate *sthāyībhāva* of the *śānta rasa.* Like other Kashmir Śaivites, Abhinavagupta considers epistemology to be key to the self-knowledge; he thus makes the *sthāyībhāva* of *śānta rasa* also an epistemological category. In Prof. Kapil Kapoor's rendering:

> *Tattvajñāna* is the means of *mokṣa*, and therefore it should be accepted as the *sthāyībhāva* of *śānta rasa*. *Tattvajñāna* is the name for *ātmajñāna* (self-knowledge or knowledge of the self). . . . This knowledge of the self, that is, *ātmasākṣātkāra* or *tattvajñāna*, is the *sthāyībhāva* of *śānta rasa*. So, *ātma*, the self, endowed with unalloyed properties . . . takes the form of the *sthāyībhāva* for *śānta rasa*. (178)

This is how the great *ācārya* Abhinavagupta traces the source of the *mahārasa śānta* to our very own self, our own true nature or *svarūpa*.

Bhakti as a Form of Rasa

Later theorists, especially of those belonging to the Vaiṣṇavite devotional school of Caitanya Mahāprabhu considered *bhakti* or fervent devotion to be the *mahārasa* or the greatest *rasa*. In a sense, *bhakti* was not a new *rasa* but a version of *śṛṅgāra*, the principal *rasa* as already identified by Bharata and reiterated by Abhinavagupta. Using the *Śrīmad-Bhāgavatam* as their key text, these Vaiṣṇavas offered a very sophisticated analysis and experience of *bhakti rasa* in their *kathā*s or performative narratives. Some of these are popular to this day.

One of the issues in the *rasa* aesthetics concerns the manner in which the art emotion or feeling is transmitted and then generalized. For a full appreciation of *rasa*, the reader or auditor must be fully in tune with the author or dramatist, almost becoming his cohort, or should I say, co-heart (*sahṛdaya*) in the process. Another important link in the theory was the idea of *sādhāraṇīkaraṇa* or the making common of the *rasa*, the process by which the art emotion gets universalized in such a manner that not just individuals, but the whole audience experiences a similar joy of relish. This fusing of the large group of people into one ecstatic mob can be seen at any good rock concert. Several theorists and commentators including Abhinavagupta likened the aesthetic experience to the spiritual one. Aesthetic pleasure was akin to spiritual bliss: *brahmānandasahodara*; both were born, as it were, of the same womb. That is why the highest aesthetic experience was also accompanied by a sense of *camatkāra* or epiphany.

The whole *rasa* aesthetics, as we have seen, is oral and gustatory rather than visual or optical. As Schechner puts it,

"Fundamentally, the attainment of pleasure and satisfaction in a rasic performance is oral . . . and the satisfaction is visceral, in the belly" (33). This is as it should be in a culture which was both pagan and sensuous but also highly sophisticated and reflective. A performance was usually a part of a feast, often a religious feast, as is the case with *Holī*. Schechner, using neuro-biology, contends that *rasa* acts on our gut, that is, on the enteric nervous system: "The gut — esophagus, stomach, intestines and bowel — has its own nervous system. This system does not replace or pre-empt the brain. Rather it operates alongside the brain, or — evolutionarily speaking — 'before' or 'underneath' — the brain" (36). While I would not go so far as to suggest that *rasa* is some kind of primitive art experience, I would argue that it is more integral and satisfying because it involves our whole being, physical, emotional, mental, and spiritual. What is more, the *rasa* aesthetic is participatory, with the audience appreciating and vocally applauding performers.

Conclusion

I would like to end by mentioning an important feature of Indian philosophical traditions, which also applies to our present discussion of *rasa*. According to the *paramparā*, there must be a causal relationship between three essential features of any given philosophical structure: *anubhava*, *ācāra* and *vicāra* or experience, conduct and thought. We consider the Vedas as the bedrock of our civilization because they are an embodiment or record of the most profound experiences of the Divine in all its facets. The *r̥ṣi*s experienced a cosmos populated with Gods and great Energies. This cosmos was not alien and separate from those who perceived it but very much a part of themselves. They "heard" the *mantra*s which they then sang and committed to memory. These *mantra*s, in turn, "produced" the Gods and gave rise to the various worlds. Without the experience quotient of the Vedas, the later systems of philosophy would be hollow. Similarly, in modern times, our tradition has been renewed and revitalized by great mystics and masters like Sri Ramakrishna. They experienced the highest truths and realities. It is upon the certitude of their *anubhava* that complex philosophical systems rest. To what avail are thought systems and philosophies to those who have no spiritual experience? Are they not empty words, devoid of substance or backing? Similarly, the great mystics, *gurus*, and sages, demonstrated in their lives that their conduct was in keeping with their experiences. Again, Sri Ramakrishna may serve as a great example. In his daily life and conduct, he lived the great truths of our tradition and his life and teachings were not only *rasamaya* but full of *vismaya*. Finally, and not all sages and mystics bothered to do so, there was an intellectual articulation of these experiences. In our tradition, any contradiction between thought and deed or precept and practice is considered a sign of imperfection, a failing. A *guru* who does not practice what he preaches is considered noteworthy of being followed or worshipped.

It seems to me that the idea of *rasa* has similarly to be experienced, demonstrated in one's daily life, and only then expounded as a philosophical or theoretical model. We must experience the *rasa* of life, experience the highest *ānanda* or bliss while being embodied, live and act as if this *rasa* and *ānanda* informs our existence, and only then speak of the theory of *rasa* as an aesthetic philosophy. This is the ideal. But more practically, our civilization expected and created an ambience where the flow of *rasa* was possible and appreciated. Nowadays, I am afraid that this high aesthetic sensibility seems to have vanished from our midst. Modern, especially urban, life seems to be marked by an unprecedented ugliness and absence of *rasa*. Ugly buildings, ugly homes, ugly vehicles, ugly pots and pans savourless food and absence of refinement in popular tastes. What is heartening, however, is that in the midst of utter squalor and wretchedness, one sometimes comes across a beautiful *raṅgolī* or decorative pattern outside the poorest of our hovels. Suddenly, in the midst of *bībhatsa* or disgust, one experiences the *camatkāra* of the *adbhuta rasa*.

Now that we are gradually regaining our prosperity as a nation, I hope that the systems and products we design, whether for the now or the future, may be full of *rasa*. They must have juice in them. They should be full of nutrition, both literarily and metaphorically. They should be able to make the consumer participate and experience a sense of satisfaction. They should be flavourful and joyful. They should not alienate the maker and the user, but integrate and connect both of them. They should, in a word, be so designed as to be tasted, relished, enjoyed, and experienced.

References

Bharata Muni, *Nāṭyaśāstra*, trans. and ed. Adya Rangacharya, Delhi: Munshiram Manoharlal, 1996.

Gopalakrishnan, Sudha, "Abhinavagupta's Interpretation of Bharata's *Rasa-Sūtra:* A Translation", *Evam* 4: 1 & 2 (2006), pp. 130-43.

Kapoor, Kapil, "Abhinavagupta on Bharata's Theory of *Rasa*", *Evam* 4: 1 & 2 (2006), pp. 144-83.

Schechner, Richard, *Rasaesthetics,* TDR 45.3 (Autumn 2001), pp. 27-50.

15

Romila Thapar on Śakuntalā

Wagish Shukla

> Methodology is much more important than phenomenology, because the principles of problem solving remain useful despite technological changes.. . . **Let us therefore pretend that we still live in that bygone era.**
>
> — Donald E. Knuth*

PROF. DR ROMILA THAPAR had published a book in 1999, *Śakuntalā: Texts, Readings, Histories*, through Kali for Women. The book contains an essay (including a translation of the story of Śakuntalā from *Śrīmad Bhāgavata*) by Dr Thapar, but has other material: A translation of the story of Śakuntalā from the *Mahābhārata* by J.A.B. van Buitenen, a translation of the *Abhijñāna-Śākuntalam*, the Sanskrit play written by Kālidāsa, by Barbara Stoler Miller, the *Kaṭṭhahārī-Jātaka*, translated by E.B. Cowell taken from *The Jātaka Stories* edited by Cowell, the story of *Kadalīgarbhā* from *Kathā-sarit-sāgara* translated by C.H. Tawney, the prefaces by William Jones and Monier-

---

* *The Art of Computer Programming,* vol. 3, p. 318 (2nd edn., 1998), Addison-Wesley, 2nd Indian reprint, 2000. Emphasis in the original.

Williams to their translations of the Sanskrit play by Kālidāsa, and an essay by Rabindranath Tagore. The endnotes list 166 items. You have photographs whose "choice is not entirely arbitrary." I quote the stated purpose from Dr Thapar's preface:

> The attempt here is to see how the theme was treated in different historical periods and why there was this difference.[1]

The concluding sentence of the book is:

> In the last two centuries we have ignored the Śakuntalā of the *Mahābhārata*, the liberated woman demanding to be justly treated, and have endorsed the more submissive Śakuntalā of Kālidāsa, a woman waiting patiently for a recognition of her virtues.[2]

Dr Thapar utilized a Senior Fellowship at the Nehru Memorial Museum and Library to write this essay.

The essay is a bundle of disservices.

I

One of the opening sentences by Dr Thapar is:

> Underlying this exercise is the suggestion that an item of literature, as a narrative, relates to history, not for what it says which is anyway fictional, but for what it might indicate as being historically significant.[3]

After a few pages, the reader is supplied with the following information:

---

1. p. vii.
2. p. 262.
3. p. 1.

> In the *Mahābhārata*, the narrative of Śakuntalā is told by Vaiśampāyaṇa[4] to Janamejaya, who in turn narrates it in the course of reciting the epic on the occasion of a major sacrificial ritual.[5]

When I was a student (of what is now called plus two), if I had written this in an examination, my teacher of History would have awarded zero marks for such information. Not satisfied with this, he would have further rebuked me for forgetting a major piece of cultural data, the fact that in any major or minor ritualistic narration, the *yajamāna* is never the narrator, always only a receiver of the narration. For, the account in the *Mahābhārata*, "fictional" though it may be, is different; Janamejaya is not the narrator anywhere. Vaiśampāyana gets the story from Vyāsa and is later ordered by him to narrate it to Janamejaya after the *Sarpasatra* (the "major sacrificial ritual" started by Janamejaya to kill all the snakes because his father Parīkṣit died due to a snakebite as a consequence of a curse) was abandoned midway on account of an intervention by Āstīka and others; *in turn*, the story is narrated by Sauti to the *ṛṣis* who had assembled for the "major sacrificial ritual" of the twelve-year *satra* by Śaunaka.

The students of today are more fortunate. Every time they are caught passing off false data as genuine, they can argue that "an item of literature relates to history not for what it says which is anyway fictional" and they can quote a distinguished historian, Dr Thapar, in their support. The generation next research scholars are still more fortunate, for as the book by Dr Thapar reveals, no consultations of the actual text are needed for attempting "to see how the theme was treated in different historical periods and why there was

4. *sic*. The diacritic below the "n" is wrong.

5. p. 15.

this difference." Unfortunate are only those general readers who will henceforward believe on the authority of Dr Thapar that Janamejaya was a narrator of the *Mahābhārata*, and enter into a quarrel with anybody who, trusting the "fictional accounts of literature," argues that the relation of ritual to narration involves the basic axiom that the sacramental character of the narration lies in the *yajamāna* being the receiver of the narration; the historical significatum ferreted out by Dr Thapar being exactly the opposite.

Here is another historical significatum, actually a set of historical significata, from the book by Dr Thapar:

> The guards are rough with the fisherman, accuse him of stealing the ring and make fun of his low caste, a vignette on normal social confrontations. (Not surprisingly, such vignettes are not included in the picture often presented of "the Golden Age" portrayed in the works of Kālidāsa.) The guards threaten to kill him but when the messenger arrives with a gift of money from the king for the fisherman, they are eager to share it. The fisherman knows that as a man belonging to the powerless lower strata, it would be to his advantage to do so. The magistrate and the fisherman, the former obviously of a high caste and the latter very low, both leave together for the wine shop to celebrate the latter's good fortune. Urban pleasures, it would seem, do not stand in the way of caste regulations — higher castes are able to consume the wealth of the lower caste in a mood of togetherness. Or else, the caste regulations were more lax than has been assumed.[6]

Let us list some of these historical significata from this passage. I will juxtapose my comments on each item under the heading "narrative significatum."

---

6. pp. 68-69.

Historical significatum: A normal social confrontation in Ancient India included making fun of the low caste of the person coming from that caste.

Narrative significatum: "Making fun of the low caste" was a punishable offence under law,[7] and this law protected the entire population in contrast to the laws of modern India which protect only selected segments. Dr Thapar is somewhat misleading in her reporting of the narrative from the play: the "caste" is not in question here, the "profession" is, seeing that "the magistrate" sardonically comments on the livelihood of the fisherman which consisted of killing fish for commercial purpose. It is of course true that the distinction between caste and profession is frequently blurred, but here at least the only issue is the killing. The caste-dimension, to the extent that it is there, is brought in by thefisherman in his immediate retort (which Dr Thapar has failed to mention) in which he justifies his livelihood saying that this profession is his by birth and parallels the killing of the fish to the sacrifice of the animals in a *yajña*, observing that the Vedic priest kills animals in a sacrifice not because he is cruel by nature and chooses to kill animals but because that is part of his ordained professional duties, adding that similarly the fisherman kills fish not because he is cruel by nature and chooses to kill fish, but because that is part of his ordained professional duties. This retort does not invite any reprisal by the "upper caste" officers of the law-enforcement agency. The fisherman hits again when after his version of how he got the royal signet ring is accepted by the king and he is released, by asking "the magistrate" sardonically: "How is my profession (to be regarded now)? Unfortunately, Barbara Miller translates this as "Master, how

7. The *Arthaśāstra* of Kauṭilya, the chapter on *Vākpāruṣya* (= verbal violence) eighteenth chapter in the third section of the book.

will I make my living now?" and since Dr Thapar relies on only this translation and not the original play for writing her essay (this will be further supported below), she has no access to what Kālidāsa has actually written. The fisherman hits again, when the money is given to him by "the magistrate." One of the "policemen" had said that his hands "are itching to fasten the garland of flowers" for the fisherman's execution, this being a reference to the custom in those times of garlanding a man just before he was to be executed. The fisherman offers now half of the purse from the king as "the price of flowers." That the "vignette on normal social confrontation" permits the fisherman to make such comments is obviously not a historical significatum according to Dr Thapar.

Historical significatum: The magistrate was "obviously of a high caste." This is so obvious in fact that this needs no investigation. Since the magistrate and the fisherman leave for the wine shop together, there are only two alternatives. Either the higher castes had no scruples in social mixing when the drinks were on the person from the lower caste, or else the entire understanding of the caste relationship, which Dr Thapar and her colleagues have always regarded as an inhuman structure so special to the uniquely oppressive hierarchical society built by the Indians of the past, has to be revised. Additionally, drinking in company was an "urban pleasure."

Narrative significatum: Let us start by noting that Dr Thapar fails to mention that "the messenger" who arrives with the money is none other than "the magistrate." This is not a triviality because Dr Thapar is introducing a *new* character in the play and a reader who believes her would not realize that the attitude of "the magistrate" has changed precisely because he himself reported the matter to the king and observed the latter's reactions. The fisherman has, howsoever indirectly, helped the king in some matter obviously far more important than the restoration of a lost valuable, a matter which makes the fisherman somehow closer to the king than the "magistrate" is, and it is obviously better to be on the right side of this fellow, just in case, by equalizing with him in a drink-house. The "policemen," who were not present in this meeting with the king, have no way of understanding the possible implications of a personal bond between the king and the fisherman and are satisfied with the "share" in the money that the fisherman offers; it is only "the magistrate" who realizes that more than the money, the comaraderie of the fisherman is a desirable in this case. When one of the "policemen" says flatteringly to "the magistrate" that he has rendered a service to the king, "the magistrate" knows well that it is the fisherman who has done the service, and so when the double-edged (because it also means "a trifle, a token" and is offered as the customary illegitimate share) offer on half of the purse as "the price of flowers" hinting at the earlier threat of "the garland of flowers for the execution" is made, *the money is not taken*. Far from being "eager to share" the purse, "the magistrate" is anxious to make friends with the fisherman, and suggests that with his "great friend," he with his force should now move to the liquor-house.

Let us now look at "the magistrate." Why is he "obviously of a high caste?" The reason Dr Thapar has in mind is not very difficult to find out. Barbara Miller's translation introduces Act Six with "the king's wife's brother, who is a city magistrate, . . . ," and obviously, "the king's wife's brother" must be of a high caste, indeed of the same caste as the king, given the endogamous caste-system of India; so argues Dr Thapar on the basis of the English translation. Indeed, the "policemen" address "the magistrate" as "sister's husband" (*āvutta*), which makes them also "obviously of a high caste" but since Barbara Miller translates this "sister's husband" merely as "chief," and does not introduce the "two policemen" as "the magistrate's wife's brothers," Dr Thapar has no comments to make on the caste of these "policemen."

Actually, Dr Thapar (and, for that matter, Barbara Miller) hasn't the faintest clue of what this "the king's wife's brother" stands for in the Sanskrit dramaturgy.

I quote from *Sāhityadarpaṇa*, a well-known fourteenth-century text on poetics which Dr Thapar mentions twice (pp. 182, 183) in her book.

> "The king's wife's brother" is arrogant, foolish and conceited. He is from a very low caste, is given power (by the king), and is the brother of a woman who the king sleeps with, but who is not married to the king. He speaks a tongue which abounds in mispronunciation.[8]

This text then proceeds to classify the king's associates and places "the king's wife's brother" amongst those from the lowest order.[9]

"The king's wife's brother" is actually a derisive term, an Aristophanesian expression. The address which "the policemen" use, namely "sister's husband," (translated by Barbara Miller as "Chief") is another device to emphasize the indecency behind the appointment to the administrative post. For, this "magistrate" is appointed only because the king, in search of pleasures to be found only in the company of a base woman, sleeps with the sister of this man. "The magistrate" has no judicial powers, but being in charge of seizure and detention, does enjoy a certain authority. In the play he is

8. *Sāhityadarpaṇa*, 3/53.

9. *Sāhityadarpaṇa*, 3/55.

called *nāgarika* which the commentary by Rāghavabhaṭṭa (which Dr Thapar recommends as being "analytic," "incisive" and "most quoted," page 183) simply explains as "being an officer of the city." The functions of this post have to be understood from the play. The two "maids at the court" whom Dr Thapar has dismissed as "decorative," are in fact controlled by this very "the king's wife's brother," they are "sent to wait on the queen" by him, which is a euphemism for being "sent for the king's pleasure." (Dr Thapar cannot identify the "the king's wife's brother" here[10] because here Barbara Miller translates simply as "the king's brother-in-law.") This character is a procurer of the women from the "lower strata of society," the strata to which he himself belongs, for the king. It is suggested that such women are brought in by consent, that they are seeking entry into the king's *harem* for comfort, leisure, and pleasure. That this is a function of "the king's wife's brother" is clearly stated in the *Sāhityadarpaṇa*,[11] where he is listed as a "*harem* associate" grouped with hunchbacks and similar socially challenged sections of the society. Abhinavagupta, who is merely "a later commentator" for Dr Thapar (page 55), regards the introduction of "the king's wife's brother" into a play as a comment on the twisted ways in which the fate works, giving power to the underserving.[12]

This, then, is "the king's wife's brother," vividly portrayed in the play *Mṛcchakaṭikam* = ("The clay-cart") by Śūdraka and given another set of colours by Kālidāsa. Some indication of this character is also obtained from Vātsyāyana's comment that with wandering women the patrolling "officer of the city"

---

10. Act Six.

11. 3/52.

12. *Abhinavabhāratī* on chapter 12 (verse 147) of *Nāṭyaśāstra*.

can carnally join."[13] That this should be an institutionalized character in Sanskrit drama, and be brought in the play by Kālidāsa as an officer appointed by Duṣyanta, the ideal king, should tell us a thing or two about the kind of "court poetry" written in Sanskrit. But when directives are received from extra-textual inputs, and juggling a few words like "upper caste" and "powerless lower strata of the society" will suffice for a scholarly analysis, why bother about the text?

Dr Thapar of course wants to prove that the Sanskrit play is a social document, a record of an oppressive society. To this end, she presses into service such remarks:

> There are women of varying status. Irrespective of this they are grouped together by their use of Prakrit which, although considered inferior as a language, was considered appropriate for the dialogue of women. . . . Language is a marker of status and identity, whereby high status male characters speak Sanskrit . . . except that there is one set of interesting reversals which suggests that language was also a strategy. The *sūta* or charioteers speak Sanskrit, perhaps to indicate closeness to the king and the ambiguity in the *varṇa* of the *sūta* . . . yet the *vidūṣaka* who was virtually on equal terms with the king spoke Prakrit. . . . The origins of the *vidūṣaka* can possibly also be traced back to the scapegoat in Vedic ritual in which case he can even take on the impurity of the king. The *vidūṣaka* is a brāhmaṇa but he speaks Prakrit. . . . Non-brāhmaṇas and those lower down in the society may well have seen some brāhmaṇas in this image — shrewd, greedy and enjoying the good things of life.[14]

There are no societies in which language is not a social marker. So we hardly get any information out of "Language is a

13. *Kāmasūtra*, 5/5/9.

14. pp. 78-81.

marker of status and identity," but what has not been noticed by Dr Thapar is the fact that what is called a "Sanskrit play" is actually a play in many languages. The concept of a play in only one language, which is the general norm in all other literatures, is generally absent in India. Unless a play is deliberately written entirely in one language (for example, a *saṭṭaka* would be entirely written in Prakrit), the multilingual play is the norm. This can be readily seen from the so-called "plays in vernacular,"[15] written by Vidyāpati, Śaṅkaradeva and others, which are in fact all multilingual plays with a substantial input of Sanskrit.

Dr Thapar seems to be at a loss in the preceding analysis; the social markers don't seem to mark all that clearly. She finds it curious that the *vidūṣaka* is prescripted to be a brāhmaṇa, and speaks Prakrit, don't the brāhmaṇas speak Sanskrit? She finds it curious that the *apsaras*es speak Prakrit, aren't the "celestial beings" supposed to speak Sanskrit, "the language of the gods?" She seems to have missed a fact in the play: *Priyaṁvadā* speaks in Sanskrit once. She is no doubt unaware of the fact that women who were well-versed in the arts (*Śilpa-kārikā*s) were supposed to speak in Sanskrit, this included courtezans. She has no idea that on occasions, the queen and women engaged in scholastic pursuits were required to speak in Sanskrit by the rules of dramaturgy. Basically, the division merely shows that highly educated sections could, though not always did, speak in Sanskrit. What is so special about that? The king could and did speak in Prakrit, the *Vikramorvaśīya* by Kālidāsa makes the king speak in not only Prakrit but also in Apabhraṁśa. The "chamberlain" (= *kañcukī*)

15. *Prācīna Bhāṣā Nāṭaka*, edited by Daśaratha Ojha and Jagadīśacandra Māthura, National Publishing House, Delhi.

speaks Sanskrit and one of the students of Kaṇva speaks Prakrit.

The remarks about the *vidūṣaka* are the most objectionable in the above extract. It will be a surprise to those familiar with the Vedas that there was a "scapegoat" in the Vedic rituals.[16] It will also be a surprise to those familiar with the classical Sanskrit literature that the *vidūṣaka* was "shrewd, greedy and enjoying the good things of life." His position is clearly stated by Abhinavagupta; he is "the friend (of the hero) in separation (from the heroine)" and is called *vidūṣaka* precisely because he intervenes contrarily (*dūṣayati*) into the separation (*vipralambha*) space. It should be educative for Dr Thapar to know that this "shrewd, greedy" *vidūṣaka* is protected by *Oṁkāra*, the Ultimate in Vedāntic thinking, whereas the hero is protected only by Indra.[17] Yes, he is not a scholar but all brāhmaṇas were not scholars. But he is not a "buffon" as Barbara Miller translates him to be. Yet another set of historical significata:

> The epic does not directly introduce Durvāsas into the Śakuntalā story, he occurs in association with Kuntī. In reassuring Pāṇḍu that she can bear sons, Kuntī explains that when she was young and in her father's house, she was required to honour visiting guests and this led her to

16. This is illustrative of the way modern scholarship operates. Apparently, F.B.J. Kuiper writes a book *Varuṇa and Vidūṣaka* in which it is suggested that because Indra was the protective deity of the hero and because "evil" is associated with Varuṇa, it must be the case that as a counterpoint to the "godly" hero we have the *Vidūṣaka* who "takes the responsibility" for the misdeeds of the hero. Barbara Miller names this as "the scapegoat function." Then Dr Thapar elevates this idiom into the status of a Vedic ritual.

17. *Nāṭya-Śāstra*, 1/97.

> welcome Durvāsas, a brāhmaṇa with an awesome reputation. He was so pleased by her attention that as a boon, he taught her a magical spell by which she could call on any god who would then be in her power, and from whom she could procreate a son. Thus she became the mother of many sons, of Karṇa and the three eldest Pāṇḍavas. Is there a hint here of hospitality including more than the customary *arghya*, the washing of feet, and the offering of food? It seems unusual that a brāhmaṇa should encourage a virgin to invite gods to procreate sons on her, merely in return for the *arghya*. Kālidāsa reverses the Kuntī episode and makes Śakuntalā neglect the required hospitality to Durvāsas. Was Śakuntalā's neglect incidental, or deliberate because it may have involved a different kind of hospitality for which she was not willing? Was this the cause of Durvāsas' wrath, or had this notion of hospitality been discarded by the time of Kālidāsa? In some societies the provision of a nubile woman, preferably of status, would have been required hospitality. The guest could be a deity in disguise or a harbinger of good or ill-fortune, and should therefore be propitiated. Above all, hospitality was an aspect of gift exchange and therefore reciprocal, demanding the recognized requirements.[18]

I will unpack this bag of innuendos into its historical significatum.

Historical significatum: The usual hospitality of the *arghya* was not sufficient for some brāhmaṇas, notably Durvāsas, who demanded that a nubile woman of the house be presented to him for his pleasure. The technical meaning of "nubile," "suitable for marriage," did not bother him, for, in spite of knowing, without being told, that Śakuntalā was already

---

18. p. 59.

married[19] (and with such divine knowledge he could not fail to know that she was also pregnant), he still wants to sleep with her as a matter of hospitality due to him, conveniently forgetting that he was a guest at the house of Kaṇva and not at the house of Duṣyanta whose wife Śakuntalā now was. Śakuntalā, knowing fully well the intentions of this lecher from the epic age, avoided meeting him and thus when Priyaṁvadā says "Śakuntalā is in her hut nearby, but her heart is far away," she is telling a lie. Though Priyaṁvadā and Anasūyā both rush to meet Durvāsas, abandoning the worship of a goddess midway, these two nubile women could not persuade him to accept hospitality from them, for his lust was set on Śakuntalā.

To sum up, the Indian society of "high culture" was a society in which the provision of a nubile woman, preferably of status, would have been required hospitality, both Kuntī and Śakuntalā belonged to this society and while Kuntī conformed by sleeping with the guest, Śakuntalā did not, not so much because she was a faithful wife, but because "this notion of hospitality had been discarded by the time of Kālidāsa."

This is nothing except a deliberate fabrication by Dr Thapar with the limited purpose of titillating the alien reader who likes to think that the Eastern women are conditioned by their

---

19. His curse, which I quote from Barbara Miller's translation since Dr Thapar must have presumably read it, is the following:

    Since you blindly ignore,
    a great sage like me,
    the lover you worship
    with mindless devotion
    will not remember you,
    even when awakened —
    like a drunkard who forgets
    a story he just composed!

culture to hop into bed with anybody who feels the need. Since no evidence and no construction are offered, no comment is possible other than the summary with an interpretation of what this sub-plot has always meant to the readers of the play by Kālidāsa in pre-modern India.

II

I start with another quotation from Dr Thapar's book:

> In the transition from the epic story to the play there is a decline in the empowerment of women. The epic emphasizes empowerment through Śakuntalā having borne the son of Duḥṣanta; in the play the romantic mood is primary — the woman of these times did not make conditions. (The importance of the son becomes a focus only later in the play.) Romantic love hides the loss of empowerment and gradually becomes a fantasy, for if Śakuntalā claims to be the wife of Duṣyanta[20] then she must behave like a *pativratā*, the ideal wife, devoted to her husband. In an upper caste, polygamous situation, romantic love is always available to a husband, but obviously not to a wife. The king's rejection of Śakuntalā does not become a moral issue: it is glossed over through the introduction of the motifs of the curse and the ring. Whereas in the epic the question of the king's morality is implicitly raised in the statement of the celestial voice endorsing Śakuntalā's claim to the truth, in the play it is not an issue. The play is a celebration of the romantic love where the woman, before she is acknowledged as wife, exercises the freedom to choose and to act. But romantic love has to be transmuted into the ideal of a *pativratā*. The conversion from one mood to the other requires the reiterating of rules which bind the woman. Romantic love becomes almost a reversal of wifely devotion.

20. Dr Thapar spells the name differently for the different "periods," namely the period of the "epic" and the period of the "play." I will come to it later in this article.

A comparison of the depiction of Śakuntalā in the epic and the play indicates the influence of patriarchy in conceptualizing the role of a woman of the upper castes, but perhaps we should tease out the nature of this change. Patriarchal norms need not always be introduced as a binary alternative. Indian society always had a multiplicity of segmented forms which makes generalizations about the totality complicated. Each segment would have experienced change and would have related to change differently. There is not only polygamy; sometimes each new marriage may be legalized through any one of the eight forms of marriage. Thus a king could be married through the most respectable form of *kanyādāna*, the gifting of a daughter by her father, or through paying a bride-price, or through a *gāndharva* marriage each form pertained to caste and custom. In such societies, the identification of a linear change in patriarchy would lose some of the nuances in the variations.

Upper caste, patriarchal attitudes to women are reflected not only in the statements quoted above, but also in the hint of ambiguity about the *gāndharva* marriage which might have been seen as something of an anachronism in the time of Kālidāsa. Deriving from the assumption that women are objects of pleasure, the *gāndharva* marriage is not generally associated with ritual: its declaration was doubtless intended more to legitimize the birth of a son than the status of the woman. Kaṇva regards it as a lawful marriage; although he might have preferred a *kanyādāna*, the gifting of the daughter, he also realized that the daughter of an *apsarā* may not have fitted that role. In a late section of the play, the king refers to Śakuntalā as his *dharmapatnī*, his lawfully wedded wife, the *kṣetra*/field in which he has planted his *bīja*/seed. This is a change from the epic reference to the woman as the sac or the bag. The simile of the field and the seed becomes more common. Indra's charioteer, Mātali, also speaks of Śakuntalā as the king's *dharmapatnī*. The ambiguity of the *gāndharva* marriage stems from Śārṅgarava's

> description of it as a secret marriage with a hint of seduction, and the rebuke that the elders were not informed. Śārṅgarava is sharp with the king and says that Kaṇva has pardoned him for his behaviour with the girl, but that he was now behaving like a thief in rejecting her. Such rebuke does make the king anxious about his own honour. But Śārṅgarava is also hard on Śakuntalā, perhaps because he resented a woman transgressing patriarchy and choosing her own husband. He finds her independence irksome. Nevertheless the legality or the morality of the marriage is not a major concern.[21]

Let us first look at certain pieces of disinformation in the above passage.

Dr Thapar says "Śārṅgarava is sharp with the king and says that Kaṇva has pardoned him for his behaviour with the girl, but that he was now behaving like a thief in rejecting her." In actuality, Śārṅgarava says, "Don't you insult the sage who has kindly given his approval to the assault by you on his daughter and thus has acted as if he turned a thief who stole his property into a worthy recipient of a gift." The "behaviour like a thief" is not in the rejection, it is in the clandestine marriage.

Dr Thapar says "Śārṅgarava is also hard on Śakuntalā, perhaps because he resented a woman transgressing patriarchy and choosing her own husband. Hefinds her independence irksome." The "independence" is a favourite translation of the word *svātantrya* which Śārṅgarava uses when Śakuntalā tries to follow them back when the rejection by the king is final; the exact sentence being, "Ah, *purobhāginī*, do you opt for this *svātantrya*?"[22] which Barbara Miller has translated as

---

21. pp. 73-75.
22. *āḥ, purobhāgini, kimidaṁsvātantryamavalambase?*

"Bold woman, do you still insist on having your own way?" It is this "bold woman" which is at the root of the analysis used by Dr Thapar. The word *purobhāginī,* however, means "fault-finder" and it is certain that "bold woman" has been used by Barbara Miller because she thinks she knows better than the traditional commentators. The logic is simple, Indian society is anti-woman. Śakuntalā chose her own husband transgressing the oppressive patriarchy, so it must be "bold woman" which Śārṅgarava means even if he uses the word "fault-finder." You first change the text to suit your intentions, then you offer that text as evidence! It is really strange that when these scholars doctor the data it never occurs to them that they are being dishonest.

So, why does Śārṅgarava call Śakuntalā a "fault-finder"? We may, with some profit, look at another use of the word in the play under discussion. This occurs when the *vidūṣaka* reminds the king who is looking at the picture of Śakuntalā and behaving as if it is a real situation, that it is only a picture he is looking at. The king asks the *vidūṣaka,* "Why did you do this fault-finding?" For reasons unknown, Barbara Miller has translated this as "Dear friend, are you envious of me?" Clearly however, the word is used for somebody who can see only the flip side of a coin.

Śakuntalā is addressed by Śārṅgarava as one such because she sees only the fact that Duṣyanta is not accepting her as a wife but not seeing that regardless of this, the wifehood, if she is speaking the truth, is already in operation and imposes certain duties on her. One of these duties is to not leave the house of the husband without permission. The law, in the present case when the husband is not permitting entry, laid down[23] that the wife in this case is to live in the house of a

23. *Arthaśāstra,* 3/4.

relative (on either side). *But as yet, no explicit orders have come from the king*. Śāradvata has said to Śārṅgarava, "There is no point in replying (to the king and prolonging the discussion)," then to the king, "This is your wife, you can abandon her or accept her, the power of a husband over a wife works in all directions" and then to Gautamī, "You please go ahead"; for some reason, Barbara Miller has cut out a stage-direction from the last part of this input and the words "You (please) go ahead" have been put in the mouth of Gautamī. Taking a cue, they start. Then Śakuntalā tries to follow. Gautamī draws the attention of Śārṅgarava to this who then turns angrily and speaks to Śakuntalā. By dropping "Śakuntalā!" which precedes the next statement (in verse), Barbara Miller has managed to convey that Śārṅgarava has spoken to Śakuntalā entirely in an angry tone, but the fact is that only the first sentence,"Ah, *purobhāgina*, do you opt for this *svātantrya*?," is in this tone, the next part is in the nature of an explanation. The reason should be clear to anybody: if Śakuntalā leaves on her own, she makes it easy for the king who is in real trouble now because he is presented with a *fait accompli*, whether he accepts or rejects, he must now do it as a husband. Anybody who reads the play should not fail to notice that when the solution is finally agreed to *by the king*, namely, that Śakuntalā should be housed with the family of the *purohita*, who incidentally is not just a "priest" but an official of the court drawing a salary equivalent to that of the Queen, the Queen-Mother, and the Heir, *they all* accompany Śakuntalā. At no point have they suggested that Śakuntalā is to fight her own battle with no support.

This last point is the clue to the "independence" part of the point under discussion. Dr Thapar dutifully quotes the much-quoted Manu: "A woman is dependent, in turn, on her father, her husband, and her son as she goes through her life-cycle." at a point[24] in her book though one could pick-up any law-giver from the Classical India and indeed any law-book from our own times from any country which has something like alimony on statutes, to the same purpose. Like all others who quote dutifully, she has not tried to understand what is being said. So let us try to understand it.

First, is a woman "independent" some time? The Indian law-givers mention a few things. She is "independent" as far as "woman-money" (= *strīdhana*) is concerned; this essentially includes dowry and gifts from the family of the husband or the family of her parents.[25] She is, after a time, free to choose a husband on her own, this roughly corresponds to the age prescribed by modern times. The basic unit of the existential according to the classical Indian vision is a married couple, not the individual. Now this married couple has a dual functionality, a functionality for this particular life from birth to death but also a functionality for the life beyond this life. Only when one has transcended the existential and merged into the non-existential, is one free.[26] For this reason, the marriage is symbolized by a knot which joins the robes that the husband and wife are clothed in and which is tied at every ceremonial occasion (not only at the time of the marriage), e.g. a bathing in Ganges. The Vedic meaning of the word *karma* is *yajña* = ("sacrifice") and the *yajña* cannot be performed by a

24. p. 76.

25. *Strī-dhana-taraṅga* of *Vivāda-Ratnākara* collects several opinions on this point.

26. Violations in favour of a single existence for the purpose of working towards this merger into non-existence are acceptable, even respectable. To take an example from the story under discussion, Kaṇva has not married, though a more highly respected sage Mārīca has.

celibate.[27] But man and woman need to live together for many reasons which are valid only for this life before death: sexual pleasure and the social obligation of producing children for the economy and the polity of the community being the major ones. Therefore, while every Indian thinker has placed the *dharma* as primary and primal basis of marriage they have provided space for any kind of living together inside the category of marriage. Marriage was thus broadly categorized into two categories.[28] One in which marriage is sacramental, with fire as witness and *mantras* from the Veda being used to sanctify the union and the other in which fire was not the witness and *mantras* were not used. The marriage of Śakuntalā was *gāndharva*, a subcategory of the second category. Purely a consequence of mutual attraction, mutual agreement and finalized by sexual union[29] the *gāndharva* has been applauded by Vātsyāyana[30] because he is writing a treatise in which love is central. Nevertheless, it always was on the basis of a covenant (= *samaya*).[31] This covenant is explicitly spelt out by the Śakuntalā of *Mahābhārata*[32] where she does not show interest in the earlier offer of jewellery, expensive dresses and state power by the king and instead makes her own condition,

---

27. This is likely to invite cries of "not true" from superficial scholars who may think that Kaṇva for example must be doing *yajña* in his hermitage.

28. Each was divided into four sub-categories. Divorce was not permitted in the first type of marriage except under special circumstances.

29. *Manusmṛti*, 3/32. Dr Thapar cites this reference and concludes that it was a "solution to the roving eye of royalty."

30. *Kāmasūtra*, 3/5/28-30.

31. *Yājñavalkya Smṛti*, 1/61.

32. Ādi Parva, 15-17.

namely that the son born of the union should be made heir. The Śakuntalā of the play also makes a condition and Dr Thapar is wrong in concluding that "the woman of those times did not make conditions." In Act 3, when the king comes out of the hiding just after Śakuntalā has composed and read aloud her letter to him at the suggestion of her friends, Priyaṁvadā requests the king to reciprocate Śakuntalā's love, and Śakuntalā says to Priyaṁvadā, "Why do you create trouble for the king who is doubtless in agitation because of being separated from his wives (for so long)." This is clearly a demand for undivided attention and a commitment from the king that henceforward he will belong to Śakuntalā alone. Unfortunately, this sentence has been translated by Barbara Miller as "Why are you keeping the king here? He must be anxious to return to his palace," a clear incongruity since the king is at the *āśrama* at the request of the ascetics and cannot leave for his "palace" before the *āśrama* is assuredly made safe from the evil spirits. This was a task which needed a long stay, long enough to accept Śakuntalā's obliquely delivered invitation to "consummate the love plentifully again and again" (not, as Barbara Miller translates, "goodbye until our joy can be renewed"). At the end of the Act, the king is being called away from his place of hiding where he is still longingly gazing at the "flowers her body pressed," by precisely this duty of being a guardsman. Priyaṁvadā is not "keeping him here," the ascetics are, and he is in no position to leave for his "palace" until they feel safe.

It is only after this pointer by Śakuntalā to the possible rivals that Anasūyā asks the "practical question." Duṣyanta answers without hesitation: he of course has many wives but the only rival Śakuntalā will have is the earth clad in the oceans. This completes the covenant and everybody is relieved.

The Śakuntalā of the play makes a condition. She is in love and she wants love in return. She does not spell out the details herself, she has friends who can articulate it more freely. This was called modesty and used to be considered a virtue, if now it merely goes to show that she belonged to the "upper castes," I have nothing to say. But as far as "independence" and "empowerment" are considered, Dr Thapar's reading of the two texts is not based on evidence.

Let me point out some of the obvious inaccuracies again. Dr Thapar is wrong in saying that Śakuntalā was "unlikely to have been subjected to rebirth"; her argument is that Śakuntalā was born of an *apsaras* and the reference is to the statement of Śakuntalā (in Act Seven) attributing her misfortunes to "something she must have done earlier which worked against her well-being," thus exonerating Duṣyanta even before the full facts about the amnesia curse are narrated by Mārīca. Barbara Miller adds the words "in a former life" unnecessarily and this is the reason for the comment by Dr Thapar who does not bother to read the original play. This apart, however, the question remains whether Śakuntalā could have said what Barbara Miller makes her say. The answer to that is that she could, and the comment by Dr Thapar would be still invalid because every form is subject to rebirth, the innumerable stories about the curses forcing the celestial beings to be born as humans that abound in Sanskrit literature should have told Dr Thapar this much. The separation of Sīta from Rāma is explained as the result of crimes done by Viṣṇu in Nṛsiṁhāvatāra,[33] the *gopīs* are the Vedic verses born[34] and Satī, after immolating herself in the *yajña* of her father Dakṣa as a protest to the insult to her husband Śiva, is reborn as Pārvatī, Vedavatī

33. *Yoga Vāsiṣṭha.*

34. *Śrīmad-Bhāgavata.*

is born as Sītā. To take an example of an *apsaras* being subjected to rebirth, Dr Thapar need not go further than the story of Satyavatī's birth she has quoted,[35] the *apsaras* Adrikā is turned into a fish because of a curse and gives birth to Satyavatī.

In the epic, nothing in the covenant says about Śakuntalā being in the court as Duṣyanta's queen, but it is unambiguous about her son being declared as the heir to the kingdom and it is necessary therefore that a promise be made that Śakuntalā will be taken to the court with proper escort at some point in future. This point is seen to have arrived when the six-year old son is seen fit because of his prodigious growth to be declared heir-apparent, only then and not before, there is a question of Śakuntalā going to the court. That Duṣyanta failed to send the promised escort does not bother Śakuntalā,[36] nor is she claiming any right for her as a wife. All she wants is that Duṣyanta should work according to the contract and declare the son as the heir. Spurned, she declares that even without Duṣyanta helping, her son is going to rule the earth. When finally Duṣyanta does accept the son as her own and the consecration as heir to the throne has been completed, Śakuntalā is no more mentioned.[37]

Dr Thapar wonders[38]: "Did the *vidūṣaka* remember the romance of the king with the girl from the *āśrama*, but prefer

35. p. 54, Dr Thapar does not provide the reference. It is from *Mahābhārata*, 1/63. verses, 58-59.

36. Although some additional verses in the southern recensions do hint at such an anxiety, these are absent in the text accepted by Nīlakaṇṭha or, for that matter, the translation by J.A.B. van Buitenen which is the basis of Dr Thapar's analysis.

37. The southern recension mentions however, that Duṣyanta took Śakuntalā to his mother and the Queen-mother accepted as her daughter-in-law.

38. pp. 55-56.

not to remind his companion of it" when there is a clear explanation provided in the play?; the king asks this very question of the *vidūṣaka* who reminds him that before sending him off to the capital (thus the *vidūṣaka* had never seen Śakuntalā in person), the king had declared that the whole talk of falling in love with Śakuntalā was merely in jest. Dr Thapar finds it remarkable that Śakuntalā writes a love letter to Duṣyanta and observes[39]: "However, as a woman of the forest she may not have been literate, nor was it necessary that such women be. Perhaps Kālidāsa assumes that all upper caste women, irrespective of where they live, have enough literacy to be able to write a love letter." Dr Thapar obviously has no knowledge that "the forest" here is an *āśrama* which functioned as the University in that culture. Ridiculous associations abound. We find, "They (*apsaras*es) are depicted as water-nymphs in the *Ṛgveda* and the goddess of speech, Vāk, is said to be born of the waters."[40] What is one supposed to infer? That Vāk can be thought of as born of an *apsarā* ? In the Vedic literature there are few things which are not said to be born of the waters, the whole world is one such. So what is born out of what ? Is this the way to read?

Texts are mingled and mauled. We find, while the play is being discussed, this information about Śakuntalā, "she is born of an *apsaras* and is initially nurtured by birds of prey, again symbolic of an innate gentleness recognized even by these birds!."[41] Gentle though Śakuntalā is, the play does not mention this. In the play, the etymological association of Śakunta to Śakuntalā is hinted at, not explicitly stated, only once, and

39. pp. 71-72.

40. p. 40.

41. p. 71.

this is in Act Seven when Bharata is asked to look at *Śakuntalāvaṇya*, the beauty of a bird, and the child associates the initial segment of the word to his mother's name. The toy bird that is actually given is the peacock. The peacock, though it eats snakes according to belief, is not famous as a "bird of prey." Dr Thapar, though she does not say so, is relying on Monier-Williams, who lists "a particular bird of prey" as one of the meanings of *Śakunta*. This "bird of prey" is actually *bhāsa*, glossed by Indian lexicographers as "vulture," a scavenger, and not a bird of prey. However, the association is untenable anyway because in the *Mahābhārata* from where the etymological association "raised/protected by *Śakunta*s" is derived, two words, "*Śakunta*" as well as "*Śakuna*," are used, not exclusively "*Śakunta*," so that only the common meaning, namely, "bird," is acceptable. "*Śakuna*" surely does not mean "a particular bird of prey" exclusively, only a bird. It now remains for somebody to improve on Dr Thapar by claiming that because "Kaṇva" also means "a particular class of evil spirits" (who actually devour the children in womb), the innate gentleness of Śakuntalā is recognized even by these spirits. I will offer my own theory on the etymological significance of the name "Śakuntalā" later in this article.

Inaccuracies are matched by pretensions. Dr Thapar uses substantial space (pp. 76-77) discussing why Śakuntalā has been called *tapasvinī*. The word is the feminine form of *tapasvī* which means "poor" as in "poor man" and is a well known, well-used term in Sanskrit found in any dictionary. She discusses the word as if it is used only in the feminine gender whereas in the play under discussion the use in the masculine gender is available in Act Six (for the trader who dies childless). One can again see why, Barbara Miller translates the word as "brave man!" Barbara Miller has in fact translated the word *tapasvī/tapasvinī* differently for each occurrence, once as "these ascetics who practice austerities" in the monologue by Anasūyā in Act Four, once as "hermit girl" in an utterance by Priyaṁvadā in the same Act. Surely *tapasvinī* also means "(female) ascetic," but if there are indeed people who believe that Śakuntalā has been called *tapasvinī* because "she was an ascetic doing penance," then it simply means that there are people who do not know Sanskrit and no discussion of their opinion should take place. You certainly do not need a research paper (endnotes 65) to find that *tapasvinī* means "poor girl" (not "ill-fated" as Dr Thapar translates). But Dr Thapar announces learnedly:

> Interestingly, the word is used in two different senses by Sānumatī, first with reference to Śakuntalā suffering from the separation (as indeed was the king) and later to mean a female ascetic.

This is not correct. In both cases the use by Sānumatī is in the same sense and it means "the poor girl." In fact, in the entire play if there is any suggestion of Śakuntalā being "an ascetic doing penance," it is at the end when the king has been finally identified as being her husband and a female ascetic tells another female ascetic that they should go and inform Śakuntalā that her days of being bound to certain rules (*niyama*) are over; these rules are those which all wives during the period when the husband was away were supposed to observe and must have been observed by other wives of the king who were in the palace. It is true however, that Barbara Miller uses the words "Śakuntalā, a female ascetic" when she translates the second use of this term by Sānumatī. Attempts at learnedness also include the referencing to the Vedic corpus. These are:

> It is said that the *apsarā* Śakuntalā conceived Bharata at Nāḍapit (which a later text[42] glosses as the location of the *āśrama* of the *ṛṣi* Kaṇva). Bharata, the son of Duḥṣanta, performed a gigantic *aśvamedha* sacrifice, where seventy-eight horses were bound near the Yamunā river and fifty-five near the Gaṅgā river, a fantasy on the pre-eminence of the Bharatas.

The "fantasy" is actually more fantastic than Dr Thapar thinks, because it is not "a gigantic *Aśvamedha* sacrifice, where seventy-eight horses were bound near the Yamunā river and fifty-five near the Gaṅgā river" that the text[43] talks about, it is a total of seventy-eight *Aśvamedha* sacrifices near Yamunā river and another total of fifty-five *Aśvamedha* sacrifices near Gaṅgā river. But the reader of Dr Thapar's book would think that only one *Aśvamedha* sacrifice was performed by Bharata. Further, he would not know that in any one *Aśvamedha* sacrifice, no matter how "gigantic," the number of horses "bound" (this is a euphemism in Vedic literature for "sacrificed") is a total of one.

"Bharata, the son of Duḥṣanta," seems to linger longer in a different kind of fantasy. Apparently, because the text talks of Bharata, the *Dauḥṣanti*, and because if there were a name "Duḥṣanta" then *Dauḥṣanti* could mean grammatically "the son of Duḥṣanta," the name "Duḥṣanta" has been invented by the scholars although it is to be nowhere found in the Vedic corpus.[44] Thus we find Dr Thapar carefully writing "Duḥṣanta"

42. This "text" is actually Hariswāmī's commentary on the *Śatapatha Brāhmaṇa*, a fact Dr Thapar could have supplied to the interested reader.

43. *Śatapatha Brāhmaṇa*, 13.5.4, pp. 11-14.

44. I will be grateful if I can be corrected on this point because I could not find the name "Duḥṣanta" in my searching of the Vedic corpus and Dr Thapar is not alone in using this name for Duṣyanta, indeed it is given without support as an older form of Duṣyanta in the dictionary by Monier-Williams.

whenever she is talking of the epic period and "Duṣyanta" whenever she is talking of the Kālidāsa play. If the reasons are deeper than the fact that the J.A.B. van Buitenen uses "Duḥṣanta" in the translation of *Mahābhārata* and Barbara Miller uses "Duṣyanta" in the translation of the Kālidāsa play, we have no clue. But the impression that is sought to be conveyed, namely that in the *Mahābhārata* the name was the "Vedic" form "Duḥṣanta" which later evolved into the classical "Duṣyanta" by the time of Kālidāsa is certainly not supported by the texts as they are found, for if you pick-up a random edition of *Mahābhārata* you will find the name as "Duṣyanta" and if you looked very carefully, you will find an edition of the Kālidāsa play in which the name appears as "Duḥṣanta."[45]

To mention another howler, Dr Thapar learnedly informs us: "Kaṇva's *āśrama* is more of the *vānaprastha* variety because it has *vaikhānasas* and *parivrājakas* rather than *saṁnyāsins*." Dr Thapar understands none of the four Sanskrit words in this sentence. She has vaguely some idea that there is a *vānaprastha āśrama*, and there is a *saṁnyāsa āśrama*, and pasted these *āśramas* which exist only in the logical space of a man's life, into the physical space of Kaṇva's *āśrama*; she also has no idea that *parivrājaka* is a category within that of *saṁnyāsin*.

III

The signet ring, its loss and the subsequent finding in the belly of a fish, and the curse of Durvāsas are the two central changes made in the story from *Mahābhārata* by Kālidāsa. We now look at how Dr Thapar looks at them.

45. The BHU edition of the works of Kālidāsa gives the variant readings of the name as "Duḥṣanta" and "Duṣṣanta." I found another variant, "Duṣmanta" in the dictionary *Śabdakalpadruma*. I am informed that this is the form accepted in Bengal and Orissa.

First, the ring. Dr Thapar, after the customary narration of how India was indebted for everything to the invasions that were made by the foreign forces in the interest of furtherance of civilization to this country of primitives, tells us that the "signet rings had become fashionable with the coming of Yavanas — the Indo-Greeks and those associated with the Mediterranean trade."[46] And then we have:

> The finding of the ring in the belly of a fish has its own meaning. . . . The ring disguises the crux of the dilemma, the question of the paternity of the child. . . . Equally important, the ring frees the king from any blame for rejecting the woman he had married.[47]

Poetry always disguises, but that of course is not what Dr Thapar means. Her position is that the ring helps Kālidāsa in avoiding "the crux of the dilemma." The fact is exactly the opposite.

For the "symbolic connections with fish," I submit that we look at the following famous simile from the Indian medical sciences:

> The form of the womb is like the mouth of the *rohita* fish. . . .[48]

It is in the mouth of the *rohita*fish that the signet ring disappears. The ring has the name of the king on it. Symbolically, Duṣyanta has entered the womb of Śakuntalā in agreement with the usual Indian understanding that "the father himself is born as the son" (*ātmā vai jāyate putraḥ*). As a poet, stating the obvious in the obvious manner was not the job of Kālidāsa, and I very much doubt that he would have ranked as high as he is if the play had repeated prose inserts proclaiming "Duṣyanta is the

---

46. p. 54.

47. p. 54.

48. *Suśruta-Saṁhitā*, Śarīra-sthāna, 5/44.

father, do not forget you readers." A much more explicit suggestion appears earlier. When, in Act Three, the two friends of Śakuntalā move out of the scene in order to create privacy for Śakuntalā and Duṣyanta, the ruse that Priyaṁvadā uses is: "this fawn is looking for its mother, let us help him meet her." A son and a mother are being united, not two lovers, when Śakuntalā and Duṣyanta meet for the first time in a private space. The title of the play is deliberately ambiguous and can be read as "recognition of Śakuntalā" or "recognition of the son of Śakuntalā," depending on which grammatical construction you use. How explicit is a poet expected to be in suggesting what "the crux of the dilemma" is?

Let us come to the curse. Dr Thapar has this to say:

> Is Kālidāsa avoiding the moral issue of condemning Duṣyanta's action in rejecting Śakuntalā and would such an avoidance not have been regarded as contemptible in those times? The epic version does at least raise the issue through the celestial voice; the play, on the other hand, introduces extraneous elements which detract from commenting on the injustice of Duṣyanta's treatment of Śakuntalā.[49]

Very carefully, this loaded question has asserted two things: (i) Kālidāsa was avoiding the issue of the injustice of Duṣyanta's treatment of Śakuntalā, and (ii) "those times" did not regard such an avoidance as contemptible. In one stroke, the poet and his times have been portrayed as having become more hostile to women than the times of the epic, and as a bonus, a conflict between the two great poets Vyāsa and Kālidāsa has been established.

The textual evidence is, however, to the contrary. *Nobody* believes Duṣyanta when he is saying that he has no memory

---

49. p. 60.

of having married Śakuntalā. Even his *purohita*, the person to whom he turns for advice and on whom the responsibility of preserving the sacramental character of the royal office rests, does not trust him. When Duṣyanta asks the *purohita* what should be done, the advice that is given is that everybody should wait till the child is born; if the child is a son and has all the signs of a *cakravartī*, then it has to be accepted that Duṣyanta is the father. This "DNA test" certainly is not suggesting that Duṣyanta is speaking the truth, it suggests strongly that he is lying. The "extraneous elements," which Kālidāsa has introduced, do not "detract from commenting on the injustice of Duṣyanta's treatment of Śakuntalā," they in fact put Duṣyanta in greater trouble.

Another quotation will help in understanding what Dr Thapar seeks to get out of the ring and the curse:

> The curse is the stereotypical impediment of the folk-tale; its object is a woman and therefore she becomes responsible for the turn of events.[50]

To the extent that all societies at all given points of time in chronology can be proved anti-woman, Indian society can also be proved anti-woman. This is empty of any information item. In the same manner, Indian society can also be proved pro-woman at all given points of time. This is also empty of any information item. I will simply indicate what the texts say. First of all, let us note that the etymology that Sanskrit lexicographers provide for Duṣyanta is from the root *Duṣ*, (= to blame) with the explanation that "he blames Śakuntalā."[51] The name Duḥṣanta also has been

50. p. 58.

51. *Śabdakalpadruma* under the entry Duṣmanta.

etymologically associated with the same root.[52] So at least the average reader of this story from Sanskrit sources remembers the male protagonist only by the injustice of his treatment to the female protagonist, and not by any virtues that might have been found in him from reading the stories.

The average reader of this story from Sanskrit sources also does not remember Śakuntalā as a "submissive woman" or a woman who was enticed by Duṣyanta into loving him. In *Mālatīmādhava*,[53] a play by Bhavabhūti, a playwright whose reputation is matched only by that of Kālidāsa, she is listed with other legendary "extremely bold" women who chose their own husbands; the two others in the list are Urvaśī who chose Purūravās and Vāsavadattā who chose Udayana. In the *Jayamaṅgalā* commentary on *Kāmasūtra*, 3/3/19, Yaśodhara cites the story of Śakuntalā as one which could be successfully used by a lover to persuade a girl to marry him on her own, without the permission of her parents. In the story of Śakuntalā from Sanskrit sources therefore, the residual collective memory believes that the male protagonist was unjust and the female protagonist was bold and assertive. This collective memory does not differentiate between the play and the epic.

Let us now come to writers.

IV

Dr Thapar follows the story of Śakuntalā through some retellings. We will begin with her translation of the relevant portion from the *Śrīmad Bhāgavata*.

1. Historians must come up with new information and so Dr Thapar dutifully informs her readers that in this "later" work,

52. The *Uṇādi-Sūtra* of Bhoja, published in the Madras Sanskrit Series and reprinted in 1993 by Navrang, Delhi.

53. Act Two.

"The ray of Vāsudeva/Viṣṇu is of course a new idea, and suggestive of the increasing association of kings with deities in the post-Gupta period, particularly the attempt to identify certain kings as incarnations of Viṣṇu."[54] Since the "association of kings with deities" is an integral component of the standard Rājasūya sacrifice, one gathers that the post-Gupta period started with, say, *Yajurveda*. Very well. After this we are presented with another piece of new information, namely, that Bharata —

> distributed lakhs of elephants each with gold-plated tusks — a wild exaggeration but in keeping with the ambience of a potlatch. The inclusion of elephants is a departure from earlier lists the elephant by now being valued not only as the animal on which the royalty rode and hunted but for effectiveness in battle and in gathering timber from the forests.[55]

"Wild exaggeration" it sure is, "but in keeping with the ambience of" the practice of treating the text with inattention, an art Dr Thapar seems to excell at. The verse is

> *mṛgāñchuklad kṛṣṇān hiraṇyena parīvṛtān*
> *adāt karmaṇi maṣṇāre niyutāni caturdaśa.*[56]

which Dr Thapar translates as:

> At Maṣnāra he donated many black elephants each with gold-plated tusks.[57]

She has been doubtless, misled by some other translators who have translated *mṛga* as "elephant" in this verse. The logic is simple: the dictionary lists "elephant" as a meaning of *mṛga*

54. pp. 172-73.

55. p. 173.

56. *Śrīmad-Bhāgavata*, 9/20/28.

57. p. 175; *sic.* the diacritic below "n" is missing.

and don't we know that elephants are "donated" and "the black buck," which would be ordinarily the meaning, are not "donated?" But what she has not bothered about is to know that Indian elephantology divides elephants in three categories: (i) *bhadra,* (ii) *mandra,* and (iii) *mṛga* (and of course there is the *miśra,* the "hybrid"), that the *mṛga* is that of the lowest category,[58] that only the best is supposed to be "donated," that accordingly the *bhadra*-class elephant is to be "donated."[59]

Bharata is not being praised for having "donated" third class "black elephants." He is being praised for having "donated the black bucks." The *kṛṣṇājina-dāna,* gifting away of the hide of a black buck, is a celebrated religious act. The word *mṛga,* normally meaning "the buck" has also been used for "the hide of a black buck" in this context.[60]

The really unfortunate part in all this is the fact that Dr Thapar has unscrupulously reassembled, relying on the ignorance of her intended readers of the Sanskrit text, the contents of the verse to suit her "gold-plated tusks." It is necessary to translate the verse literally in order to see what she has actually done. The verse says:

> He gifted fourteen million[61] "black bucks," covered with gold, and with silver-plated teeth, at Maṣnāra in a sacrifice.

The *kṛṣṇājina-dāna* mentioned above says exactly this: the hide is to be presented with "silver-plated teeth," the horns and some other parts to be covered with gold.[62]

---

58. For details, *Arthaśāstra,* 2/31.
59. *Vidhāna-Pārijāta,* Part 3, p. 189.
60. *Vidhāna-Pārijāta,* Part 3, p. 363.
61. or "fourteen hundred thousand," the word *niyuta* means one of these depending on the particular textual practice.
62. *Vidhāna-Pārijāta,* Part 3, pp. 355-64.

The word *śukla* is obviously the reason she has done this doctoring: it usually means "white"; since "white teeth" does not seem a reasonable construction here, it must be "gold-plated!" But *śukla* does mean "silver" (when used in the neuter gender).

This then is the methodology. You decide that "by now," that is, in "the post-Gupta period," the importance of the elephant had increased and that the Vedic Sacrifice is a "potlatch,"[63] that Bharata therefore must be praised for this potlatch and not something which has value in India which is named after him, that therefore he must have given away elephants in gift, and well, the verse mentions gold and teeth so to hell with Sanskrit grammar and syntax, it must be "gold-plated tusk." This the reader is supposed to consider a scholarly work.

One retelling is being discussed as follows:

> In the *Matsya Purāṇa,* a brief reference states that Duṣyanta became the father of a world conqueror through his wife Śakuntalā. In the next verse we are told that a disembodied voice proclaimed the legitimacy of his son, comparing inexplicably, the mother to "a pair of bellows." This was a variant on the more frequent description of the mother being simply a bag or a sac and the son belonging to the father alone, since the father is responsible for the seed/birth — an echo of the statement in the *Mahābhārata.*[64]

---

63. The potlatch is a festival of northern Amerindians in which the host gifts away large amounts of wealth and destroys his property in a show of wealth, the guests later attempt to surpass it. This meaning I have taken from the Random House dictionary, and I do not share the tenor. But the use of the word does tell us what Dr Thapar thinks of the Vedic culture, a culture which she is so infirmly equipped to approach.

64. p. 172.

The only thing "inexplicable" about this "variant" is how Dr Thapar found it since the *Matsya Purāṇa* uses the same word, *bhastrā* for the simile which *Mahābhārata* does, in fact the verse is essentially the same verse. But then may be it is not so inexplicable, the word *bhastrā* does mean "a bag or a sac" and also "a pair of bellows." What has clearly happened is that the translation that Dr Thapar has seen of *Mahābhārata* translates *bhastrā* as "a bag or a sac" and the translation that Dr Thapar has seen of *Matsya Purāṇa* translates *bhastrā* as "a pair of bellows." This is the variation on the theme Dr Thapar is talking about. The same verse appears in the story of Śakuntalā as given in the *Śrīmad Bhāgavata Purāṇa* of which we have a translation supplied by Dr Thapar herself, and she translates *bhastrā* as "pouch." Another variant?

The metaphor isomorphing the mother to the *bhastrā* is very important in the analysis by Dr Thapar; she in fact bases the differential from the epic of the play on the differential between the two metaphors, that of the *bhastrā* in the epic and that of the "earth" in the play. It should be relevant therefore to see what the verse actually says.

The line in question is:

bhastrā mātā, pituḥ putro, yena jātaḥ sa eva saḥ[65]

The mother is bellows, the son is from the father, he is he by whom he is born.

The word *bhastrā* has been translated by J.A.B. van Buitenen as "water-sack," his translation is: "The mother is the father's water sack — he is the father who begets the son." Dr Thapar bases her analysis on the basis of this translation. Just how did this particular translator arrive at this particular word, "water sack?" Exactly in the same way that he arrived at the

65. *Mahābhārata*, I/1/74/110.

particular orthography "Duḥṣanta" for the husband of Śakuntalā, by going to the "Vedic" usage. How does one know that the "Vedic" meaning of the word *bhastrā* is "water-sack?" Well, the word occurs twice in *Śatapatha Brāhmaṇa*, its occurrence in 1/1/2/7 has been translated by J. Eggeling as "leathern bag," its occurrence in 1/6/3/16 has been translated by J. Eggeling as "skin bag." Thus have the scholars concluded that *bhastrā* means "bag," and well, don't we carry a water bottle or a purse with us?

The verse needs careful attention. I have supplied my translation, the supportive reasoning follows.

Science is not an activity which is decontextualized from culture. In spite of the hyped dissociation of Western sciences from the Church, certain paradigms are still theological in character. The Indian medical sciences relate themselves explicitly to the theories and opinions which are not "secular." Thus they have to answer certain questions which are not relevant to the modern medical sciences. In particular, they need to discuss the following: (i) how is it, if it is accepted that the *jīva* (the atomic unit of life) is the same in all its rebirths, and can be born as a human, an animal or a plant, if it is accepted that as long as the *karma*s are not completely erased there is a Life distributed into lives punctuated by deaths, that the *jīva* is born as a human or as an animal?, (ii) if the Vedic theory is accepted and the entire dynamics of the Cosmos, whether macro or micro, is *yajña* (= sacrifice, for want of a better word and in deference to the long-established practice in translation), that we can think of reproduction as sacrifice? The solution is a metaphor; the female input is *agni* (= "fire"), the male input is *soma* (= a "plant-juice"), and the sexual union is the *agnisoma* sacrifice, whose gods are Agni and Soma.[66] The metaphor simultaneously answers the other question: just as the melted ore forms into the shape of the mould into which it is poured, so is the *jīva* formed according to the *yoni* (= female reproductive organs) into which it is placed.[67] Now it is well known that fire is blasted using bellows, which in its shape can be said to resemble the female reproductive organs as popularly summarized into the word "womb"; indeed, etymologically, the two words, "bellows" and "belly" (= womb) even in English come from the Old English "belig/belg" which means "bag." The "bag" that the mother is therefore, serves as a "fire-blaster," it is thus bellows, and the female input, the fire, melts the essential existence (= *sattva*) of the *jīva* into the "bag," the mould that the mother is. For a fully detailed discussion of all this, including a complete synthesis into the Vedic remarks on the topic, the *Caraka-Saṁhitā*, with the commentary *jalpa-kalpa-taru* by Gaṅgādhara is an excellent source.

Thus we can reasonably argue as follows: The word *bhastrā* in this verse stands for the female genitalia interpreted as the "bellows" which blasts the "fire" that is the femininity in both the sexual and the reproductive functionalities, and melts the male input into a life form which matches her own; the process is after the *agnīṣoma* sacrifice.

This reasoning is supported by the fact that in the *Aṣṭādhyāyī* (7/3/47) of Pāṇini, we have a word *a-bhastrā* (as a derivative example). This is to mean "a woman without the bellows," which admits of no explanation other than "a woman whose reproductive organs are dysfunctional." The word itself, together with its two connotations, survives in contemporary

66. *Suśruta-Saṁhitā*, Śārīrasthāna, 3/3, 4.

67. *Aṣṭāṅgahṛdaya*, Śārīrasthāna, 1/4.

Bhojapuri, an associate language of Hindi, in which *bhāthī* means "bellows, the re-blasting leathern machine," and *bhathiyāna* means "the female genitalia."

But the real problem is that Dr Thapar mixes two contexts and in the process does not hesitate in doctoring what the text of the play says. The *bhastrā/kṣetra* dichotomy is actually a dichotomy in law and it is discussed in the context of the legitimacy of a son. With semen banks and surrogate wombs, the dichotomy is also under debate in our times. Specifically, Kauṭilya[68] discusses two opinions about the legal paternity of a child who is born to a mother who is not wedded to the father. According to the theory "The mother is *bhastrā,*" the child belongs to the one who has contributed the semen. The other theory "The mother is *kṣetra,*" says that the child belongs to the one who is legally wedded to the mother. Kauṭilya says that the child belongs to both and therefore should inherit from both.

An example is provided by the case of Bharadvāja. Instead of simply mentioning him as the "adopted son" of Bharata, Dr Thapar should have read the chapter she has translated from *Śrīmad Bhāgavata Purāṇa* to the end; this would have given her the opportunity to examine the *bhastrā/kṣetra* dichotomy in some detail. To narrate the story briefly, Mamatā was the wife of Utathya and was pregnant with his child when Bṛhaspati, the younger brother of Utathya, impregnated her with his semen. The child in the womb expelled this new drop forcibly from the womb and was cursed by Bṛhaspati for this. As a consequence, he was born blind. This is Dīrghatamas, who "anointed Bharata" to use words from Dr Thapar. The reading by Dr Thapar we shall discuss later though the

---

68. *Arthaśāstra*, 3/7.

connection here is missed by her. The expelled drop was a child who was a subject of hot dispute between the mother and the father regarding support. The mother argued for the theory "The mother is *bhastrā,*" and wanted the father to support and raise the child; the father opted for the theory "The mother is *kṣetra*" and wanted Mamatā (by extension Utathya also) to take the responsibility. "A disembodied voice" here intervenes to ask them both to support and raise the child; the name "Bharadvāja," literally, "support this born of two," refers to this instruction. The end result is curious: they both abandoned the child who was then raised by the Marut-gods. This is the "adopted son," called "meaningless" (= *vitatha*) for more than one reason, who succeeds Bharata.

The other example, also related to the "Puru lineage," which Dr Thapar insinuates was "invented for those who had power, wealth to bestow on the creators of genealogies, and the ability to protect their clansmen," relates to the "androgynous Iḍā," who does not merit more than this adjective from Dr Thapar. Tārā was the wife of Bṛhaspati and Soma (= Moon) impregnated her, the son was, according to the theory "The mother is *bhastrā,*" accepted by the Moon as his son and this is the origin of "the lunar dynasty" to which Bharata belongs. This son was called Budha and with him as father and Iḍā as mother, Purūravās was born from whom the "dynasty" starts with the *apsaras* Urvaśī as the mother.

Dr Thapar makes no attempt to examine why the heftily paid creators of genealogies chose to create genealogies which have such ancestors and why those who had power, wealth to bestow on the creators of genealogies, and the ability to protect their clansmen accepted such genealogies. She looks at these data with the same amused contempt that the post-Christ West looked at the stories of gods from Homer and

Hesiod when it appropriated the pagan Greece in search of a heritage, with the same feeling of "Thank God we have progressed beyond all this numbo-jumbo," and for the same reasons, summarized in "Thank God" or its clone "Thank Marx." Is it believable, if the *Mahābhārata* is written by creators of genealogies in search of monetary rewards, that the famous ancestor, Purūravās, would be presented as one, who out of greed and arrogance, robbed brāhmaṇas and was consequently destroyed by a curse?[69] We shall come to this later in this article; we must now look at what Vyāsa and Kālidāsa have to say. The question in the epic is that of the custody of the child, of inheritance and support, and of legitimacy in terms the acknowledgement by the father. Ultimately, the "The mother is *bhastrā*" theory prevails and Bharata is accepted to be the son of Duṣyanta as Bhāradvāja is accepted in the literature as the son of Bṛhaspati. Vyāsa must be grateful to Dr Thapar that this meets with her approval and empowerment of women is being channelled through giving the custody of the child to the father. There are others though, who would argue exactly in the opposite direction. I prefer not to intervene.

Kālidāsa changes this. Bharata is etymologically explained in *Mahābhārata* as being named so because of this question of his support, specifically, because Duṣyanta is to support him, (*bhṛ* = "to support") and Kālidāsa explains, using the same root, that the child is to be later called Bharata because he will support the people as a king. The question of the custody of the child is not important now because if Duṣyanta was refusing to acknowledge, it was because of the curse.

---

69. *Mahābhārata*, 1/1/75, verses 20-22. I have little doubt, however, that with the convolutive reasoning process used by modern scholarship, this will be interpreted as an input by the genealogists to warn their benefactors against interfering with the wealth of brāhmaṇas.

It is important to note that though Dr Thapar incorrectly says that Duṣyanta has replaced the *bhastrā* by the *kṣetra*, he has not. He says, to quote precisely:

> Although I planted myself into my lawfully wedded wife, I abandoned her, the seat of my family, exactly as a man hoping for a rich yield, plants a piece of earth which holds all wealth, and then abandons it at the exact time it is ready to yield the crop.[70]

There is no *kṣetra* here, he is not talking about abandoning or accepting the son, only the wife who is compared to *vasundharā*, the name for earth when one refers to its capacity to yield riches. The *kṣetra*, in the context of a son, always refers to a woman who is another man's wife (unless preceded by *sva* = "own") which is why the son out of such a woman is called *kṣetriya*, the one who is born out of the field, in contrast to the *aurasa*, the one who is made of breast. This in fact is the way it has been used by Duṣyanta when he starts rejecting Śakuntalā in the court. To quote exactly, he says:

> Ascetics, Even after deep searching my memory, I do not recall accepting (into my bed) this lady. So how can I accept her, seeing that she is obviously pregnant and thus accepting her would turn me into an owner of the *kṣetra* (which is cultivated by somebody else with my approval).[71]

The word, *aurasa*, is the word Duṣyanta uses when he looks at Bharata (Act Seven) for the first time, when he now knows that he "accepted" Śakuntalā. Words are important, words by poets are more important, words by poets like Kālidāsa

---

70. *Abhijñāna-Śākuntalam*, Act Six, verse 24. Barbara Miller introduces overcorrectively "the holy ground" here because she thinks "lawful" not holy enough.

71. *Abhijñāna-Śākuntalam*, Act Six, between verses 19 and 20.

are most important. You have to approach them with reverence to understand the import. The major problem with scholars like Dr Thapar is that they are arrogant. They think a half-heartedly consulted beginner's dictionary compiled for use by missionaries will tell them what a poet like Vyāsa or Kālidāsa intends. They laugh at these poets because they have no respect for the work they are studying. They act as anthropologists from an external civilization, not students who are studying a literature which can tell them what their country is. And so we have:

> The name Dīrghatamas — literally, deep darkness — supports the legend that he was born blind, and in later life set adrift in a river which took him to the Aṅga country where he married outside the social pale. The son Kakṣīvanta was therefore a *dāsīputra brāhmaṇa*, by birth a *brāhmaṇa* of lower status, but an established category nevertheless. The association of Bharata with Dīrghatamas is somewhat unexpected, since it hints that the hero was befriended by a priest who may have access to non-orthodox rituals and shamanistic practices. If such practices were a recognized alternative ritual, then the hero would be drawing on more than one culture.[72]

Dr Thapar seems to be a little behind the times, the last in-word among the Indian Historians was "sub-altern," not "alternative." But the perspective is constant and has been best articulated by Eggeling who described (the *Brāhmaṇa* textual material of the) Vedic literature in the following manner:

> For wearisome prolixity of exposition, characterized by dogmatic assertion and a flimsy symbolism rather than by serious reasoning, these works are perhaps not equalled anywhere; unless indeed, it be by the speculative vapourings

72. p. 11.

> of the Gnostics, than which, in the opinion of the learned translators of Irenaeus, "nothing more absurd has probably ever been imagined by rational beings."[73]

So we have everything needed by the historians thrown in, non-orthodox rituals, shamanistic practices, and pluri-fragmented, not pluriform, culture. We will have to come to this again.

Another retelling Dr Thapar discusses is in *Padma Purāṇa*. As seems to be the habit with her, she does not consult the source she cites. Thus we find:

> Closer to the Kālidāsa version is the story in the *Padma Purāṇa* which has been quoted in the controversy regarding the date of both texts. A longer narrative is given in the later *Bhāgavata Purāṇa*.[74]

The narrative in the *Padma Purāṇa* is as a matter of fact considerably longer, running into more than 340 verses, compared to the narrative consisting of 25 verses in the *Bhāgavata Purāṇa*.

And Dr Thapar wrongly cites it into the Uttara Khaṇḍa of *Padma Purāṇa* (in her endnote 76), it is in fact in the Svarga Khaṇḍa, and that too, only in the Bengal recension.[75] A brief look at the narrative in the *Padma Purāṇa* is needed. I will do so now.[76.]

---

73. Introduction to the translation of the *Śatapatha Brāhmaṇa* by Julius Eggeling, Part I.

74. p. 172.

75. Thus for instance in the Svarga Khaṇḍa of the *Padma Purāṇa* reprinted under a scheme of the Govt. of India in 1986, the story of Śakuntalā is absent.

76. I am following the text as published in The Svarga Khaṇḍa of the *Padma Purāṇa*, edited by Prof. (Dr) Asoke Chatterjee Sastri, All India Kashiraj Trust, 1972.

Since the days Viharilal Sarkar brought to the attention of the scholars that there were similarities between the story of Śakuntalā as given in the Svarga Khaṇḍa of the *Padma Purāṇa* and *Abhijñāna-Śākuntalam* by Kālidāsa, the Purāṇic account has been tied down to the "date of Kālidasā" and little else. The limitations of this "historical" approach to literature are obvious; thus a scholar like the late M.R. Kale, in a single piece of writing, observes "The author appears to paraphrase sometimes even the wording of Kālidāsa," and then again "Lastly it is significant that the story of Śakuntalā in *Padma Purāṇa* shows no familiarity with the language of Kālidāsa.[77]

However, the interesting part of the overlap is some variation from the Kālidāsa version. The first is something which should have satisfied Dr Thapar, if she had cared to read the Purāṇic account: Priyaṁvadā does go to the court with Śakuntalā, although she is not able to convince Duṣyanta, indeed her speech is confined to informing Śakuntalā in a whisper at the exact moment that the ring is asked for by Śakuntalā, that she (Priyaṁvadā) lost the ring. Priyaṁvadā then fades from the scene and is not mentioned. Kālidāsa has introduced an additional friend, Anasūyā, and explicitly not included the two friends in the train that goes to the court of Duṣyanta with Śakuntalā. The Purāṇic account places the departure of Śakuntalā in an advanced stage of her pregnancy (seventh month), this is somewhat curious because travel in such a condition is prohibited in conventional households even now. In the Purāṇic account, Śakuntalā asks for the ring as a part of the covenant which is otherwise the same as that in the *Mahābhārata*. The second major variation is in the role of the *purohita* of Duṣyanta. In the Purāṇic account, the *purohita*

77. *The Abhijñāna-Śākuntalam,* edited by Prof. M.R. Kale, 1977, reprinted by Motilal Banarsidass, p. 48, p. 62."

intervenes on his own, apparently tired of the invectives hurled at Śakuntalā by the king who repeatedly calls her a slut, and suggests that Śakuntalā should live in company with the women of the royal family, till the child is born. The king refuses, fearing that the company of Śakuntalā would tempt the women of the royal family to be unfaithful. The *purohita* then says that he will accommodate Śakuntalā in his own family since he is sure that Śakuntalā is not a woman of bad morals. Other than these elements, the narrative in the *Mahābhārata* has been more or less completely incorporated by the *Padma Purāṇa*, several verses being included verbatim.

It is quite clear what Kālidāsa has done from these variations in his version from the *Mahābhārata* and the *Padma Purāṇa*. His art is understatement; where a word, or the absence of a word, is eloquent enough, he will not use sentences. Situational changes hone up what was intended in a telling manner. Thus, Priyaṁvadā is unambiguously placed as a person in her own right, and not an appendage to Śakuntalā, by a simple statement of Kaṇva that the two friends of Śakuntalā are to be given away in marriage. The variants in the statement of the *purohita* are equally significant. The *purohita* in the *Padma Purāṇa* is more aggressive on the surface, but less contextualizing. The suggestion of the placement in the royal quarters was certainly not a good one, this being a well-known method of procurement for a king.[78] The offer of a shelter for a woman who has no shelter is a complex offer. The *purohita* in the *Abhijñāna-Śākuntalam* has come up with a solution which has a Vedic background. In the *Rājasūya* sacrifice, the king expels from his kingdom, as a ritual, a woman who is not supported by her husband or son. This is an impossible punishment, seeing that by definition of the *Rājasūya*, the

78. *Kāmasūtra*, 5/5.

kingdom of the king extends to the entire earth. The woman is then asked to live in the house of a brāhmaṇa,[79] because the reign of the king does not extend to a brāhmaṇa's house.

No society in recorded history can claim to have treated women with fairness, but the Vedic ideals were the nearest to meeting the requirements of feminist activism without a confrontationist character. Kālidāsa, to the extent that a poet does any social modelling at all, is a poet for those ideals. He avoids therefore, a lover who does not love or a husband who is more a king than a husband, by introducing the curse. Therefore, Duṣyanta is placed in a Hamlet situation, to accept or not to accept. As he says,[80] the choice before him is between being an abandoner of a lawfully wedded wife (a serious crime in ancient Indian law and a religious misdeed), or be defiled by admitting the wife of another man as his own (a serious misconduct for a conscientious king). At every possible occasion, Kālidāsa emphasizes the central and pivotal role of a wife in the family, his favourite simile[81] is that the wife is "the trust in the Vedic *dharma*" (*śraddhā*) and the husband is "the executive authority" (*vidhi*); the two are the constituent units of a Vedic sacrifice. It is only in accordance with these ideals that he refers to Bharata by his matronymic, a practice which was the rule rather than the exception in the Vedic literature and was never entirely discarded in the traditional culture. Even here the sense of balance is heeded to, when Kaṇva speaks to Śakuntalā (Act Four), the son is "the son of Duṣyanta," when Mārīca speaks to Duṣyanta (Act Seven), the son is "the son of Śakuntalā."

---

79. *Kātyāyana-Śrautasūtra*, 15/3/21, with the *saralā* commentary by Vidyādhara Śarmā, Acyuta Granthamālā, Kāśī, 1930.

80. *Abhijñāna-Śākuntalam*, Act Five, verse 29.

81. *Abhijñāna-Śākuntalam*, Act Seven, verse 29; *Raghuvaṁśam*, 2/16.

A significant reference is the passing mention in the *Padma Purāṇa*, not in the Svarga Khaṇḍa which is frequently referred to in the introductions to the various editions of *Abhijñānā-Śākuntalam*, the play by Kālidāsa but in the Pātāla Khaṇḍa. Since to my knowledge, this passage has not been discussed by any modern scholar, nor is a citation to be found, I will quote the passage in full (in translation).

Kuśa and Lava say to Sītā after they have defeated the army of Rāma and brought his horse intended for his *Aśvamedha*:

> We have defeated that king (Rāma) and his forces fighting according to the code of the kṣatriyas. We did not have anything else in mind, all we thought was that one should fight as the code of the kṣatriyas dictates. The sage Vālmīki has narrated to us while we were studying, that in earlier times, Bharata had fought against Duṣyanta capturing the latter's horse meant for the sacrifice when it came near the *āśrama* of Kaṇva. Therefore, even a son should fight against his father, a younger brother against his elder brother, a student against his teacher. There is no sin in that. Now that you order us to return this noble horse, we shall do so.[82]

We have thus the story of Śakuntalā placed in a standard framework in Indian story-telling: A man insults his wife, the son avenges by defeating the father and then the wife pardons the husband. The frame is popular with the Sanskrit writers. The most important and the most well-known story is that of the *Rāmāyaṇa*,[83] but there are others. A major story is that of Arjuna and his son Babhruvāhana[84] where Arjuna is defeated

---

82. Chapter 64, verses 71-74.

83. According to Vālmīki, his work, the *Rāmāyaṇa*, is "the story of Sītā" (Bālakāṇḍa, chapter 4, verse 7).

84. *Jaiminīyāśvamedha-parva.*

and killed, later to be brought to life by his wife (actually two of his wives, but this is no place to record the story in full). The occasion is that of the *Aśvamedha*, when the father is at the maximum of his authority and wants a public attestation of his invulnerability. So while Rāma has some other things by which he is remembered, Vālmīki[85] has framed the story in the context of the killing of the male *krauñca* bird. As Govindarāja (on Bāla Kaṇḍa, chapter 4, verse 7) explains in his celebrated commentary *Bhūṣaṇa*, "The name of the epic is *Paulastyavadha* = "The killing of Rāvaṇa." This killing of Rāvaṇa however, is only an artifice employed to tell the actual story in which the major component is the story of Sītā, the story of Rāma being a minor component. The work is called *Rāmāyaṇa* because one can reach Rāma by reading it (and not because it is the story of Rāma)." Duṣyanta has only his neglect of Śakuntalā to be remembered by.

This particular mention in the *Padma Purāṇa* is however, not found in the text under discussion, namely *Abhijñāna-Śākuntalam* and the particular case of Kālidāsa has to be discussed by what he has written, so we must turn to the work of this poet. Since he has also written *Raghuvaṁśam*, an epic in which the story of Sītā appears, we may examine his account with some relevance.

The Śakuntalā of *Abhijñāna-Śākuntalam* reminds one of the Sītā of *Raghuvaṁśam* in the way she receives the news of the banishment. All she says is: Lakṣmaṇa, please tell that king on my behalf the following, "You abandoned me, who was

85. It is a settled matter, however, which one is the more important indicator in the mind of the Sanskrit narrator. There is nothing special in the *Rāmāvatāra* about removing a scourge, this is common to all the *avatāras* of Viṣṇu. The one distinguishing feature of the *Rāmāvatāra* is the injustice to Sītā, something which is clear to any classical reader of the *Rāmāyaṇa*.

purified by fire before your very eyes, simply because the people spread canards about me. Is that in accordance with the norms of your well-known family?," and in the very next verse, she says "Or, maybe, I should not suspect an arbitrary exercise of the will in you to whom no thoughts except the good ones come. This intolerable experience is doubtless a culmination of the evil deeds I did in my other births."[86] The statements of Śakuntalā in the court of Duṣyanta and later in the *āśrama* of Mārīca can be taken as expansions of these statements. A few verses later, we have Vālmīki saying:[87] "Although Rāma has wiped out the scourge of the entire cosmos (= Rāvaṇa), although he is true to his word, and although he does not boast idly, still, when he has behaved in this wrong manner towards you, I have nothing but anger for him" This we can take to be expanded in the *Abhijñāna-Śākuntalam* in the statements of Śārṅgarava (and the silent agreement of everybody else). Even the unsuccessful appeal to be received by the mother earth and the doctrine of the impossibility of a daughter who has sullied the reputation of her parents are common.[88] It is clear that the parallel exists between the two in the mind of the poet; when one episode is analysed, so is the other.

We need to discuss the curse which is common to both the cases. Since the story of the curse in the case of Rāma is not reported by the modern scholars, I will have to do so. It is given in the *Rāmāyaṇa* itself,[89] just after Rāma decides to send Sītā to exile. To summarize, Viṣṇu had killed the wife of Bhṛgu, and Bhṛgu cursed him to the effect that he will have to suffer

86. *Raghuvaṁśam*, 14/61, 62.

87. *Raghuvaṁśam*, 14/73.

88. *Raghuvaṁśam*, 14/54, 55.

89. Uttar Kāṇḍa, Chapter 51.

the separation from wife and be born on earth to experience this. There is little doubt that Kālidāsa has got the idea of introducing the curse of Durvāsas from this.

The next question is: Who in fact has been cursed? It will be easily seen, the moment one reads the play carefully, that the curse is on Duṣyanta. It is he who gets the amnesia and commits an act for which only his name is etymologically remembered. This in fact is said in so many words by Mārīca near the end of the play.[90] One may well ask: What is his crime? It is the well-known fault of many great persons: Pride. It is he who was proud of his memory, promising to Śakuntalā that before she can finish counting the letters of his name on the signet ring at the rate of one letter a day, his messenger will reach her to take her to him. These are big words, and big words, as the last chorus in the *Antigone* reminds us, are always punished. These are not in fact words of a lover, these are words of a king. This is *hamartia*, and instead of being the "romantic comedy" that *Abhijñāna-Śākuntalam* is made out to be, it is a tragedy comparable to thefinest that there is in the world literature.

V

But let us discuss the "empowerment" question. It will be necessary to correct a misreporting. Dr Thapar says:

> In his rejection of her, "Duṣyanta" is uncomplimentary about women whom he describes as designing, shrewd and with an untaught cunning such as that of the cuckoo laying her egg in another's nest. This contrasts with the epic

90. Act Seven, verse 32. Mārīca says to Śakuntalā: Because of the curse, your husband's memory was blocked and having become devoid of love, he had rejected to you. Now that the darkness has been lifted from him, yours is the word which will hold sway over him.

> version, where Duḥṣanta is abusive towards Śakuntalā and her parentage, but not about women in general. In the play there is scant mention of her illegitimacy or the charge of immorality against her parents.[91]

In fact the very first words "Duḥṣanta" says in the epic when he starts abusing Śakuntalā are, "all women are liars, who will trust you?" But we know by now that Dr Thapar is least bothered about a suppression or two when it helps her "scholarly" investigations. That is the way she thinks history should be written. This quotation reveals something else.

Dr Thapar has, in a candid moment, confessed that "the Kālidāsa play had to be read for a Sanskrit exam, an activity which destroys sensitivity to poetry."[92] The damage seems to be permanent, because in the epic, "Duḥṣanta" is not abusive towards the parents of Śakuntalā. In fact, what he is saying is exactly the opposite. He is saying,

> (What you have just said to me amounts to saying that) your mother Menakā is a cruel slut who abandoned you and your father Viśvāmitra, who was aspiring for attaining the position of a brāhmaṇa was actually overpowered by lust ! (But I know that both the things are impossible because) Menakā is one of the highest *apsaras*, and Viśvāmitra is one of the highest *maharṣis*. They surely are incapable of such deeds as you blame on them. Therefore you are lying. How could you be the daughter of (such illustrious) parents as these (when) you speak like a trollop! That great *maharṣi* and that great *apsaras* and (their daughter) a pitiable *tāpasī* (= poor woman) like you! (impossible). . .

Of course, the words in the parentheses have to be inserted by the reader mentally. This is a dramatic delivery and

91. p. 73
92. p. ix

Duṣyanta is faking incredulity. Even the translation which Dr Thapar has included in her book and which presumably she has read even if she is not familiar with the original, should tell her that she is wrong. I quote that part in full:

> Duḥṣanta said:
>
> I do not know that this is my son you have born, Śakuntalā. Women are liars — who will trust your word? Menakā, your mother, was a merciless slut who cast you off like a faded garland on a peak of the Himalayas! Viśvāmitra, your merciless father, who, born a baron, reached for brahminhood, was a lecher! Menakā is the first of the *apsaras*es, Viśvāmitra the first of the seers — how can you call yourself their daughter, speaking like a whore? Are you not ashamed to say such incredible things, especially in my presence? off with you, evil ascetic! An ever awesome seer, an *apsaras* like Menakā — are related to you, a wretch that wears a hermit's garb! Your son is too big, and he is strong even while still a child, how can he have shot up like a *śāla* tree in such a short time? Your own birth is very humble, and you look like a slut to me. So Menakā happened to give birth to you from sheer lust? Everything you say is obscure to me, ascetic. I do not know you. Go where you want![93]

It should be clear that "Duḥṣanta" is trying to show that he is sceptical about Śakuntalā's claim of being born of the parents that she mentions and no adverse comments are made on Menakā or Viśvāmitra. In the epic, to use Dr Thapar's own words, "there is scant mention of her illegitimacy or the charge of immorality against her parents."

In fact, neither illegitimacy nor the charge of immorality are relevant here if Duṣyanta admits that he believes Śakuntalā is born as she claims she was. He is trying to show that he does not think Śakuntalā is speaking the truth. The only harsh

93. pp. 31-32.

comment against Menakā was made by Śakuntalā herself, in the presentation which precedes Duṣyanta's remarks; explicitly, she says "she abandoned me as the children born out of wedlock are abandoned by unfaithful women."[94] Duṣyanta is using these words in his reply as a righteous defender of Menakā.

So much for the reading of the epic. Let us see how the play is being read. In the play, it is quite true that the parents are not mentioned explicitly. But in a way, the barb here is much more cruel. First, a clarification. The cuckoo in the folk wisdom, does not "lay her eggs in another's nest," she puts them in the nest of another bird, namely, the crow. The play explicitly mentions this. Duṣyanta is saying:

> Not to speak of women who are equipped with reasoning power (this power is supposed to be exclusively a human faculty, other life forms getting knowledge from intuition or other devices), even the females not descended from Manu (=belonging to species other than human) are clever without any training. Look at the cuckoo, before they fly up in the sky, they leave their offsprings to be cared for by other birds.

This is as literal as I could make it. But the verse leads to many directions because of the words used. First, there is an obvious second meaning: Menakā is an *apsaras*, and therefore a woman who did not descend from Manu, Śakuntalā was raised by birds (*Śakunta* means "bird"), so the verse refers to the desertion of Śakuntalā by Menakā. The word that has been used for "bird" in the verse is *dvija* which means also brāhmaṇa, so the fact that Śakuntalā was raised by Kaṇva is also hinted at. Next, the word used for cuckoo is *parabhṛta* (= supported

94. In the Chicago translation included in the book by Dr Thapar, this has been translated as "abandoned me pitilessly and went, as if I were another's child."

by others), precisely because of the supposed raising of the cuckoo by the crow but because the root *bhṛ* (= to support) used here has *bhartā* (= supporter) as a derivative and because *bhartā* means "husband," the offspring becomes "begat by another" which refers to the temporary character of the alliance of Śakuntalā's parents. Finally, as noticed by the commentator Sriniwas, essentially the same applies to Bharata; he is also raised by other brāhmaṇas, namely Mārīca, and before Duṣyanta went to the sky (to help Indra) he in fact got his child supported by Mārīca.

VI

Dr Thapar is somewhat contemptuous about *kanyādāna*, the gifting of the daughter, clearly because this is seen by modern scholarship at par with the gifting of a domestic animal. It will be necessary to make some comments on the concept of a Vedic marriage.

It is quite true that it was regarded as a responsibility of parents to get their children married. But it was not only in the case of a daughter. In the play under consideration, when Śakuntalā wants to know when she will return to the hermitage of Kaṇva, she is told that she will come back after she has got the "son of Duṣyanta" married.[95] The reference is to the practice of handing over the responsibility of the house to the son and daughter-in-law and moving into the next logical space of *vānaprastha*. This may not be compatible with the "freedom to

95. *Abhijñāna-Śākuntalam*, Act Four, verse 20. Barbara Miller has not translated correctly here, because she does not know the meaning of the word *niveśya*. So she has translated ". . . raised Duṣyanta's son. . . ." The word *niveśya* however means precisely "after completing the marriage rites (of a ward)," and has been used by Kālidāsa (*Raghuvaṁśam*, 11/57) when Daśaratha is returning from Mithilā after the marriage of his four sons has been completed.

decide about one's own life" but the so-called "arranged marriage" has been the norm in India and there is nothing in it which discriminates between a daughter and a son.

The next question is about the mode and model. One basic issue is that of what modern scholars call "the bride-price."[96] There has to be a "bride-price" since the groom's family is getting the means of continuing the family line and nothing in this world is free. Kauṭilya,[97] who has to discuss the legislative aspects of the situation in terms of the involvement of the State, says that in the first four categories which are in the category of the *dharma-vivāha*, it is the father who is entitled to the "bride-price."

But it was regarded as fragile, not because it was illegal or immoral but because it was not sanctified before fire. The entry of Kaṇva in the play is programmed to emphasize this aspect. First, he blesses Śakuntalā by saying that she should be to her husband as what Śarmiṣṭhā was to Yayāti, a verse which Dr Thapar discusses[98] but which as usual, she does not understand. The comparison with Śarmiṣṭhā is apt because Śarmiṣṭhā was visited by Yayāti in secret, and the legally wedded wife, Devayānī comes to know of these visits by her husband to her maid Śarmiṣṭhā only after the three sons to Śarmiṣṭhā are already born. Now both Devayānī and Śarmiṣṭhā have been married to Yayāti under the *gāndharva* sub-category of marriage with one basic difference, Devayānī's choice was later approved by her father Śukrācārya and consecrated so that in spite of the fact that the legality and

96. The so-called "dowry" is an aberration, the only gifts enjoined from the parents of the daughter are to the daughter and form part of *strīdhana*.

97. *Arthaśāstra*, 3/2, 4/12.

98. p. 73.

morality of the *gāndharva* in the case of Devayānī are more problematic than that of the *gāndharva* in the case of Śarmiṣṭhā (Devayānī was a brāhmaṇa by birth whereas Śarmiṣṭhā was the daughter of the *asura* king Vṛṣaparvan who was thus a kṣatriya in this context),[99] we find that it is Devayānī who is the lawfully wedded wife. The next step that Kaṇva takes is to remedy the situation somewhat by making Śakuntalā walk around the fire.[100] Only then, and not before, does he call his students to take their "sister" to her husband's house. Now that the marriage has been witnessed by Fire, no matter how anachronistically, Śakuntalā is the *dharmapatnī* of Duṣyanta. We may note here, that many modern scholars think that Kaṇva makes Śakuntalā walk around the fire because it was considered auspicious to do so before the start of a journey and they quote in support a passage from *Raghuvaṁśam* (2/ 71). But the Indian understanding is what I have reported, the example explicitly appearing in some rule-books on ritual.[101]

In all this there is no suggestion that Śakuntalā has done anything wrong. The message that is delivered on behalf of Kaṇva in the court to Duṣyanta uses the root-word *upayam* (= to appropriate) for "marriage" which emphasizes the enticement, seizure and the sexual consummation, king's acts of doubtful morality which are all forgiven in the message; a bit later however, the moment the king wants to know what exactly is required of him, the "marriage" starts being

99. *Mahābhārata* and the only argument that Śarmiṣṭhā can put forward to persuade an unwilling Yayāti to treat her as a wife is that the husband of a girl's girl-friend (= *sakhī*) is also husband for the girl.

100. Act Four.

101. *Vidhāna-Pārijāta*, Asiatic Society of Bengal, reprinted 1992 by Krishnadas Academy, Vārāṇasī, Part I, p. 691.

discussed in derivatives of the root-word *pariṇī* (= to walk around the fire in the marriage rites).[102] Earlier, Gautamī has said that all she has to say is that there is nothing for her to say because in this matter neither Śakuntalā nor Duṣyanta consulted the kinsmen.

The reason Sakuntalā's people are upset is not that they "resented a woman transgressing patriarchy and choosing her own husband." They are worried because they fear that she has trusted Duṣyanta who was under no obligation to acknowledge her as a lawfully wedded wife. All forms of marriage, including the *gāndharva* had to be sanctified later by proper rites which involved the consent of the families of the bride as well as the groom and a proper witnessing by fire if this had not been done earlier. Śakuntalā's case is even weaker than that of Śarmiṣṭhā because there is some substance in the argument of Śarmiṣṭhā that she was a wife to Yayāti because she had come as a companion-slave to Devayānī and Devayānī was a wife to Yayāti. We may recall that the reluctance of Yayāti is only because of an explicit injunction from Śukrācārya that he should not take Śarmiṣṭhā to bed and this reluctance is over once Śarmiṣṭhā points out that it was the king's right and duty to take a maid of his queen to bed if the maid was demanding it.[103]

Dr Thapar is incidentally missing a significant pointer when she remarks: "it is quite likely that had Priyaṁvadā accompanied Śakuntalā to the court, it is quite likely that she would have convinced Duṣyanta of the legitimacy of the marriage." In the first place it is not due to the lack of proper legal representation or pleading that Duṣyanta is not

102. Since Barbara Miller fails to translate correctly, I supply the correct translation of the relevant passage here.

103. *Mahābhārata* = Ādi Parva.

convinced, it is because he does not remember. But more significantly, Śakuntalā does want to know whether her friends are not accompanying her to the court and Kaṇva says "No" with the reason,[104] "these two are also to be given in marriage," implying that the import of sending them with Śakuntalā will be to send them as "companions" which entitles the king to treat them amorously, a subtlety which obviously Śakuntalā does not understand. The noted Hindi poet, Jayashankara Prasada makes the same mistake when he wants, in his poem *Vanamilana*,[105] which is a post-script to improve on Kālidāsa by sending the two friends to the court.

VII

The compulsions of the Rāma of *Rāmāyaṇa* and the Duṣyanta of *Mahābhārata* are quite obvious; both are kings in a hereditary system of monarchy in which the right to succession depends on public acceptance. The heir to the throne has to be recognized as a genuine claimant. Even in a cardboard monarchy like that of UK in our day, the question whether a princess whose child would one day ascend the throne had a right to act as her heart dictates could not be settled to the satisfaction of anybody with a stake. In ancient India, the definition of a son was fairly inclusive; with proper sacramental authority, the father could be somebody other than the king. But it was not arbitrary and it was certainly not within the right of the king to pass on the kingdom to anybody he liked. In particular, it was not open to him to accept as wife a woman whose faithfulness to him was, no matter how unjustly and no matter how remotely, in question or likely to

104. Act Four.

105. *Prasāda Granthāvalī*, vol. 1, Lokabhāratī Prakāśana, Allahabad, 1985, pp. 17-22.

be in question in the minds of a section of the people, no matter how insignificant that section was. Nowhere in the *Rāmāyaṇa* has it been suggested that Rāma himself was in doubt, nowhere in the *Mahābhārata* has it been suggested that Duṣyanta himself was in doubt. Yet they act in the harshest possible way, till there is an incontrovertible *public* proof that the wife is speaking the truth. Such a proof was provided by the Sītā of *Rāmāyaṇa* by an extremal oath: "If my words are true, let the Mother Earth receive me." In the case of the Śakuntalā of *Mahābhārata*, the proof was provided by the Divine Voice.

In *Abhijñāna-Śākuntalam*, the question is not the same. Here, Duṣyanta is essentially on his own and has nothing to rely on except his sense of the right. As I have indicated above, there is little doubt in the mind of anybody that Śakuntalā is speaking the truth, the only question was why Duṣyanta is telling a lie. I will now proceed to discuss *Abhijñāna-Śākuntalam* independently of what Dr Thapar has written.

VIII

We should perhaps first concentrate on the name itself. *Abhijñāna-Śākuntalam* is made of two word-units, *Abhijñāna* (= Recognition) and *Śākuntala* (= of/by/from Śakuntalā). They can be grammatically constructed and combined in more than one way. Two of these combination possibilities I have already indicated. They are, (i) the recognition of Śakuntalā by Duṣyanta, which is the most popular understanding of the play, and (ii) the recognition of the son of Śakuntalā by Duṣyanta, which is not so popular an understanding of the play but is not exactly unknown and is amply supported by the contents. Let us briefly support this second reading. When Duṣyanta is accosted by the students of Kaṇva in the first Act, they bless him by saying, "May you beget a son who is a *cakravartī*,[106] that is one whose kingdom extends to the entire earth unchallenged." Now this may be thought of as a regular, exaggerated, encomiastic blessing extended to a patron[107] but the crucial role becomes clearer as we proceed. The identification of Śakuntalā rests on it, because as the *purohita* states, if she gives birth to a child who is having the marks of a *cakravartī* then it is she and not Duṣyanta who speaks the truth. Later, the theory is translated into practice because the pieces of evidence which conclusively build the identity of Bharata as the son of Duṣyanta include these marks. Thus there is a dimension to the play which suggests the centrality of the recognition of the son (and thereby the recognition of the mother).

I submit however, that there is a *third* dimension of the play and it is the recognition of Duṣyanta by Śakuntalā. There is almost a clear statement to this effect in the play. In Act Seven, when Duṣyanta is seen by Śakuntalā, she *fails to recognize him* for a moment; Duṣyanta then says that even his cruelty to her has yielded a lucky ending because he "now" (after this momentary failure) sees that Śakuntalā recognizes him. This contrasts with the behaviour of Duṣyanta when Śakuntalā was in his court; now that the tables are turned, Śakuntalā does not reciprocate in kind and behaves nobly. Naturally, Duṣyanta falls at the feet of Śakuntalā, an act which is permitted in poetry

---

106. Barbara Miller has totally misunderstood this word and translates it as somebody who "turns the wheel of the empire" because *cakra* does mean wheel. However, *cakra* means "kingdom" also and that is the relevant meaning here. A *cakravartī* is one who is in his kingdom (no matter where he is), that is, whose empire extends to all of this earth. It is a very distinguished term from political science and there is a complete list of the *cakravartī*s given in many Indian texts, usually ending with Yudhiṣṭhira.

107. I have little doubt that scholars like Dr Thapar think so.

only in the amorous mood, when the wife is angry with the husband for his showing partiality to another woman and the husband is requesting her to forgive and forget. This is not an occasion of that nature and by introducing this scene, Kālidāsa has brought in a situation of genuine regret on the part of Duṣyanta, elevating Śakuntalā to a status no other wife in Sanskrit literature has risen to. To understand this fully, we should contrast it with the scene in *Mahābhārata*; Duṣyanta is not at all apologetic there and "forgives" Śakuntalā for her harsh words to him! The difference between the Duṣyanta of the epic and the Duṣyanta of the play is of the same character as the difference between the Urvaśī of the *Ṛgveda* and the Urvaśī of the play *Vikramorvaśīyam* by Kālidāsa. The Urvaśī of the *Ṛgveda* is harsh and calculating, detailing the exact number of times she can be sexually touched by Purūravās (thrice a day), and stating clearly that the hearts of women are like those of the hyenas, never expect a soft corner in them for anybody. Kālidāsa has changed it to a situation when Urvaśī falls in love with Purūravās. The Urvaśī of the *Ṛgveda* conspires with her people, the *gāndharvas*, to frame the king into a situation when he is forced to break her word to her and thus she can leave him with all the blame on him, the Urvaśī of the play does not want to leave the king. There is a method in this of course, but that method is not gendered; if there are shortcomings in the Duṣyanta of the epic which have been now mended by the device of a curse, there are shortcomings in the Urvaśī of the *Ṛgveda* which have been now mended by the device of a curse.

One may still ask: what constitutes a "shortcoming"? What is wrong in a woman who negotiates and sets terms for her favours whose power she understands, is it not a better world for a woman if she knows the actual value of her services and is not willing to submit in exchange with a few words of flattery? As a matter of fact, a comparison between the epic and the play is not called for because the two are dealing with two different problematics.

We may start by noting that the *apsaras* is associated to water and is seen (in a group) as a bird (= *āti*), in the famous story of Purūravās and Urvaśī.[108]

The word *āti* has been interpreted by Sāyaṇa as "water-bird," which may or may not mean "swan" as is read by many. But they are usually in a group because the word *apsaras* standing for a single individual of the race, is a grammatical exception, the actual word is *apsarasaḥ*, always in the plural. One may therefore imagine a group of water-birds near a lake/river, a scene not unnoticed in nature, as *apsarasaḥ*. Next, we may note that the *apsaras* always "abandons" her child after birth. The two famous sons of Urvaśī, the *ṛṣi* Vasiṣṭha (from Mitra and Varuṇa) and the king Āyu (from Purūravās) as well as the two daughters of Menakā, Pramadvarā and Śakuntalā, are both abandoned in this manner. All are raised by *ṛṣis* who share a common name with birds: both are *dvija*. Dr Thapar notes, while speaking of the Śakuntalā of the epic, her being a "counterpoint to the notion of the *pativratā*," a phrase she repeats while speaking of the *apsaras*.[109] This is to be contrasted with her observation that "The play is a celebration of the romantic love where the woman, before she is acknowledged as wife, exercises the freedom to choose and to act. But romantic love has to be transmuted into the ideal of a *pativratā*."

---

108. As given in *Ṛgveda*, 10/95 and the *Śatapatha Brāhmaṇa*, 11/5/1.
109. pp. 39 and 41.

Appendix
The Mystery of the Little Princess

Vasu-Lakṣmī is the daughter of King Agnimitra, the hero of the play *Mālavikāg nimitram* by Kālidāsa. In a number of important entries, including the edition by M.R. Kale and the dictionary by Monier-Williams, she has been called a sister of Queen Dhāriṇī, thus making her a sister-in-law of Agnimitra. The confusion, I think, arises from the following: In the beginning of the First Act, when Bakulāvalikā is narrating how Mālavikā has been seen by the king although the queen tried to hide her from his amorous eyes, she mentions that while the king was looking at a group picture, he enquired, and to use the words from the translation by Edwin Gerow, Vasu-Lakṣmī piped up, saying "Papa, this is Mālavikā." The word for which Edwin Gerow has correctly used "Papa," is found in different editions in two textual variants, *Ajja* and *Āvutta*. These are Prakrit words, the first is rendered *Ārya* in Sanskrit and can be regarded as a general term of address when speaking to a senior person; the second of course means "sister's husband" (and is counted as a Sanskrit word). Now anybody who follows the *Āvutta* reading is bound to conclude that Vasu-Lakṣmī is a sister-in-law of Agnimitra.

This has led to certain curious situations. The Nirṇaya Sāgara edition follows the *Āvutta* reading in the text but disregards the fact that the commentary by Kāṭayavema, printed in the same edition, follows the reading *Ajja* because he renders it *Ārya* in Sanskrit. The BHU edition in the first version follows the reading *Ajja* without any indication that there is a variant reading but switches to the *Āvutta* reading in the second version and the editor for both the versions, Pandit Rewa Prasada Dvivedi, personally confirmed to me in a telephonic conversation that (i) he preferred the *Āvutta* reading, (ii) the revised reading is based on the Nirṇaya Sāgara edition; and (iii) Vasu-Lakṣmī is a sister-in-law of Agnimitra. The most confusing reading is that of a modern Sanskrit commentary (published by Śrī-Nivāsācārya from Chennai in 1950) which follows the *Āvutta* reading and concludes that in Prakrit, *Āvutta* is the form of address to elders because Vasu-Lakṣmī is using it for her father Agnimitra!

That Vasu-Lakṣmī is the daughter of King Agnimitra and Queen Dhāriṇī is conclusively apparent on any reading of the play. She is consistently being referred to as *kumārī*, a word which in the royal household refers to the daughter of the king and the queen (just as *kumāra* refers to the heir to the throne) since the Vedic times[110] to this day. In the Fourth Act, when she is frightened by a monkey and is shaking uncontrollably in the lap of the queen it is the king who is called to go and console her back to normalcy.

The only possible explanation that I can suggest is that the *Āvutta* reading is an error of the redactors and the actual word must have been *Āvuka* which means "father" in dramatic dialogue just as *Āvutta* means "sister's husband". In a transfer from manuscript to print, such a mistake is possible and since *Āvuka* is less frequent (in fact I have found it only in the popular lexicon *Amarkośa* and not in a play), the reading *Āvutta* may have been taken as the "logical" possibility.

I submit this for the consideration of readers and editors of *Mālavikāgnimitra*.

> Reasoning is a bridge between young common sense and old common sense — Nichita Stanescu
>
> — epigraph for chapter 7, *Network Algebra*, Gheorghe Ştefanescue, Springer, 2000

110. See for instance the dialogue between the Kumārī and the Adhvaryu in the *Aśvamedha yajña, Śatapatha Brāhmaṇa.*

Author's Note

There is no point in proceeding further for that would only mean replicating the examples of methodological and substantial failures in Dr Thapar's study of Kālidāsa.

List of Contributors

PANCHANAN BHOI is working as Senior Research Fellow, Nistha Foundation, New Delhi. He has been awarded a PhD from the Centre for Historical Studies, Jawaharlal Nehru University, New Delhi and also is an alumnus of Indian Institute of Mass Communication, New Delhi. The author has specific interest in epigraphy and palaeography especially on writing materials and writing instruments with interlinking ethnographic research in that horizon [**address**: 134 Extension, Brahmaputra Hostel, Jawaharlal Nehru University, NEW DELHI - 110 067; **e-mail**: <dr.pancha.bhoi@gmail.com>, <panchabhoi@yahoo.com>].

MARIA KRZYSZTOF BYRSKI (1937–), joined Banaras Hindu University in 1959 as a research student of the Paderewski Foundation (USA). In 1966, he was awarded PhD Degree in Ancient Indian History, Culture and Archaeology for a thesis entitled "Concept of Ancient Indian Theatre". In 1978, Byrski was awarded the Degree of *doctor habilitatus* (D. Litt.) for the thesis entitled "Methodology of the Analysis of Sanskrit Drama". In 1990, he became the first ambassador of Poland to India. Mr. Lech Walesa, President of Poland, awarded him the title of professor. He has also been awarded by the President and the Prime Minister of India [**address:** Smolna Street 8, Apt. 58, 00-375 - WARSZAWA, (Poland); **e-mail**: <m.k.byrski@uw.edu.pl>].

LOKESH CHANDRA, is presently the Director, International Academy of Indian Culture and a renowned scholar of Tibetan, Mongolian and Sino-Japanese Buddhism. He has to his credit over 400 works and text editions. Among them are classics like his *Tibetan-Sanskrit Dictionary, Materials for a History of Tibetan Literature, Buddhist Iconography of Tibet* and the present *Dictionary of Buddhist Iconography* in 15 volumes. Dr Chandra was twice nominated by the President of India to the Rajya Sabha in 1974-80 and 1980-86. He had been the Vice-President of the Indian Council for Cultural Relations and Chairman of the Indian Council of Historical Research [**address:** J-22 Hauz Khas Enclave, NEW DELHI - 110 016].

TATIANA ELIZARENKOVA, Late Doctor of Philology, main research-worker of the Institute of Oriental Studies of the Russian Academy of Sciences Moscow, (ul. Ihdanova, 12). Tatiana has Translated the *Ṛgveda* (in three volumes) into Russian. Dr Elizarenkova was awarded Padmashri by Government of India. [**address :** Institute of Oriental Studies, Russian Academy of Sciences, A-315, ul. Sameda Vurguna, d 5, RV, 49, MOSCOW - 125 315 (Russia) **e-mail**: <msalganik@yandex.ru>].

BINA GUPTA, PhD, is a Curators' Professor, Professor of Philosophy, and Director of the South Asia Language and Area Program at University of Missouri, Columbia. She is either author or editor of ten books written on subjects like Indian philosophy, Buddhism, Feminism and Comparative Philosophy. Some of her important works are: *Perceiving in Advaita Vedānta, The Disinterested Witness: A Fragment of Advaita Vedānta Phenomenology*. From 1998 to 2001, Professor Gupta served as the President of the Society for Asian and Comparative Philosophy, an international alliance [**address:** Curators' Professor, Professor of Philosophy, Director, South Asian Studies Program, 418 General Classroom Building, University of Missouri, Columbia, MISSOURI - 65211 (USA); **e-mail:** <guptab@missouri.edu>].

PANKAJ S. JOSHI, PhD, is a Professor at the Department of Astronomy and Astrophysics, at the Tata Institute of Fundamental Research in Bombay. He has undertaken several important foreign assignments, including the National Science Foundation research position at the University of Pittsburgh. Prof. Joshi had been a Member of the National Advisory Committee to the University Grants Commission, India, for the subjects of Gravitation and Cosmology. He has received many Prizes and Awards, including the Gravity Research Foundation, USA, for his research work on the "Final Fate of Gravitational Collapse" and a Nuffield Foundation Fellowship to work at the Cambridge University. He has authored many books including *Global Aspects in Gravitation and Cosmology* (1993) and *Gravitational Collapse and Spacetime Singularities* (2007) [**address**: Department of Astronomy and Astrophysics, Tata Institute of Fundamental Research, Homi Bhabha Road, Colaba, MUMBAI – 400 005; **e-mail**: <psj@tifr.res.in>].

KAPIL KAPOOR, (1940-), has been Professor of English, Centre for Linguistics & English Studies and concurrent Professor at Special Centre for Sanskrit Studies, Jawaharlal Nehru University, New Delhi. He was also Dean of the School of Language, Literature and Culture Studies, from 1996-99 and Rector of the JNU from 1999-2002. His teaching and research interests include literary and linguistic theories, both Indian and Western philosophy of language. He has been teaching for almost forty-five years now. *Dimensions of Pāṇini Grammar: The Indian Grammatical System; Text and Interpretation: The Indian Tradition*, (both 2005); *Canonical Texts of Literary Criticism* (1995); and *South Asian Love Poetry* (1994) are among his publications [**address**: B-2/332, Ekta Garden, 9, Indraprastha Extension, NEW DELHI – 110 092; **e-mail**: <kkapoor40@yahoo.com>].

NICOLAOS KAZANAS studied English Literature at University College, Economics and Philosophy at the School of Economic Science and Sanskrit at the School of Oriental and African Studies — all in London. A post-graduate from Deccan College, Pune, he taught in London and Athens and since 1980 has been Director of Omilos Meleton Cultural Institute. Nicholaos has many publications in the West and India and is on the Editorial Board of *Adyar Library Bulettin* (Chennai) [**address**: 50-52, Aetideoan Str. Holargos GR 15561 ATHENS (Greece); **e-mail**: <nk@omilosmeleton.gr>].

VICTORIA LYSENKO is a Research Professor at Center of Oriental Philosophies, Institute of Philosophy, Russian Academy of Sciences and also a member of *Societé Asiatique*, Paris since 1993. She obtained her PhD on "The Vaiśeṣika Atomism" in 1982 and D. Litt. on "Continuity and Discontinuity in Indian Thought — the Vaiśeṣika and the Grammatical Philosophy" in 1998. Her published books in

Russian are: *Philosophy of Nature in India — Atomism of the Vaiśeṣika School* 1986); *Early Buddhist Philosophy* (1994); *Early Buddhism — Religion and Philosophy* (2003); *Universum of Vaiśeṣika* (2003); and *Padārtha-dharma-saṅgraha of Praśastapāda with Nyāyakaṇḍalī of Sridhara* — Translation from Sanskrit into Russian, Introduction, Historico-philosophical commentary, Notes and Indices by Victoria Lysenko (2005) [**address:** Avtozavodskaya Street, 6, Ap. 183, 115280 - MOSCOW (Russia); **e-mail:** <vglyssenko@yandex.ru>].

R. Nagaswamy (1930–), is former Director of Archaeology, Tamil Nadu and the Ex-Vice Chancellor of Kanchipuram University. He obtained Masters Degree in Sanskrit language and literature (Madras) and PhD in Indian arts (Poona). His fields of specialization include Art, Archaeology, Architecture, Ancient law, Palaeography, Temple rituals and philosophy, etc. Dr Nagaswamy was acknowledged International Expert on "South Indian Bronzes and appeared as an Expert Witness in the London High Court, in the London Nataraja case. The case was won and the Bronze returned to India. Hon. Justice Ian. Kennedy, the Judge of the London High Court in his judgment mentioned that "RN is an unequalled expert in his field". RN's publications include *Art and Religion of the Bhairavas* and *Timeless Delight,* on the great bronzes in the collection of Sarabhai Foundation in Ahmedabad [**address:** 11, 22nd Cross St., Besant Nagar, CHENNAI - 600 090; **e-mail** <nagaswamy@msn.com>].

K.T. Pandurangi (1918-), is presently the Chairman and Honorary Director of Dvaita Vedanta Foundation, Bangalore. He received education at Mysore, Annamalai University and Banaras Hindu University and obtained the traditional titles of Vidvān in Vedānta and Śiromaṇī in Vedānta. Prof. Pandurangi was a Reader and Professor from 1948-79 with Bangalore University. *The Prakaranapañcikā*, a Prabhākara Mīmāṁsā work and a volume on *Pūrvamīmāṁsā* are both edited by him. He has also edited over two dozen Dvaita Vedānta works and four Pūrvamīmāṁsā works with detailed introduction in English, published by Dvaita Vedanta Foundation, Bangalore. He received Rashtrapati Prashasti in 1989 and Mahamahopadhyaya title in 1997 [**address:** 132-4, 2nd Cross, III Block, Jayanagar, BANGALORE – 560 011; **e-mail**: <achut@absindia.net>].

Makarand Paranjape is Professor of English at the Jawaharlal Nehru University, New Delhi. He is the author-editor of over twenty-five books including *Decolonization and Development: Hind Swaraj Revisioned; The Penguin Sri Aurobindo Reader*; and *English Studies: Indian Perspectives.* He is founding editor of a multi-disciplinary international journal — *Evam: Forum of Indian Representations,* and a trustee of the Saṁvād India Foundation, a non-profit trust that promotes cross-cultural dialogue [**address**: Chairperson, Centre for English Studies, School of Language, Literature and Culture Studies, Jawaharlal Nehru University, NEW DELHI – 110 067; **e-mail:** <makarand@mail.jnu.ac.in>].

Wagish Shukla (1946-) teaches mathematics at Indian Institute of Technology, Delhi. He is a student of the Indian Classical Mind as revealed through Sanskrit, Persian and Hindi literature. He has published more than fifty articles in English and Hindi on these subjects. He is closely associated with the Special Centre for Sanskrit Studies at JNU as a member of several committees and is Associate Chief Editor of the *Encyclopedia of Indian Poetics*, an ongoing project of the Sahitya Academy, New Delhi [**address**: Deptt. of Mathematics, Indian Institute of Techonology, Hauz Khas, NEW DELHI – 110 016; **e-mail:** <wagishs@yahoo.com>].

Walter Slaje, PhD (Vienna), has been the Chair and Director of the Indological Institute in the Department of Ancient Civilizations, Halle University (Germany), and Member of the Academy of Sciences and Literature, Mainz. Slaje, the Associate Editor, *Zeitschrift der Deutschen Morgenländischen Gesellschaft* (ZDMG) and Editor, *Studia Indologica Universitatis Halensis* (Monograph Series) has Over 100 publications on the intellectual and cultural history of pre-modern India, on Kashmiri Sanskrit literature and historiography [**address**: Harmann-Loens-Str. 1, D-99425 WEIMAR (Germany); **e-mail:** <slaje@t-

online.de>].

G.U. Thite (1944-) is Curator and Editor at Bhandarkar Oriental Research Institute, Pune, and has been a Professor and Head of the Department of Sanskrit, University of Pune, Pune. His publications are: *Sacrifice in the Brāhmaṇa texts; Medicine: Its magico-religious aspects in the Veda; Music in the Veda; Āpastamba-Śrautasūtra:* English translation and *Kātyāyana-Śrautasūtra*: English translation [**address**: Bhandarkar Oriental Research Institute, PUNE; **e-mail:** <boril@vsnl.net>].

Index